THE INNER LIFE OF THE EARTH

THE INNER LIFE OF THE EARTH

*Exploring the Mysteries of
Nature, Subnature & Supranature*

CHRISTOPHER BAMFORD
DENNIS KLOCEK • DAVID S. MITCHELL
PAUL V. O'LEARY • MARKO POGAČNIK
ROBERT POWELL • RACHEL C. ROSS

PAUL V. O'LEARY, EDITOR

SteinerBooks

2008

2008
STEINERBOOKS
PO BOX 749, GREAT BARRINGTON, MA 01230
steinerbooks.org

La chute des anges rebelles (*Fall of the Rebel Angels*)
by Pieter Brueghel the Elder (c.1525–1569): Musee d'Art Ancien,
Les Musées royaux des Beaux-Arts de Belgique (photo by David S. Mitchell)
Temptation of Saint Anthony (detail) by Mathias Grünewald
From the Isenheim Altarpiece: Musee d'Unterlinden, Colmar, France
(photo by David S. Mitchell)
Cover and book design: William Jens Jensen
Cover background image: *Abstract Julian Flame* © by Werg

LIBRARY OF CONGRESS CATALOGING-IN-PUBLICATION DATA

The inner life of the earth : exploring the mysteries of nature, subnature, and supranature / Christopher Bamford ... [et al.].
    p. cm.
Includes bibliographical references.
ISBN 978-0-88010-595-8 (alk. paper)
1. Earth—Religious aspects. 2. Earth—Miscellanea. 3. Nature—Religious aspects. 4. Nature—Miscellanea. I. Bamford, Christopher, 1943–
BL438.2.I56 2008
299'.935—dc22

2008018001

PRINTED IN THE UNITED STATES

CONTENTS

"THE SILVER-SPARKLING BLUE BELOW, arising from the depths of the Earth and bound up with human weakness and error, is gathered into a picture of the Earth Mother. Whether she is called Demeter or Mary, the picture is of the Earth Mother. So it is that in directing our gaze downward, we cannot do other than bring together in Imagination all those secrets of the depths that go to make up the material Mother of all existence. While in all that is concentrated in the flowing from above, we feel and experience the Spirit Father of everything around us. And now we behold the outcome of the working together of the Spirit Father with the Earth Mother, bearing so beautifully within itself the harmony of the earthly silver and the gold of the heights. Between the Father and the Mother we behold the Son."

—RUDOLF STEINER, *The Four Seasons and the Archangels*

Introduction

Paul V. O'Leary

IF YOU COULD ASK an angel, "What do you find remarkable about human beings?" the likely reply would be, "We are fascinated that humans are split in two, that they live their lives divided within themselves. How do they stand it? How can they manage all that conflict? And how do they live without knowing their purpose, without knowing why they are alive?"

From the angelic viewpoint, humans present themselves as an immediate and obvious duality. Angels are not divided beings; they are unitary and not composite, as we are. Angels and the other Hierarchies of Good exist apart from, yet have their reflection or counter-pole in, the Hierarchies of Evil. Together, both echelons of spiritual beings comprise a duality, but not separately. The Hierarchies of Good can do good, or do better, but they cannot harbor a good and evil thought at the same time, as we humans can. The Hierarchies of Evil have a similar but polar perspective. Neither group is both good and evil, as we are, who bear our polaric sides within the same being—ourselves: hence, the uniqueness of specifically human conscience.[1] Only human beings can experience freedom.

Angels stand in awe of our normal, everyday situation, where we can intuit multiple, yet contrary, ideas, motives, and emotions at the same time. Have you ever had a powerful experience in which your reactions run the gamut from fear, anger, revenge, and shock to bewilderment, confusion, compassion, forgiveness, and willingness to sacrifice? Have all these thoughts and emotions happened almost or actually simultaneously? Of course, you have; you are a human being. Angels, archangels, and so forth have no experience of this; it is outside their realm. Schizophrenia belongs to human beings and to human beings alone. It is unique to the human condition.

Our dual nature is a primal phenomenon, an Ur-phenomenon of our very being. It is our signature and marks us out for what we truly are: the microcosm of the macrocosm. The split of the universe into spirit and matter, inner and outer, darkness and light, or the "matter" and "anti-matter" of contemporary physics, is reflected in our inner nature in the duality of percept-concept, mind-body, thought-will, good-evil, life-death, and so on. "There is an important occult axiom: every quality has two opposite poles. So, we find, just as positive and negative electricity complement one another, so we have warmth and cold, day and night, light and darkness, and so on."[2]

Everyone has a "dark side," a "shadow," which is revealed in every sphere of life. Saint Paul famously describes the division in his soul: "For I do not the good that I wish, but the evil that I do not wish, that I perform ... unhappy man that I am!"[3] The poetic form of the same lament is Goethe's famous "Two souls, alas, reside within my breast; the one from the other would be parted."[4] It is you and it is I, every time we act less morally than we know to be our best. It is the rift manifest in the twin opposites of higher self and lower self. Why we cannot *be* as "good" or as "moral" as we can *think;* and why our thoughts, emotions, and actions are out of sync with one another: these issues reveal the fundamental problem. On the other hand, we experience our ego most intensely precisely through the encounter with our own polarity.

"One does not usually notice that a human being is a duality," notes Rudolf Steiner. Nevertheless, we are doubtlessly a duality. Moreover, that fact pervades the spiritual-scientific worldview from anthroposophic medicine to biodynamic agriculture, from the description of the constellations of the zodiac to the description of the various members of the human being. With its sister concepts "polarity" and "metamorphosis," this dynamic drives evolution itself through the cultural epochs and from ancient Saturn to future Vulcan. It stands behind the esoteric mantra: "That which is above is like to that which is below, and that which is below is like to that which is above."[5] This is true within the human being as well.

Continuing from the quote on duality, we learn from Steiner that what appears in the lower part of one's organism always corresponds to something in the upper part of the organism; that certain organs could not come into being in the upper part unless parallel organs—in a certain sense, opposing organs—were able to have a place in the lower part as the opposite pole; that there is an inner relationship between the form of the intestine and the form of the brain and that the intestinal organs are truly the reverse side of the brain.[6]

The macrocosm and microcosm mirror each other. The phenomenon of the human being's dual nature is shown by the Earth as seen floating in space. The Earth has no light of its own, but receives its light from the Sun and stars and from the reflected light of the Moon. Half of the Earth is always in darkness, while the other half is flooded with light. From a Goethean point of view, where physical facts simultaneously represent spiritual reality, this picture portrays the essence of polarity. For Goethe, natural phenomena are living expressions of the theory (idea) that created them. "The best of all would be to realize that every fact is already theory. The blue of the sky shows us the principals of color. We need not look for anything behind phenomena; they themselves are the doctrine."[7] If the phenomena are the theory, then the dark and light Earth revolving through space perfectly expresses both the dynamic of polarity and our human nature.

What has all this to do with the subject of this book, the realm of the subterranean spheres and the interior of the Earth?

The goal of human evolution is that we develop an independent, free "I," or self. We are to evolve from created beings to creative beings, motivated and permeated by love, an energy that will be comprised of the transformed wisdom we have learned through our many incarnations. This new form of love will be an objective, cosmic force, universal in scope and not subjective, personal, and limited as it is now. To that extent, we must acquire self-knowledge. "Know thy Self" is the profound esoteric mandate of the past, present, and future. At the event known in the Bible as the Fall, Lucifer provided our initial self and imbued humankind with a selfish nature in our astral body. This permeation by selfishness, or egotism, however, also provided the basis of our freedom; "freedom and evil have the same original source."[8]

Selfishness transforms and reappears in the ether body as falsehood and lying, and descends further into the physical body, where it manifests as sickness and death. These forces, originating from selfishness, are found within the human subconscious, the subterranean spheres, and are the sources of evil. In order to transform these forces and overcome the Fall, we must first recognize them, acknowledge their existence, and bring them into full consciousness. We are slaves to our own nature and to the karmic web we live in because of our past lives. Freedom, as such, is currently not possible within the sphere of human will; freedom is possible only within the realm of thinking. Free thought can lead to freedom from enslaving emotions, urges, and passions. Free thought is the precondition for the moral transformation needed to become a free personality. To the degree we lack self-knowledge, we are controlled by our subconscious life. Steiner noted that where self-knowledge ends, self-love begins...and vice versa. Descent into the subterranean spheres is a descent into the lower self and the forces of egotism. Enhanced understanding of these forces is a prerequisite to increasing self-knowledge and facilitating purification and spiritualization of one's all-too-human nature. Otherwise, we cannot avoid "the catastrophe of the lower nature."[9]

Our very "I"-consciousness is possible because the mineral earth—the first layer of the interior of the Earth—and the other chthonic regions exist. Our human nature is a reflection of the subearthly and supraearthly realms that comprise the macrocosm and the microcosm. "The true meaning of the microcosm–macrocosm analogy is not that the human being is a little cosmos, but that the cosmos is a big human being."[10] From this perspective it makes complete sense that the subterranean realms described by spiritual science live within the deepest realms of our human nature and subconscious life of darker feelings and will.[11] Deep within the human being, they radiate into the shadows of thought. This region is more familiarly known as Hell, Hades, or the Abyss. The subterranean spheres, then, are the Earth's "dark side." This perspective is clearly Manichean.

The energies that feed our irrational side pour forth from these depths. We can view human history, or simply everyday life, as a constant battle between the irrational and rational. We humans, individually and collectively, have a "self-destruct" impulse deep within our nature, whereby we destroy the things we hold most dear and kill those things we most love. Historical events since the dawn of the Age of Light in 1900, as well as the daily news headlines, provide overwhelming proof of this. Money, power, sensuality, and violence enthrall human beings. What was culturally unacceptable forty or even twenty years ago is now normal. The gradual, manifold, and seemingly inevitable degradation of cultural norms, sliding progressively down into the abyss, needs no additional documentation for the reader of this book. Thoughtful people question whether we should classify human beings as "rational creatures" at all. "A bevy of experiments in recent years suggests that the conscious mind is like a monkey riding a tiger of subconscious decisions and actions in progress, frenetically making up stories about being in control."[12] Robert Kagan, a professor and historian at Yale, recently commented, "To me, the deepest message, the most tragic, is [Thucydides'] picture of civilization as a very thin veneer. When you punch a hole in it, what you find underneath is hollow, the pre-civilized characteristics of the human race—animalistic in the worst possible way."[13] More appropriate to this particular book is a picture of human nature as a volcano fueled by ancient energies from the subterranean spheres, capped and (ideally) controlled by the developing and newest member of human nature: the nascent ego, or "I."

Two paths are available to penetrate the maya of existence toward genuine spiritual reality: the outer path through the outer world, and the inner path via one's inner life. Tracing the chthonic energies to their source is, obviously, part of the inner path. Steiner warns of the dangers for those who would follow this path.[14] One can observe human beings who have become addicted to the lower passions through perverted sexuality, drugs, greed, gambling, the lust for power, and even rape and murder. The washed-out addict or serial killer appears hollow, an empty shell; the self is devoured while that person devours others by indulging in, or being dominated by, the passions. The depths of the subterranean realm eventually lead to the source of black magic, which Steiner defines as "magic based on egotism."[15]

From a more global perspective, the Earth, as a planet within the solar system, is very much a living being. It was only with the advent of modern natural science that the Earth began to be seen as a dead, lifeless ball floating in the vacuum of space. Natural science knows less about the depths of our oceans than it does about the depths of outer space, and even less about the interior of the Earth. The materialistic worldview has reached its zenith; since the middle of the last century, new-age scientists and spiritually minded people have initiated countervailing concepts that the Earth has qualities of life,[16] or even that it is a "self-regulating, living being."[17] For spiritual science "the evolution of the human being and the evolution of the Earth are a single process."[18] They each condensed into physical substance through the same event—the Fall, also characterized as the fall into matter. Moreover, they mutually depend upon the same polar event—the Mystery of Golgotha—for their transformation and spiritualization.

For those readers who wish to penetrate more deeply into the anthroposophic worldview concerning the interior of the Earth, two recent publications are useful. Sigismund von Gleich's *Transformation of Evil*[19] provides an excellent summary of the spiritual-scientific picture of the interior of the Earth, the corresponding energies of evil and their counter-pole in the nine Beatitudes of the Sermon on the Mount. The other, *The Interior of the Earth: An Esoteric Study of the Subterranean Spheres,*[20] offers Rudolf Steiner's only five lectures that address the topic directly. In addition, it contains relevant excerpts from five other lectures by Steiner, as well as material from Adolf Arenson and Countess von Keyserlingk. The present collection may be considered the third in that series.

In brief, the nine layers of the subterranean spheres are numbered and named as follows:

1. The mineral or solid earth (the Earth's crust)
2. The fluid (soft) earth
3. The air (vapor) earth
4. The form earth
5. The fruit earth
6. The fire (passion) earth
7. The mirror earth (earth reverser)
8. The fragmenting (splintering, or explosive) earth
9. The earth core

According to Rudolf Steiner, "the ninth layer, immediately around the Earth's center,"[21] encloses a tenth layer, the true center of the Earth, where Christ, the planetary spirit since the Mystery of Golgotha, has his abode. The true center of the Earth is made of gold.[22] It is the place where, at a subterranean altar, the spiritual Sword of Michael, is being forged.[23]

The subterranean spheres, whose forces are found within the human subconscious, are likewise the realm of the Apocalyptic beasts.[24] What frequently passes for "self-knowledge" is really a form of reflected self-love plus a collection of images from the outer world. Although artistic portrayals abound in literature, painting, and film, few persons have the strength and courage to penetrate these dark realms. The inner life of most people is really just the outer world poured into them, sitting atop a base of primal self-interest.

> Ordinary consciousness, however, emerges only from what actually originated in outer sensory impressions and has been transformed by feeling and will. One finds only the reflections, or mirror images, of outer life, when looking into one's inner being with ordinary consciousness; and, although the outer impressions are transformed by feeling and will, humankind still does not know how feeling and will actually work. Consequently, people often fail to recognize what they see in their inner being as a transformed mirror image of the outer world, taking it, perhaps, as a special message from the divine, eternal world. This is not the case, however. What appears to the ordinary consciousness of modern human beings as self-knowledge is only the transformed outer world, which is reflected out of the inner human being into one's consciousness.
>
> If people really wished to look into their inner being, they would (I have often used this image) have to break the inner mirror.... We can no more gaze into the inner human being with ordinary consciousness than we can look behind a mirror without breaking it.... For the purpose of developing the human, thought-filled "I," we all bear within us—below the memory mirror—a fury of destruction and dissolution in relation to matter. There is no self-knowledge that does not point with the greatest intensity toward this inner human fact.... Humankind is the sheath for a source of destruction, and, in fact, the forces of decline can be transformed into the forces of ascent only when human beings become conscious of this—that we are a sheath for a source of destruction;...

the world that manifests as a source of destruction lies within, behind the memory mirror.[25]

[handwritten margin note: Look @ the evil When is to know your Self,]

This "source of destruction" originates in the subterranean spheres. These enormously powerful, terrifying, and overwhelming subearthly forces arose at the very beginning of our cosmic system, at humanity's conception.[26] Steiner identifies these transformations of previous planetary evolutions as Goethe's "realm of the Mothers" from Faust.[27] He "described the Mothers as personifications of the pure life force in its different aspects as it originated on ancient Saturn, ancient Sun and ancient Moon respectively:

> Let us ask ourselves what the Greeks looked for in their three Mothers, Rea, Demeter, and Persephone. They saw in these three Mothers a picture of the forces that, working down from the cosmos, prepare the human cell. These forces, however, do not come from the part of the cosmos that belongs to the physical, but to the suprasensory. The Mothers—Demeter, Rea and Persephone—belong to the suprasensory world. No wonder then that Faust has the feeling that an unknown Kingdom is making its presence felt when the word *Mothers* is spoken. . . . All the forces that are in Saturn, Sun, and Moon are still working—working on into our own time.[28]

Ancient Saturn was comprised of warmth (fire or warmth ether). The ancient Sun developed both light (ether) and air (gas). Sound (ether) and water arose on the ancient Moon. Solid earth, along with its corresponding life ether, arose on Earth.[29] All of this is a further expression of the Law of Polarity.[30]

The deepest three layers of the subterranean spheres are the province of the Asuras and comprise a reverse or anti-Upper Devachan. The middle three chthonic layers comprise the realm of Ahriman, and are the counter-reflection of Lower Devachan. The upper three subterranean spheres, a counter Astral World, belong to Lucifer.[31] These realms are energized by ethers of which are polar to light, sound, and life—which we know as electricity, magnetism, and forces of super-destruction (including nuclear energy). Electricity is "fallen" light "which destroys itself within matter." Magnetism is the "fallen" chemical ether. The polaric counterpart to the life ether finds expression in nuclear energy, although its full expression has yet to be realized.[32] Yet all these forces may also be found within ourselves. "All that is light, sound and warmth is then akin to our conscious life, while all that goes on in the realms of electricity and magnetism is akin—intimately akin—to our unconscious life of will."[33]

The telluric regions which lie below Nature are the province of God the Father. Steiner paints this picture:

> Imagine we have Nature: then above it leads to a circle; below, it leads to a circle; and what is above joins to what is below. If we draw the circle larger and larger and continue to draw it larger, we finally get a straight line. A piece of circle that continues on, after it has gone into infinity, comes back from the other side. This shows that the terms "upper" and "lower" should not be understood as signs of rank, but simply as different ways that the gods come to human beings. They have been thought of as working in equal rank with one another, of striving to unite at a point in infinity....
>
> When we understand this we are able to bring into our own modern age what was present in human consciousness in olden times. If we ask what can be identified in modern consciousness with the realm of the lower gods, the answer must be: the Being whom we call the Father, when we think of the Divine Trinity. The Father belongs in the most eminent sense to subnature.... When we sleep, we enter the realm of the Father God, we enter subnature—the realm of the Father....
>
> So we see that the human being is organized on Earth in such a way that one is able to go out from nature in two directions: in the direction of subnature to the Father, and in the direction of supranature to the spirit. Since the Mystery of Golgotha, Christ has been the mediator for both worlds.

Shannon

He is the one who permeates the world of nature, the one who permeates normal human existence. He has always to create harmony between subnature and supranature. [34]

The interior of the Earth is the realm of the Father forces within the Trinity, as Steiner notes in his opening lecture on the Foundation Stone Meditation: "For the Father-Spirit of the Heights holds sway / In the Depths of the world, begetting life." These are "forces surging in the Depths, from the interior of the Earth, the forces working in our limbs."[35]

The purpose of this collection of essays is to broaden the view on the whole topic of the earthly and subearthly worlds. The goal is to "put into play" facts, concepts, and ideas that contribute to filling out the spiritual-scientific worldview, so that its historical emphasis upon the suprasensory and celestial is balanced by additional considerations of the subsensory and terrestrial. It is time to extend the search for "self-knowledge" into our own subconscious and into our home planet. Expansion of our awareness of our Earth planet as a spiritual being, which has hidden depths rarely discussed, will lead to greater clarity and comprehension of our own subconscious life, which is permeated by forces streaming upward from those same depths. Here is the juncture where the inner meets the outer; self-knowledge becomes world knowledge, and visa versa.

Through the wide world there lives and moves
The real human being.
While in the innermost human core
The mirror image of the world is living.

The "I" unites the two
And thus fulfills the meaning of existence.[36]

SUBTERRANEAN ESSAYS: A BRIEF REVIEW

We ought to praise the seven authors of the essays contained herein, if only for their courage in tackling so daunting a subject. As Steiner observes, "Even among esotericists, it is considered one of the most difficult things to speak about the mysterious configuration and composition of our planet Earth.... These things are part of the most advanced knowledge in esotericism." [37] These seven articles stand on the leading edge of spiritual research. Several contributors are well known in their fields and have published numerous articles and books. Others are familiar only to their immediate colleagues. None would claim infallibility, however; all are open-minded to discover and share new insights and approaches to comprehend these mysterious realms.

It would be convenient to categorize these essays as addressed to one or another facet of the Earth's interior—to the planetary aspect or to what one encounters along the path of inner development. However, these essays, like the topic itself, are more complex than that, and each addresses both aspects at various junctures.

David Mitchell offers a poetic yet philosophical exploration of the many phenomena he has discovered and experienced in science, art, and religion, which may be interpreted more profoundly by awareness of these terrestrial energies. In "Evil: Our Dance Partner through Life," he leads us on a personal journey with and through the sub-terrestrial.

Dennis Klocek and Marko Pogačnik emphasize the planetary aspect of the Earth as a living being, though from very different viewpoints. Klocek is an artist, scientist, gardener, and genuine alchemist. He has spent decades conducting scientific research into the behavior of clouds, cyclones, wind, and all the phenomena of weather against the background of planetary and celestial influences streaming in from the unfathomable distances of outer space. His studies reveal that the Earth's energy bodies, which extend hundreds of miles above the Earth's crust, have parallels and reflection in the nine subearthly layers first described by Rudolf Steiner. His findings are on the frontier of spiritual-scientific research, and he presents them in his essay, "As Above, so Below—as Below, so Above."

Marko Pogačnik has an international reputation as a conceptual artist and geomancer. In "Portals to the Inner Earth," he reports on his direct encounters with suprasensory phenomena. He has discovered "interdimensional portals" that lead to the Earth's past, to antediluvian civilizations and their inhabitants, and to beings who reside within the subearthly regions. His research opens up communication with prehistoric civilizations that suffered destruction through natural catastrophes, offering the potential for our culture to learn from their experiences.

Robert Powell's essay, "Subnature and the Second Coming," shows the transition from the outer to the inner, from the consideration of the Earth as planet to the Earth, the interior life of which forms part of our own inner life. The law of polarity[38] is exhibited in the dynamic interplay of resurrection forces emanating from the etheric return of Christ, which give rise to corresponding counter-forces issuing from the depths. Powell carries this theme of "call and response" from the onset of the etheric Christ in 1933, through the decades of the last century, and to future events prophesied in the Apocalypse and in the writings of Rudolf Steiner. He documents archetypal cultural and spiritual phenomena associated with the various layers of the subterranean spheres, as each is penetrated by solar energy according to the twelve-year Jupiter rhythm. Apocalyptic events are foreordained by the penetration of the etheric return of Christ through the interior of the Earth.

In "Transforming Subearthly Energies through Eurythmy," Rachel C. Ross, an educator and eurythmist of wide experience, provides us with a fresh look at the art and therapy of eurythmy. She probes the deeper reasons for the advent of eurythmy in the second decade of the twentieth century and gives concrete examples of specific exercises designed to connect the suprasensory with the subsensory. It should be of great import to serious students of these matters that eurythmy can be employed as a means of therapeutic transformation and purification of the subearthly forces permeating our physical, etheric, and astral sheaths.

The Mineral Earth—the first terrestrial layer—is the focus of Paul O'Leary's article, "The Mineral Earth as the Gateway to Freedom and the Subterranean Spheres: The Ministry of Jesus Christ." He explores the connections between the Earth's crust, the realm of death, "I"-consciousness, evil, and freedom, as exemplified by scenes from the earthly life of Jesus Christ.

The perspectives found in Christopher Bamford's "Paradoxical Thoughts on Christ and Sophia in the Human Mystery of the Earth" are all-encompassing. Long experience with such topics and genuine erudition are required to pen such a piece. The parallel and unified (though seemingly separate) evolutions of the ideal human being (Anthropos), the Sophia, the Earth, and our cosmic system, are traced in a majestic panorama. There is much to ponder here, which is more meditation than essay.

Although these seven essays are extraordinary in their breadth and depth, they merely scratch the surface of esoteric truths concerning the regions known as the subterranean spheres. Their transformation lies within humanity's collective mission as a whole. Yet their nature remains dark, as do the depths of our own subconscious will life. Their essence will be increasingly unveiled as we progress into the future. An extensive quote from a lecture on color by Rudolf Steiner reveals their comprehensive significance:

> The cosmos, seen from inside, is light and, seen from outside through spiritual perception, is thought. The human head, seen from inside, is thought and, seen from outside, is light....
>
> If I were to get outside the world, outside the light-filled world, and see it from beyond, I would see it as a thought image, a being consisting of thought. You see, light and

thought belong together; light and thought are the same thing, seen from different sides.

Now our thoughts are actually the part of us that comes from the past. They are our most mature aspect and are the result of earlier incarnations. What was once the will has become thought, and, as thought, it appears as light. You will be able to feel from this that where there is light there is thought. However, what is its nature? Thought is a world that is perpetually dying away. A past world dies away in thought, or we could say that a past world dies away in light. This is one of the world's secrets, or mysteries. We look out into the universe, and it is flooded with light. Thought lives in light, but it is a dying world that lives in this thought-filled light. The world is perpetually dying away in the light....

The will element is in our limbs. As I have often mentioned, our experience of will is the same as our experience of the world when we sleep. We experience the will element unconsciously. We are asleep to our will. Is there some way of looking at this element of will from outside, as we did with thought?... What does will look like when we see it with the developed power of clairvoyant vision? In this case, too, we can experience something externally. When we see thought with the power of clairvoyance, we experience light, luminous light. When we see the will with the power of clairvoyance, it condenses and becomes substance, or matter. On the inside, matter is will, just as, on the inside, light is thought. On the outside, will is matter, just as, on the outside, thought is light.... If you delve into the nature of will, you will discover the true nature of matter.... Moreover, in matter—that is, in will—you discover finally a continually beginning and continually germinating world.

You look out into the world, and there you are surrounded by light. In this light, a past world is dying away. You tread on hard matter, and the world's strength bears you up. Beauty shines forth as thought in the light. In the shining of beauty, the world of the past dies away. The world rises in its strength and its power, but also in its darkness. The worlds of the future rise in darkness, in the element of matter and in will.... The future actually lies in the strength of matter. The past radiates in the beauty of light....

We cannot understand what we ourselves are unless we see ourselves as seeds of the future enveloped in what comes from the past, the light aura of thought. We can say, from a spiritual point of view, that we are in the past to the extent that we have an aura of beauty; yet this aura of the past is enveloped in the darkness that accompanies the light from the past, and this carries us forward into the future. Light is the element that shines toward us from the past, and darkness points toward the future.... It must become very real to us today that the world, including humankind, is composed of a combination of thought-light, or light-thoughts, and will-matter, or matter-will, and that these, in innumerable variations and combinations, constitute the real world that confronts us. We must think about the cosmos in a qualitative way, not merely quantitatively; in this way, we will come to understand it. This cosmos is composed of both elements: a continual dying away—past dying away in light—and a future arising out of darkness....

So you see there are these two world entities: light and darkness—light with its living thought and dying past, and darkness, in which the will germinates and the future comes into being.... Light contains death, a dying world. Light can give us a feeling of cosmic tragedy. Thus, we get away from mere abstraction, mere thought, and come into an element of movement. And in darkness we can see part of the future that is coming into being.[39]

NOTE FROM THE EDITOR

This volume of essays was solicited and compiled by the editor. None of the contributing authors was privy to the essays of the other authors during or after their composition. No inference should be drawn that the individual authors agree or disagree with the views expressed by the other authors. Each essay should be read independently and judged solely upon it own merits.

Chapter 1

Evil: Our Dance Partner through Life

Living under the Influence of the Earth's Subterranean Spheres

David S. Mitchell

A soft breeze wafted through the maroon curtain in the bedroom window and made it dance an airy flutter. Dappled light played against the wall, and the young, pre-kindergarten boy rested in a bed for his daily nap. The sheets were crisp and cool. Thoughts rolled through his mind and he questioned: Why am I me? Where do my ideas come from? Why am I unable to think my father's thoughts?

Nature was his sanctuary, and observations brought him joy. In the out-of-doors, he reconnected with his spiritual home. He rejoiced in every detail—from the smell of a soft breeze in the springtime, the patterns that eddies form around rocks in a river, and the feeling of oneness in a forest when mottled sunbeams filter through to the ground, to the bursting spray and rainbow a wave creates when it explodes over a partially submerged boulder on the Maine coast. Life filled him to the brim. His family laughed when they went to the beach and the boy spent more time under the water than on top of it. "But there are so many interesting and mysterious things down there to discover," he replied.

As he grew and became a teenager, he was visited by dark thoughts and wondered from where they came. He explored them, but the greater part of him was in fierce opposition. They forced him to struggle with himself. As he grew in strength and stature, the force and power in his body sought domination over others in athletics while at the same time his tender heart longed for his "Beatrice."[1] This polarity awakened a striving to find meaning through religion. While his friends sampled drugs, he visited a synagogue, a mosque, a Catholic Mass, and delivered the youth sermons at his granite, Protestant, New England, white-spired Congregational Church. Contemporary religion did not bring fulfillment, but intense prayer brought him several profound inner experiences and intensified his inner striving, his knowing that there were more important things to be discovered by diving into himself, just as there had been in diving beneath the surface of the ocean. The more he dove the more he had to deal with passion, anger, competition, lust, the struggle to hold fast to integrity, and various other evils that arose within from some uncharted depths. He puzzled over the source of those dark forces.

As with the subjects he studied in school, he felt there was something more meaningful and important behind the outer religion than what he met on the surface. There was something that could provide meaning to life. He sought out the roots of his personal evil quagmire and for the ability to navigate through what came to him from this dark region. Now as a senior citizen, he has made a fragile peace with the dark side of existence and has learned to appreciate evil as a necessary companion. The struggles, rebuked temptations, and tamed lusts have transformed the iron into steel within his soul. Of course, the struggles still continue, but wisdom, trust, and self-patience provide the ability to endure.

What exactly is evil, where does it originate, and how can we be part of its redemption, if, in fact, evil can be redeemed at all? Rudolf Steiner said, "Evil is nothing but the chaos that is within humankind by necessity, which is projected outward. From this necessary chaos, which not only must be present, but also must remain in humankind as the central seat of evil, in this the human

'I,' or Ego principal, must be tempered."[2] Thus, humanity is in a blacksmith's forge, within which spiritual forces first intensely heat us and then place us on an anvil to hammer upon our malleable souls. What part does the intense demand for freedom play in this smithy of my soul? It was through esoteric Christianity, spiritual science, and literature that the young man found the first hints for understanding. The playwright Christopher Fry, a participant in the Religious Drama Movement in England (which also launched T. S. Eliot as a dramatist), wrote about a world untarnished by original sin. "Between our birth and death, we may touch under-standing, / As a moth brushes a window with its wing." But even a brief brush brings hope and shows that the pathway upon which to ramble is worthwhile.

In his play, *A Sleep of Prisoners,* Fry says through Meadow, one of the soldiers:

> Thank God our time is now when wrong
> Comes up to face us everywhere,
> Never to leave us till we take
> The longest stride of soul men ever took![3]

Yes, thank God we are alive at this time of the consciousness soul, when we have capacities to aid us in our pursuit of truth in light of the evil with which we must contend. Steiner proclaimed that the whole world "is a riddle, a riddle of existence, and human beings themselves are its solution."[4]

In order to gain insight into evil, let us consider some of the stories and myths about the creation of the world. The following one comes from the Christian tradition.

THE WORLD'S BEGINNING

Long ago, there was no Earth. There were no clouds and no stars, no, not even a sun! Darkness was everywhere. No animals bounded, and no birds flew. How could they have, since there was no Earth?

Did anything exist at all? There was a Heaven, an upper world, high above our stars. In Heaven, God's eye shone like a sun. Small angels could not look directly into God Father's shining eye, for it was much too bright. It shone more brightly than our Sun and would have blinded them. The great angels, however, could look for a moment into God Father's eye. They could even come near his throne when they wanted to tell him something. All heaven rang with beautiful music. Flutes, violins, and harps resounded, and angels sang long songs. Whenever one concert came to an end, a new one would begin. Some angels sewed golden stars upon God Father's mantle of blue, while others caught light beams and kneaded them into precious stones. All was splendor and a great wonder.

Once, two great angels knelt in prayer before God Father's throne. As they rose, they flew together downward through the heavens, for God's throne stood high and steep like the peak of a mountain. All at once, an angel named Lucifer stood still. He gazed upon the splendor of heaven and upon his own shining garment and thought to himself, "How nice it is, to be such a god. My garment is almost as bright as that of God Father! Indeed, it is bright enough that I might sit in God's place."

As Lucifer thought this, a wispy, gray cloud gently hovered before his forehead. It floated toward his heart and there made a spot upon his garment. Lucifer was frightened when he saw this and quickly covered the spot with his wing. As he went on his way through heaven, he met Michael. Michael asked, "Lucifer, what is wrong? Are you ill? You have a spot upon your garment!"

"My heart aches a little, that's all," Lucifer answered. He quickly flew to the lesser angels and said to them, "Make a fiery red mantle for me. I must cover something." They made the mantle, and when he put it on, the spot could be seen no longer.

Lucifer stayed with the lesser angels and asked them, "Will you help me build a throne? I will sit upon it and be your god. You are not permitted to go to the highest throne, but to my throne you may always come." Many angels were frightened at these words.

The Fall of the Rebel Angels
by Pieter Bruegel, c.1527–1569 (photo by the author)

Others, however, liked Lucifer so much that they agreed. These angels ceased singing and making music. They also ceased sewing stars upon God Father's mantle.

Now Michael saw what Lucifer was doing. Filled with dread, he brought the news to God Father that Lucifer was building a throne for himself. God Father spoke, "Tell Lucifer to destroy his heart. I will give him a new, shining heart. If he will do so, bring him to me. If he will not do so, he shall have his throne, but not in heaven. If he refuses to heed my words, take your sword and cast him out of heaven." Thus God Father spoke.

All this Michael told Lucifer. However, Lucifer had stirred up many angels; he did not want a new heart. The angels ceased singing. Loud voices shouted in confusion. Thunder rumbled through heaven and a fiery wind blew. Michael took up his sword. Bolts of lightning flashed from it. He called out with a mighty voice, "All those who will be true to God, stand by my side."

Lucifer shouted, "Those who would go with me into the new heaven stand by my side!" Thus, the spirits separated into two groups. Michael's group was above, Lucifer's below.

Now Michael struck against the wall of heaven with his lightning sword. Loud crashes resounded, and a deep gash appeared. Lucifer and his angels fought desperately, for they did not want to go into the darkness below. But God Father's light no longer shone upon them. The beautiful colors in their garments and wings paled and faded. Their faces became gloomy and ugly. Claws grew out of their fingers. They howled and wailed but were forced to give way before Michael and his hosts. Lucifer and his followers were cast from heaven. They plunged down into the deep, dark depths.

The evil spirits made a small fire out of their own light, for they were cold. They danced around it and it grew into a huge fire. They forged a throne for Lucifer and placed it upon the fire that he should always be warm. Michael closed the cleft in heaven, but a scar remained where it had been.[5] Since that time there has existed a dark, lower world.

LUCIFER AND AHRIMAN

In late Medieval Christian and modern thought, Lucifer is usually identified as Satan, the embodiment of evil and the enemy of God. Steiner, however, divides the devil between two beings, Lucifer and Ahriman, and informs us that neither is intrinsically bad; each has a necessary spiritual influence on humankind, and each provides gifts to human beings that further our evolution. However, each human being must learn to balance appropriately the forces they inject into our individual lives. Otherwise, chaos and one-sidedness prevail.

Lucifer appears in the Bible in the fourteenth chapter of the book of Isaiah, at the twelfth verse, and nowhere else:

> How you have fallen from the heavens
> O morning star, son of the dawn!
> How you are cut down to the ground,
> you who mowed down the nations!

You said in your heart:
　"I will scale the heavens:
Above the stars of God
　I will set up my throne;
I will take my seat on the Mount of Assembly
　in the recesses of the North.
I will ascend above the tops of the clouds;
　I will be like the Most High!"
Yet down to the nether world you go
　to the recesses of the pit! (Isa. 14:12–15)

The Rosicrucians spoke of the prince of the adversarial powers as *Deus inversus,* or the reversed god, who works on humanity through the spheres of evil to destroy it with their help. The prince of darkness, the ursurper prince, they called Ahriman.

We first learn of Ahriman (Angra Mainyu) from the ancient Persian religion of Zoroastrianism. The Zoroastrians believed in a completely dualistic form of religion. The Avestan language name is the hypostasis of the "destructive spirit." Ahriman was the foremost enemy who opposed Ahura Mazda (the Sun spirit). Ahriman is thought to be the first personification of the "Devil." Steiner identified the biblical "Devil" with Lucifer and "Satan" with Ahriman.

In a lecture on January 1, 1909, Steiner first referred to Ahriman, whom he associated with materialism and the unconscious aspects of technology.[6] He stated that Ahriman fulfills the role of influencing and undermining events that occur in contemporary society. Steiner wrote that Ahriman, the biblical Satan, and the demon Mephistopheles in Goethe's *Faust,* can all be considered the same entity. According to Steiner, the biblical forces of evil, Mammon and Beelzebub, are Ahriman's associates, while the demonic Asuras are the army. The Asuras enter the human "I" when it becomes vacant or weak.

According to Steiner, Ahriman's spiritual assignment is to alienate human beings from their spiritual roots, while inspiring materialism and heartless technical control of human activity, so that we will see one another in terms of machines and parts of machines. As such, his influence is highly relevant to present-day Western culture. Myths tell us that the ahrimanic beings did not want to live in the sphere in which they were destined to live by the higher hierarchies. They wanted to conquer the Earth, but had no bodies, so they entered the Earth by permeating salts and minerals. As human beings metabolize salts and minerals, ahrimanic beings enter our bodies. While in our bodies, they represent what we call our "double," which lives beneath the threshold of our conscious life and is nothing less than the author of our organic illnesses. In this manner, the double acts as a karmic conditioner. The double is threefold: there is a luciferic double present in our astral body; an ahrimanic double in our ether body; and an asuric double in our physical body. In this section, I am confining myself to the discussion of the ahrimanic double.

The ahrimanic double wants human beings to forsake their spiritual nature, to develop only the cold parts of their intellect, to reject all spiritual knowledge for earthly knowledge, to reject their souls. The role of the double is to help human beings into incarnation by placing their lower nature in an affinity with the Earth. Different parts of the Earth are more influential in this regard. The double chooses to relate itself to the forces that radiate from the Earth. These forces are clearest in the North American continent, so they exist there.

The double is in our unconscious and cannot be driven away. It leaves us only some weeks before we pass through the threshold of death. Magnetism enhances the double and makes it more prominent. Steiner relates that as the inherited physical body is about to die, the double journeys back to the mountains and reenters the mineral world through the salts to begin the process again.

The intellect in Europe needed to be protected from those forces. Steiner points out, along with Professor Barry Fell,[7] that many journeys across the Atlantic took place to study the diseases that

occurred in Native American cultures because of their special relationship with the double (see note 19). The remedy was found in high
silica-bearing leaves and herbs available only in North America.

This concept of the double appears throughout literature.
Contemporary authors who have written of the double include
Feodor Dostoevsky in *The Double;* Oscar Wilde in *The Picture
of Dorian Grey;* Nathaniel Hawthorne in *The Birthmark* and *The
Scarlet Letter;* Edgar Allan Poe in *William Wilson;* and Robert
Louis Stevenson in *The Strange Case of Dr. Jekyll and Mr. Hyde.*

Consider the double and the ruthless will activity of the
American settlers moving west—not, as a river of humanity, as
is often described in history books, but as a confluence of human
bulldozers. They allowed nothing to stop them. They could engage
in any action without being called to task. Mightily influenced by
Lucifer and Ahriman, the characteristics of these spiritual beings
represent two poles, each of which is detrimental in the extreme
but needed for the possibility of human freedom. Thus, inclinations
toward evil are present, whether consciously or subconsciously, in
every human being. It is the tripartite or middle ground where we
need to find our inner balance.

Lucifer:	Ahriman:
self-absorbed	self is irrelevant
ideas	ideology
frenzy	boredom
generalization	diversity
life is unimportant	life is too important
pulled from the Earth	pulled into the Earth
flaky/spaced out	anal retentive
seeker of spiritual truths	seeker of statistics
qualitative	quantitative
freedom becomes license	rules exist to be obeyed
lives in fantasy	lives in concrete reality
spiritually based cosmology	mathematical laws
soft and malleable	sclerotic
hazy light	cold shadows

Other ancient religions such as Manichaeism also are based on such polarities. In the ancient Gnostic religion of Manichaeism, one striking principle was dualism. Dualism is a view of life that proposes two principles are always at work in the universe. Mani postulated two natures that existed from the beginning: light and darkness. The realm of light lived in peace, whereas the realm of darkness was in constant battle with itself; the universe is the temporary result of an attack by the realm of darkness on the realm of light, created by the Living Spirit, an emanation of the light realm, out of the mixture of light and darkness. Manacheans viewed suffering as a manifestation of evil.

THE HUMAN BEING IN BETWEEN

Let us leave the realm of mythological and poetic imagery and veiled suggestions and consider a spiritual-scientific description of evil.[8]

Lucifer has his domain in the light above the surface of the Earth, while Ahriman has retreated to the darkness of the Earth's core. Humankind lives in the middle, on the Earth's surface. Thus, we have the polarity of supranature and subnature interacting through us (nature). One's individual soul is the battleground upon which those polarities meet. Our strengthened "I" becomes the decisive factor in how the uniqueness of our being represents those forces outwardly.

Our "I" being demands that we find our center so that we can establish ourselves properly in life. If we do not find the center, the "I" goes to the outside and appears as egotism, which opens us up to evil. We do not have to reach up to the supranatural world, but we cannot avoid the influences on us from the subnatural world.

Rudolf Steiner was interested in the evolution of the human being; he recognized the human being as both spiritual and physical, and he brought a pathway to train human thinking to Western civilization.[9] His published works on spiritual science provide exercises and activities that one can practice, out of freedom, to gain

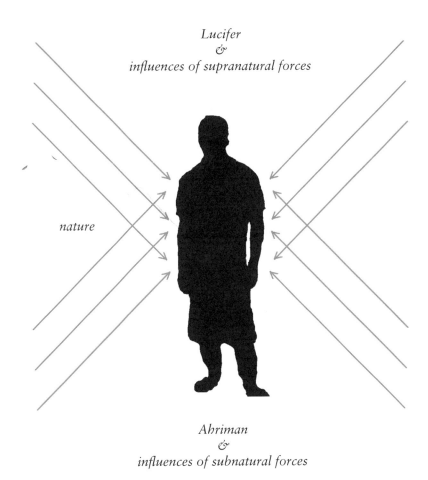

Lucifer
&
influences of supranatural forces

nature

Ahriman
&
influences of subnatural forces

higher perception. Individuals possessing such higher consciousness and its resultant loss of egotism are able to serve others.

As long as we remain within the limits of ordinary consciousness,
we retain memories of impressions of the world, but this is as far as
we can go. We receive impressions from the world, we transform
them into experiences through our senses and our understanding,
and they affect and imprint themselves upon our soul. As time
passes, we are able to recall pictures of what we have experienced.
Steiner says that this process acts as though we have a mirror deep
within our body. The pictures are held within us; they are the stage
setting for our inner life.

What lies behind that mirror, even deeper within our being? If we look behind the mirror, we might gain some insights. We see beyond the mirror by pausing our outer activity, by focusing on bringing harmonious regulation to our breathing, and by constructing meditative images that in turn release us from temporal existence. We can strive to reach the center of our being, or we can expand to the center of the universe by using meditative road maps described by Steiner in his books *Theosophy* and *How to Know Higher Worlds.*

From his spiritual research, Steiner describes how and why evil has been at work in human history, using not philosophical theories but facts. Such descriptions are not easy for most people to comprehend; one needs courage and imaginative self-knowledge. In his lecture "Suprasensory Aspects of Historical Research,"[10] Steiner points out that the inclination to all possible evil exists in every modern human being. "There is no crime, however dreadful, that we...do not have the propensity for. Whether this tendency actually leads to a crime or evil action in an individual case depends upon wholly different circumstances, not upon the propensity itself."[11]

Even when we are willing to see this, it may evade our recognition unless we can trace quickly the connection between great things and small ones, unless we can form pictures sufficiently vivid and mobile to illuminate them both. We could never form the concept "good" if we did not recognize its opposite concept, "evil."[12]

POLARITY AS A FUNDAMENTAL PRINCIPLE OF CREATION

A polarity is a pair of diametrically opposed principles, ideas, or qualities. We experience polarities all around us, in the rhythms of day and night, in sleep and consciousness, in birth and death, in illness and health, in the geocentric and heliocentric qualities in plant life, in the contraction and expansion in plant formation, and in gravity and dark energy.[13] ["When one force begins to work in the universe, another force, opposed to the first, arises at the same moment. Everything that happens in the world is subject to the law of polarity."[14] It is the overarching concept which is the fundamental principle of creation itself.[15] Polarity even exists in our thoughts. "The forces of polarity work through the human soul, the lowest as well as the highest."[16]

While studying at the university, the young man we met in the beginning of this chapter found guidance in the words Goethe gave to Faust:

> Two souls, alas, are housed within my breast,
> And each one will wrestle for the mastery there.
> The one has passion's craving lust for love,
> And hugs a world where sweet the senses rage;
> The other longs for pastures fair above,
> Leaving the murk for lofty heritage.[17]

"Man must reconcile the polarities which created him."[18] We could never form the concept "good" if the opposite concept were not known to us. In so doing we become the tripartite which is essential to every polarity, like the fulcrum to a seesaw at the playground.

The cosmos above us consists of light, and, like the heliotropic quality within plants, most of us are drawn to this realm in our spiritual seeking. It is comfortable to work in the light and to focus our prayers on the heavenly heights. Here we can also find the realm of white magic. This sphere has obvious influences on us even to the point of physical sensation during periods of atmospheric low-pressure systems or the smell of ozone in the air during a lightning storm.

The polarity of supranature is the dark sphere of the subnature or the subterranean realm. Usually we shun these forces. Yet they too influence our being. They rise to live in our subconscious as uncontrolled passions, hatred, animal-like urges, confusion to the point of chaos, and self-loathing. This dark realm is the realm of evil, and here we find the source of black magic.

Therefore, we must become acquainted with nature forces that exist within the Earth. A task in life for the spiritual seeker is to penetrate our inner being, not with head-forces but with heart-forces fructified and motivated by a moral will that leads us to a deeper, more profound wisdom about both ourselves and the world.

To penetrate the depths of our inner world of soul requires immense courage and truthfulness because the abyss of our own soul darkness is revealed, and we come face to face with all the beasts we may recognize from Matthias Grünewald's painting *The Temptation of Saint Anthony*.

Most people become afraid and retreat in the face the perils they find, preferring to stay on the surface of their consciousness and attend to the call of material life. This disembodies us, leaving us unable to relate fully to our own bodies. In the extreme, it can lead to cutting, piercing, and bodily mutilations practiced by some of today's youth.

For balanced self-development and spiritual research, the higher one's penetration reaches into the suprasensory, or spiritual, worlds, the deeper one's penetration and transformation must go into the sub-sensory, or subterranean, worlds; otherwise, one's spirituality assumes a dominant luciferic character. Therefore, it is time to pull up our moral socks, stand with both feet on the ground, and keep in mind that investigation into this realm can make us ill. When entering the dark realm to gain spiritual insight, we must also work diligently to armor ourselves in moral and ethical truthfulness.

The very existence of humankind in the age of modern civilization consists in receiving into ourselves the tendencies to evil. The poet W. H. Auden (1907–1973) said, "Evil is unspectacular and always human, / And shares our bed and eats at our own table." How does the Earth beneath us affect our soul life, if in fact it does? How can we introduce a new ecology based on a spiritual perception of the Earth?

Detail of The Temptation of Saint Anthony *by Matthias Günewald*
(photo by the author)

DEVELOPING A SENSE OF PLACE

Perhaps the first thing every human being needs to do in developing an understanding of the Earth's subterranean sphere is to gain a "sense of place" of where we are at the present moment on the Earth's surface. Does our place in geography affect us physically and spiritually? How does geography express living forces, and how can we become aware of these forces in our daily tasks as striving human beings? We can gain comprehension by developing an understanding and consciousness of the place where we live. We can study the physical land (geography, geology, mineralogy) to determine the physical character; the bioregion (botany, water,

influences of the light and warmth) to determine the etheric character; the cultural heritage (history, indigenous peoples, struggles
and wars, and the qualities of pleasure and pain) to determine the
astral character; and the question of human destiny (the biography of one's school or business, the influence of the double, and
questions coming from the future) to determine the "I" nature of
the place.[19]

When we transform our place of dwelling, we transform our
self at the same time. "When a person spiritualizes himself, he
spiritualizes the Earth as well"[20] By working through the research
on these four major topics, we can come to an imagination of
the being of our unique location. By developing consciousness of
this being, outer events will no longer surprise us. Rather, we will
be able to understand them in light of the greater whole. In this
way, we can use our consciousness to rise above the environmental
forces. (For more on the comparison between the living Earth and
the structure of the human being, see chapter 9 in Kees Zoeteman's
amazing book *Gaiasophy: The Wisdom of the Living Earth.*[21])

THE LIVING EARTH

Scientific thought has replaced superstition, the "old" religions,
and atavistic practices. The scientific revolution of the seventeenth
century asserted that nature is not a fallen orb, but an amoral,
unconscious entity to be studied, dissected, and understood if possible; thus, "ignorance" was to be eradicated through the knowledge acquired. Scientific thinking has led to ease and comfort in
our lives; it has released power from the Earth in the forms of gas,
petroleum, and electricity. Through science, we have penetrated
the atom to find infinitely small matter: neutrinos, quarks, and
other nano-particles. With the Hubble space telescope, we have
remarkable photographs of distant galaxies never seen before.[22]
Nevertheless, a great many questions remain unanswered, and
many scientific blunders, even catastrophic mistakes, have occurred.

Having gone to the boundaries of nothingness and the expanse of infinity, many heretofore-agnostic physicists are now returning to the question of God. Several physicists have suggested that it might even be possible to discover the ultimate laws of nature—what physicist Stephen Hawking calls "knowing the mind of God."

In his *The Tao of Physics,* Fritjof Capra describes the journey of physics as an essentially spiritual journey. "I was sitting by the ocean one late summer afternoon, watching the waves rolling in and feeling the rhythm of my breathing, when suddenly I became aware of my whole environment as being engaged in a gigantic cosmic dance."[23]

Few physicians in the twentieth century have been able to bridge the gap between science and literature as well as Lewis Thomas (1913–1993), who wrote, "The greatest of all the accomplishments of twentieth-century science has been the discovery of human ignorance."[24]

Carlos Castaneda (1925–1998) wrote a series of books that purport to describe his training in traditional Mesoamerican shamanism. His controversial and popular works, which describe practices that enable increased awareness, spoke of areas of the Earth that emanated power to him (chthonic forces). Perhaps many of us who love the wilderness can extol certain geographic points that we return to frequently and experience as "powerspots." Nature does indeed have the power to give us strength and renewal, which is why we travel to the mountains and seashore for our restorative vacations.

James Lovelock views the Earth as a self-regulating, living being and defines life as "an open and continuous system that is able to lower its internal entropy, a measurement of chaos in a system, at the cost of free energy which is taken from the environment.[25] Life can only exist as an open system which receives the energy required for life from the outside—in our case from the Sun."

Far from being the lifeless product of past chemical and mechanical actions, as modern science describes it, the Earth is alive and filled with soul and spirit, just as one's physical body is worth much more than the value of ingredients as determined by a chemist. The trace quantities of fluorine, silicon, manganese, zinc, copper, aluminum, and arsenic together amount to less than one dollar. Our most valuable asset is our skin, which the Japanese invested their time and money in measuring: our fourteen-to-eighteen square feet of skin is worth about $3.50. The full monetary value of the body amounts to $5.00. On the black market body organs, DNA, bone marrow (the most valuable, at present), stem cells, and antibodies dramatically raise the total value to $45 million.[26] It makes us shudder to think of the human body as a farm for salable commodities, but we frequently think of the Earth in this way.

The Earth is more than minerals and ores to be harvested. The Earth breathes through the seasons; the atmosphere is replenished; and the air circulates. About 1.9 miles above the Earth, there are atmospheric rivers—five in each hemisphere—420 to 480 miles wide and 4,800 miles long, from equator to the poles. Many different gases make up the air we breathe. They are invisible. Similarly, spiritual forces are all around us, but we do not perceive them unless we have developed clairvoyant vision. Spiritual forces imbue the Earth itself.

The scientific paradigm is shifting. We have come near the end of facts. There is significant evidence that we are destroying the planet we live on. Is it time now to explore a different, more spiritually based phenomenological thinking?[27] The state of the Earth and the condition of humanity cry out for something new to serve a healthy evolution of both the Earth and her inhabitants. Goethe stated that it is in the anomaly that the archetype can be revealed. Without devaluing the old wisdom or depreciating the strides of modern science, today's humanity needs to penetrate Rudolf Steiner's spiritual science and revolutionary ideas. "At the core, they offer a new understanding of evil and its role in human evolution and a more comprehensive picture of the human being, a more profound concept of the Earth."[28]

Steiner contends that spirit permeates all matter. It permeates the human being; it permeates nature; and it permeates the Earth upon which we evolve. Neither the Earth nor human beings are physically immortal; because we live, we must die. Our human body serves us in life because it includes death among its processes; likewise, the Earth serves humanity and planetary evolution because it embodies destructive forces. The fact of death allows us to become conscious beings. Nonetheless, people generally see nothing holy in death, but consider it a curse imposed by force; we simply must endure it. People expect to go through death kicking and screaming while holding onto life.

Goethe wisely stated, "Nature invented death in order to have so much life."[29] Steiner said that the Earth's dying is a necessary tragedy. Moreover, the solar system needs a healthy Earth to fulfill its destiny. Our present task is to insure that the Earth does not die prematurely. Global warming occurs when the Earth's biosphere is diseased by its digestion; humankind must learn to develop more in harmony with the essence of the Earth.

Al Gore proclaimed, "The Earth warming is a moral crisis—it cannot be solved with concepts." We might think that our mechanical and physical excesses harm the atmosphere, but our lack of spiritual discipline does far more harm. The Earth has a spiritual task to evolve regardless of human evolution. Each, however, can retard the evolution of the other. Human beings have now become responsible for the evolution of the Earth, and that is because, through our freedom, we have developed Earth consciousness.

Natural science has met its limits in some areas. Our knowledge of how the Earth's interior formed is incomplete. Much of that knowledge, which comes largely from speculation and assumptions based on seismic-wave reflections, is frequently redefined.

Recent scientific findings about the interior of the Earth include:

- The continental plates rest atop a magma sea. In the October 1997 issue of Scientific American, geophysicists acknowledged that, at the center of our Earth, there is a spinning crystalline structure the size of the Moon. Immense pressure on the inner core has solidified the iron and caused it to take on a hexagonal crystal form, which has inherent directional, physical properties. Some unknown force seems to keep all the hexagonal iron crystals in close alignment. The single gargantuan crystal is more than 1,491 miles across. The internal stress caused by the Earth's rotation is strongest along the north-south axis. Thus, the hexagonal iron that constitutes the inner core could crystallize in parallel with the spin axis, as do mica flakes that form in rocks squeezed by tectonic forces. The tumultuous churning of the outer core's liquid iron creates the magnetic field, but the inner solid core is needed for proper stability.[30]

- In 2007, scientists reported a giant blob of water the size of the Arctic Ocean, hundreds of miles beneath eastern Asia. Researchers found the underground "ocean" while scanning seismic waves passing through the Earth's interior.

- Researchers have found evidence of bacteria thriving in volcanic rocks more than 4,000 feet below the island of Hawaii. They also found DNA and RNA, the two molecules needed for life. Both showed little or no degradation, demonstrating that these tiny organisms have been active recently, possibly even on the day the sample was taken from the drill hole.[31]

At astonishing depths within the Earth, researchers recently found endoliths (organisms that live inside rock or in the tiny pores between interlocking mineral grains), which eat rock. Thousands of different species have been found, including representatives of bacteria, archaea, and fungi. Endoliths have been found inhabiting the Earth's crust at depths up to nearly two miles, far from

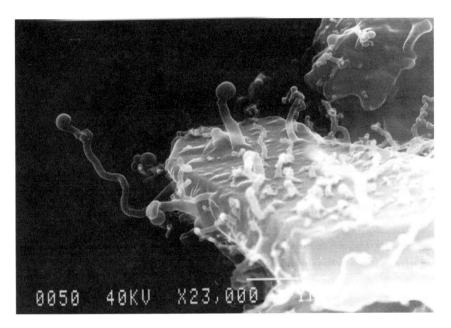

Dr. Philippa Uwins found nanobe structures in Australian sandstones.
(Photo courtesy of Philippa Uwins and the Nanoworld Image Gallery.)

sunlight. Owing to the costs of digging so deeply into the Earth, it is unknown whether they live at deeper levels. They appear to survive by feeding on traces of iron, potassium, or sulfur. Whether they metabolize these directly from the surrounding rock or excrete an acid to dissolve them first is also unknown. Many endoliths are autotrophs, organisms that generate organic compounds needed to survive independently of inorganic matter. Others may incorporate inorganic compounds found in the rock substrate, possibly by excreting acids to dissolve the rock. Such organisms have a very slow procreation cycle, since water and nutrients are sparse in the endolithic environment. Early data suggests that some engage in cell division only once every hundred years. Most of their energy is spent repairing cell damage caused by cosmic rays. Many are autotrophs, while other varieties feed on the organic substances produced by the autotrophs, giving rise to microscopic underground communities known as SLiME (Subsurface Lithotrophic Microscopic Environments).

Imperfections and impurities determine many of the "interesting" properties of minerals and rocks. Rubies, sapphires and other gems, for example, derive their colors from chemical impurities.[32]

- Under a microscope, slices of rock known to be some of the oldest have revealed the remains of former living organisms.

- The magnificent gorge of the awe-inspiring Grand Canyon is but a mere scratch on the Earth's surface; it may be compared to a fingernail scratch on glass. We have drilled gas and oil wells, but even the deepest are mere pinpricks in the Earth's mantle. Near Murmansk on the Kola Peninsula, Russians attempted to drill a super-deep "Mohole," a hole through the Mohorovic Discontinuity, the layer that separates the crust from the upper mantle. It is a ten-mile hole into the Earth's crust in search of answers to conflicting questions. After nineteen years, Project Mohole was halted, having achieved a depth of only 7.5 miles. The data gathered are contrary to many longstanding assumptions by geologists. For example, temperature increased with depth more dramatically than anticipated; a body of ore was located at a depth where none was thought to exist; and fluids and gasses, including hydrocarbons, were found circulating through the rocks of the crust at depths where high pressure would hypothetically rule out cracks and fissures in the bedrock. Had the project been completed, the Mohole would have examined only one four-hundredth of the distance to the center of the Earth. Inevitably and clearly, our understanding of the Earth's interior is far more a matter of conjecture than knowledge.[33]

- Much of what we "know" about the Earth's interior has been inferred. The interior of the Earth is not a "solid" as we understand the term, but in a semi-plastic state that allows ions to migrate (more or less) at will.[34]

The dream of many geologists is to observe the Earth's interior directly. They yearn to see the churning in the core that generates the Earth's magnetic field; to take temperatures below the mantle; to probe the roots of continents; and to understand the true makeup of the Earth. The reality, however, is that science knows relatively little about the makeup of the Earth's interior.

Our so-called knowledge of the Earth's interior is based on physical and mechanical extrapolations. "It is becoming clear that Earth's interior is rich in complexity," said Edward Garnero of Arizona State University. "Earthquakes, volcanoes, and large pieces of Earth's outermost layer or 'plates' slowly move, grinding and shifting. All of these point to a dynamic system within the planet."[35]

If we can consider the Earth to be alive, what are its spiritual realities? To investigate this, one needs to develop clairvoyant capacities or rely on the spiritual observations of someone like Rudolf Steiner, who possessed such capacities. First, however, we must heed his advice: "Penetration into the subterranean realms without moral and spiritual development leads only to acquaintance with the most destructive forces."[36] We must be morally prepared to enter into the subterranean worlds. If we are not, insanity can be the result. The gesture of morality is the seed of the human being, the "I AM." Whereas it is relatively easy to gain clairvoyant awareness of the astral and devachanic planes, another kind of initiation is needed to explore the interior of the Earth.

THE SUBTERRANEAN SPHERES IN THE INTERIOR OF THE EARTH

The Earth is the arena of human existence. On Earth, we stand between two opposite poles. Above are the heavenly spheres, which radiate forces connected with everything calculable and orderly in earthly existence—the regularity of the ocean's tides, the alternation of day and night, and the passage of the four seasons. The other pole radiates from the center of the Earth, and what lives there is chaotic. "Wind, weather, thunder and lightning, earthquakes, and volcanic eruptions—they are all reflections of what takes place in the interior of the Earth."[37]

As we bring the following observations into our imagination, we must try not to think of physical substance and instead picture the descriptions of a spiritual investigator describing qualities of soul concentrations in the Earth's inner layers. "We must think of the Earth as consisting of a series of layers not completely separated from one another, like the skins of an onion, but that merge gradually into one another," says Steiner.[38] The Earth mediates between supranatural and mechanical laws.

The following illustration from the Harvard Seismology Lab shows its three-dimensional seismic tomographic study (like a CAT scan) of the Earth. To see how the layers interpenetrate one another from a physical perspective,[39] when we look at heat convection moving upward from the Earth's center, we see that a huge plume seems to feed a spread at the East Pacific Rise directly from the core. Most of the heat released from the interior of the Earth emerges at the fast-spreading East Pacific.

Steiner's spiritual investigations show, in esoteric terms, that the solidified Earth consists of nine soul layers that merge into one another, perhaps in a way similar to this image. Each layer has a distinct effect on humankind; as we approach the center, farthest from the sun, their effects become more malevolent.[40] However, human evolution offers the possibility that human beings can transform the center of the Earth and spiritualize it.

In the interest of clarity, I have recast the names for the nine layers to reflect spiritual rather than physical properties. Moving inward, they can be characterized as follows:[41]

1. **Spiritual-binding Layer:** This layer acts like a rigid membrane to hold in all of the spiritual forces in the eight layers beneath

Image from the Harvard University Seismology Lab

it. This is where the forces within mineral substances and ores exist. It holds the Earth's will forces. From this layer humankind has released the subnatural forces of electricity, magnetism, and radioactive radiation. Modern science is most concerned with this realm. This layer is relatively thin and can be penetrated by the forces from below.

2. **Spiritual-viscous Layer**: This is relatively glutinous in a spiritual, but not a physical, sense. Steiner called it the "life layer," or soft earth, where substance begins to have spiritual characteristics. It is actually a polarity to life—spiritually, this layer always wants to expand and take over, even destroy the essence we refer to as life (as opposed to our physical body of bone and tissue). This layer would spiritually consume or repel everything; it has powerful expansive forces, yet a defined boundary. It exists only because it is held in place by tremendous pressure.

3. **Spiritual-awareness Layer:** This layer is full of spiritual forces. Steiner referred to this layer as the vapor earth or steam earth. Contrary to the second layer's inclination to shatter, this layer is contained throughout. It is the layer of inverted consciousness, and soul astrality is transformed into its counter-pole. Here joy is experienced as sorrow and pain is felt as pleasure. All feeling sensations are extinguished and transformed into their opposite.

4. **Spiritual-reversed Astral Layer:** This layer consists of spiritual substance that cannot be perceived with outer senses since they are all in an astral state. Here physical objects are given negative images. The spiritual-reversed astral layer materializes everything that has happened spiritually in devachan. Steiner referred to this layer as form earth or water earth. Here, the counterpart to everything that happens in the spirit realm is transformed into its opposite while the original is left empty.

5. **Spiritual-harvest Layer:** This layer fairly bursts with exuberant spiritual energy and expansive growth such that spiritual forces multiply vigorously and are kept in check only by the layers above it. It contains soul as well as the archetypal source for all terrestrial life. Here we find the spiritual seed of life in its most original state. Steiner called this level the fruit earth, seed earth, or growth earth. If it were to reach the surface of the Earth unfettered it would reproduce madly and then vanish into the cosmos.

6. **Spiritual-passion Layer:** This layer is composed of pure, spiritual will forces in constant motion. It is the seat of passion, the fount of all pleasure and pain. Steiner referred to this layer as fire earth, or passion earth. It is a highly sensitive zone and the source of extreme, unharnessed passions. It holds everything that exists as drives and instincts. According to Steiner, this area reacts strongly to excesses of human will. It can burst via channels to the zones above it, transforming spiritual forces into physical forces such as earthquakes,

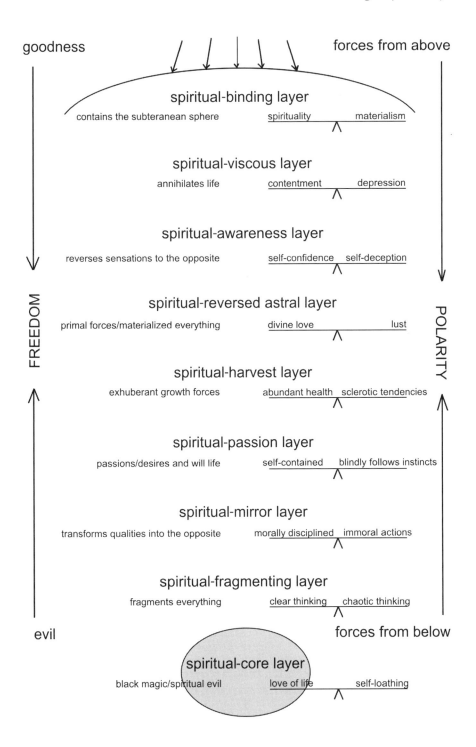

goodness — forces from above

spiritual-binding layer
contains the subteranean sphere — spirituality — materialism

spiritual-viscous layer
annihilates life — contentment — depression

spiritual-awareness layer
reverses sensations to the opposite — self-confidence — self-deception

spiritual-reversed astral layer
primal forces/materialized everything — divine love — lust

spiritual-harvest layer
exhuberant growth forces — abundant health — sclerotic tendencies

spiritual-passion layer
passions/desires and will life — self-contained — blindly follows instincts

spiritual-mirror layer
transforms qualities into the opposite — morally disciplined — immoral actions

spiritual-fragmenting layer
fragments everything — clear thinking — chaotic thinking

evil — forces from below

spiritual-core layer
black magic/spiritual evil — love of life — self-loathing

FREEDOM

POLARITY

tsunamis, and volcanic eruptions. To overcome the spiritual-passion level, human beings can train their breathing in a way that promotes life. Ahriman predominates in this layer, in the eighth layer, and in the ninth layer. In terms of the spiritual hierarchies, Ahriman is an exusiai who now works as an archai. The consequences of his spiritual presence envelope the whole Earth and the Moon.

The rays that link the core at the center of the Earth with the surface connect the various layers. A great number of subterranean cavities are linked to the sixth, or spiritual-passion, layer.

7. **Spiritual-mirror Layer:** Like a mirror, this level transforms all spiritual qualities into their inverse. Steiner called this layer the earth-reflector layer. It reverses everything spiritual on Earth to a negative, reversed form, much like a prism splits and refracts. Here we find all the forces of nature, but transformed in spirit. Like magnetism, this is an inorganic effect. An emerald, for example, would appear red in the spiritual-mirror layer.

In this layer, we meet the counter-principle of the divine "I" being. The reversed god, mentioned earlier, is most active when sowing confusion in thinking. The action in this layer projects distortion and illusion on Earth; problems that human beings encounter are shifted to where they do not belong, the result of which is false analysis, imprecise synthesis, and erroneous conclusions.

8. **Spiritual-fragmenting Layer:** This layer brings the substance of evil up into the world. Spiritually, it projects unhappiness, dispute, disharmony, hatred, and division among nations and people on Earth. The school of Pythagoras named it the "number creator sphere," because it endlessly multiplies all single entities. We can understand its basic gesture by contemplating fractals and the Mandelbrot set.[42] Consider the inner laws that create similar leaves throughout an elm tree, in contrast to a

maple tree or a Ponderosa Pine. They hold onto and reproduce the same form.

Steiner called this layer the slicer, "dismemberer," or splintering level. It fragments everything of a moral nature. In the Bible, Cain slew his brother Abel, and with this act evil manifested on Earth. The word Cain means "individual thinker" or "expert." It appears in the names of legendary blacksmiths: Vulcan (Vul-Cain) and Thubalcain, the master smith of brass and iron. (Thubalcain is also the secret code and name of a Freemason handshake.)

Also called the "explosive" Earth, we can witness its power in the persuasive speeches by such demagogues as Hitler, Mussolini, and, on a smaller scale, Charles Manson. This layer exists so that human beings will have to develop peace and harmony for themselves and thereby neutralize the forces projected by the fragmenting level.

9. **Spiritual-core Layer**: This central layer functions as the seat of power of spiritual evil. Ahriman has retreated to this innermost dark place in the Earth, the most inaccessible for human thought to penetrate, according to Steiner. This may be because Ahriman directs his activity primarily toward human cognition. Steiner stated that the spiritual-core layer contains two great mysteries: First, we can compare it to the human brain and heart as the domain of the Earth's planetary spirit. Second, it is the source of power for spiritual evil as well as the forces that lead to black magic.

The origin of all disruptions and destruction lies in the subnatural regions. For every heavenly force, there is a subterranean polarforce. Now is the time for all spiritual seekers to work with the forces that stream toward us from below with the same earnestness with which they accept the blessings that radiate from above. Evil exists in every one of us by necessity, and the interior of the Earth influences our nature to a remarkable degree, although we

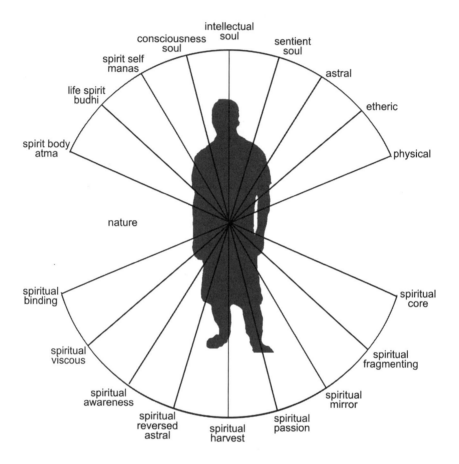

SUPRANATURE

intellectual
soul

consciousness
soul

sentient
soul

spirit self
manas

astral

life spirit
budhi

etheric

spirit body
atma

physical

nature

spiritual
binding

spiritual
core

spiritual
viscous

spiritual
fragmenting

spiritual
awareness

spiritual
mirror

spiritual
reversed
astral

spiritual
harvest

spiritual
passion

SUBNATURE

may be unaware of this in daily life. We must heed Steiner when he says, "Our age needs knowledge that rises above nature, because it must deal inwardly with a dangerous life content that has sunk below nature."[43] We must also acknowledge that the Earth has a planetary karma to fulfill, and human beings must not accelerate or hinder this evolution. As Steiner warns, "We must realize that a universal karmic law operates at every level of existence, over and above the karma that belongs to every individual human being."[44]

Questions such as, "Why does God allow bad things to happen to good people?" and, "Why does God allow suffering?" are
merely temporal and sentimental. Once we understand the need
for such polarities in human and earthly evolution, we will not ask
such questions. Instead, we will see how God has provided both
goodness and evil so that we can determine our own destiny in
freedom.

SUBNATURE AND ENERGY:
ELECTRICITY AND PETROLEUM

The destiny of North America is connected with the ultimate mastery of force. In our modern world, America experiences the destiny of force—whether economic, military, or technological—as its
own. This force arose from the conquest of the continent's aggressive and resistant geography. The land imbues those who live on it
with certain qualities. North America's nature and its landscape
are not soft or comfortable, but offer opposition. The land fosters
a pioneering spirit and inspires such human characteristics as courage, tenacity, perseverance, and self-reliance. It also evokes reck-
lessness, thoughtlessness, and ruthlessness.

Force requires strengthening the will life. We experience the
will of North Americans through the many scientific discoveries
made on this continent—most strikingly through the history of
electricity and its technical applications. It would be shortsighted
to discuss the subterranean forces without considering the sub-
forces of electricity and magnetism, which are especially strong in
North America. The Earth's magnetic north pole is in the Western
Hemisphere in northwestern America, which makes North America
the electromagnetic continent. This predisposed human minds
there to discover the secrets of magnetism and electricity and other
forces of the physical, material world.

Electricity is the Earth's light, the opposite of sunlight. It is
generated by the combustion of coal, gas, and oil, which are forced

to reveal their hidden light. Electricity is the force derived from matter. In the human organism, electricity is connected with the physiological processes behind activities of the will. No muscle movement is possible without electrical current, nor is breathing or beating of the heart. Normally, we regulate the electricity within us, the result of which is movement.

Magnetism also seems to be connected with brain activity. In his experiments with mediums, Paul de Rochas found that, through the application of a magnet, the thoughts of one person can be conveyed to another. Commercial catalogs throughout North America today offer magnet-equipped pads, belts, and shoe inserts, all claiming to redirect the body's energy and relieve pain.[45]

Static electricity, which occurs in low humidity, is the phenomenon of stationary electric shocks produced by friction. Static electricity is especially prevalent in North America. It is so plentiful in Washington, DC, that many federal office buildings employ rubber door handles to prevent shocks.

Salt ions in the human body create electrical forces that permeate the nervous system. These salts, imbued with elemental forces, originally come from the Earth.

The deepest basement rock of the North American continent's crust is in the Granite Gorge, Grand Canyon, Arizona, and bears an inspired name: Zoroaster granite, named for the first to name Ahriman as the destructive prince of darkness.

The Earth produces forces that can overwhelm us and create imbalances if we do not meet those forces with wakeful consciousness. An electric shock is aggressive and can shake and contort our muscles and limbs. Electricity also has an esoteric quality that emerges from hidden depths of nature, filled with tension and potential violence. Liberated from subnature, electricity gave rise to new technologies and changed human life on Earth. Michael Faraday (1791–1867) linked magnetism to electricity and studied the magnetic field around a conductor carrying direct current, thus establishing the basis for a magnetic field concept in physics and the electric motor. Thomas Edison (1847–1931) arranged a delicate carbon filament in a vacuum and produced incandescent light. Thus, subnature was harnessed for technology.

We can experience electricity directly as a force, though we cannot understand it easily through the concepts of ordinary experience. Radiations of the atomic world are even less accessible. As with Edison's light bulb, they emerged into direct physical appearance as a new light—a light of terrifying intensity and power that first spread across the desert of New Mexico in July 1945 with the first detonation of an atomic bomb. Its overwhelming power led Robert Oppenheimer, the scientific director of the project, to quote a phrase from the Bhagavad Gita: "I am become Death, the shatterer of worlds."[46]

Petroleum raises different and very contemporary questions. Because it takes millions of years to form, we call petroleum a nonrenewable energy source. A fossil fuel, it formed from the remains of organisms that died millions of years ago. We find petroleum in porous rock formations in the upper strata of certain areas of the Earth's crust, and owing to its high energy density, it has become the world's most important source of energy since the mid-1950s. Oil wells average five thousand feet deep and may eventually go below twenty thousand feet.

In his 2006 State of the Union address, President George W. Bush proclaimed, "America is addicted to oil, which is often imported from unstable parts of the world." He announced that it was time for the United States to "move beyond a petroleum-based economy and make our dependence on Middle Eastern oil a thing of the past." His stated goal was "to replace more than seventy-five percent of our oil imports from the Middle East by 2025."[47] The growing scarcity of petroleum in the world is leading to increasing war and violence, making it a substance with "evil" inclinations.

> Where do the wars and where do the conflicts among you
> come from? Is it not from your passions that make war within

your members? You covet but do not possess. You kill and envy but you cannot obtain; you fight and wage war. You do not possess because you do not ask. You ask but do not receive, because you ask wrongly, to spend it on your passions. (James 4:1–3)

Many of the materials we use daily—dyes, antiseptics, plastics, pharmaceuticals, and perfumes—contain compounds derived from coal, yet another product mined from the Earth's crust. Even nylon stockings come from a transformation of coal; nylon was the first commercially successful polymer and the first synthetic fiber made entirely from coal, water, and air. Saccharine, an artificial sweetener, comes from coal tar derivatives. "Fashion" and "artificial sweetness" owe fealty to subnature.

The Need to Achieve Balance

This chapter describes the quality of evil and explains that it is needed in human life so that we can live in freedom and decide how to balance the uprising forces from the Earth. Owen Barfield commented, "Mechanical causality has reduced man himself, man the spirit, to a kind of zero. But by the very fact of doing so, it had made him free."[48] Human evolution implies a transformation of the spiritual forces streaming from the Earth's interior. We are here on Earth because there is a mineral Earth and because there are the subterranean spheres. The upward rush of forces from the abyss is in full swing, and the counter-realm of subnature is active among us.

We are "shells" inasmuch as we remain only in the life of ideas; once we sever ourselves from nature, all we can do is talk about her. However, those who penetrate their own inner "kernel" and experience the very center of their soul will discover that they are also in the very innermost of nature; they are experiencing nature's inner being.

Nature is neither kernel nor shell,
She is both in one, she is one and all.
Look in your own heart, man, and tell
If you yourself are kernel or shell!
                                        — Goethe[49]

To balance our self-development and spiritual research, the higher we penetrate the suprasensory spiritual worlds, the deeper we must penetrate and transform the sub-sensory, subterranean worlds. With each new level we ascend, we must consciously descend as well to maintain the balance of the middle. Our task is to acquire the strength of spirit to transform the forces from the subterranean realms into benevolent, healing impulses. Human beings facilitate the Earth's evolutionary process. After we die, we leave behind transformed forces created by our actions on Earth. Those changes are the result of developing the human individuality. Human beings are the media through which extrasensory forces continually seep into the physical world. Written just before his death, Steiner said:

> By far, the greater part of what functions in modern civiliza-
> tion through technology and industry, within which human
> life is so intensely woven, is not nature at all, but subnature.
> It is a world that emancipates itself from nature, emancipates
> itself in a downward direction.... Human beings needed this
> relationship with the purely earthly to unfold the spiritual
> soul. Thus, in the most recent times, a strong tendency has
> arisen to realize in everything, and even in the activities of
> life, the element into which human beings must enter for their
> evolution. Entering the purely earthly element, we encoun-
> ter the ahrimanic realm. With our own being, we must now
> acquire the right relationship to the ahrimanic.[50]

Nevertheless, in this age of technology, finding a true relationship to the ahrimanic master plan has eluded us. We must find
the strength, the inner force of knowledge, to avoid domination
by the subterranean forces in our technical civilization. We must

try to understand subnature for what it really is. We cannot do this unless we rise in spiritual knowledge at least as far into extra-earthly supranature, as we have descended in technical sciences into subnature. Our age requires knowledge that transcends nature; its inner life must come to grips with a life that has sunk far beneath nature and whose intention is dangerous.

What do we enter when we are immersed in physical pain, mental anguish, and spiritual listlessness? Is suffering a substance in the world? Nothing deepens the soul as much as suffering does. In suffering, a person has to grow inwardly, and this leads to the formation of a fruit that has the quality of multiplying. Experiences wrought in pain endure. Through concentration, we deepen our experience so that it remains part of us—not just as a fleeting mood, but present in our consciousness. This consciousness is wisdom.

The harvest of suffering and pain is concentration, deepening, inwardness, and finally individualized experience. The pain that Christ suffered at the end of his ministry was inconceivably great. Because of his suffering, he became profoundly great. Through his sacrifice, renunciation, and contraction he could approach every pain with an attitude that says, "I know this at a deeper level, this is not new to me. I have gone through this at more intense levels, and my spirit has survived." Christ suffered in total freedom. He could have escaped but chose not to; he was selfless and pure for the sake of humanity and the Earth. Generally, we try to avoid suffering; but when we willingly take on evil and recognize the necessity of suffering, it transforms us, becomes fruitful, and leads to a spiritual metamorphosis of pain. The poet Novalis said, "Out of pain the new world will be born." The meaning of Christ's ministry on Earth may very well be to teach us how to endure pain and allow it to transform us. "The Passion of Christ is not redemption from suffering, but redemption to suffering, the womb for the birth of the new human."[51]

Another powerful phenomenon of Christ's mission was his descent into the subterranean worlds after the crucifixion ("the

harrowing of Hell," or *Sheol* in Hebrew and *Hades* in Greek).
For us, this descent is a powerful representation of life "in the
in-between." The final phase of his mission on Earth was, indeed,
a supreme event. It was prefigured in the lives of several gods
and semi-divine heroes of antiquity: Osiris, Horus, Isis, Ishtar,
Demeter, Hercules, Theseus, and Orpheus, all of whom descended
into subnature. Some of the apocryphal gospels describe Christ
vividly storming Hades and vanquishing its ruling powers. The key
passages of Scripture that speak of Christ's descent into the subterranean realm are Colossians 2:15 and 1 Peter 3:18,19, as well as
the Apocryphal Gospel of Nicodemus and the "Apostle's Creed,"
which was once considered throughout Christendom as equal to
the Bible itself.

> And, behold, suddenly Hades trembled, and the gates of
> death and the bolts were shattered, and the iron bars were
> broken and fell to the ground, and everything was laid open.
> And Satan remained in the midst, and stood confounded and
> downcast, bound with fetters on his feet. And, behold, the
> Lord Jesus Christ, coming in the brightness of light from
> on high, compassionate, great, and lowly, carrying a chain
> in His hand, bound Satan by the neck; and again tying his
> hands behind him, dashed him on his back into Tartarus.
> (Nicodemus, 16, 19)

Christ's purpose was threefold. First, he sought to redeem the
earthly karma of human souls. Second, he sought to bring redemption to the living Earth for the evil it had to harbor. An image of
this is Christ saving the souls of those who were doomed there for
eternity. Third, he sought to prepare the eventual assault to over-
throw death and Hell, which will come at the end of time.

According to the Gnostic view, Christ's redemptive mission did
not begin on Earth, nor is it confined to humankind. His mission
began when evil began, and his work on Earth is part of a longer,
drawn-out work of salvation. When he came onto the Earth, he
came to fulfill a specific mission for every form of creation—for the

Earth itself, the fallen angels, the eons, the archons, human beings, and so on, down the hierarchy of beings. He goes to other worlds in the remotest spheres of the universe to heal. In the Naassene Psalm, Christ says, "All the worlds shall I journey through, all the mysteries unlock."

The Gospel of Philip states that Christ always revealed himself in a way that all would be able to see and understand. To the great, he appears great; and to the small, he is small; to the infirm he is a healer. To the immature, he appears as a youth, and to the mature, he appears as a sage. To all, he is a teacher who teaches us how to endure and transform pain.

On Palm Sunday, many churches sing the hymn "Lord of the Dance":

> I danced on a Friday and the sky turned black;
> It's hard to dance with the devil on your back;
> They buried my body and they thought I'd gone,
> But I am the dance and I still go on.

Now, in the twenty-first century, we certainly need a mood that is not trivial, one that can lift us out of muddy obsession and despair. Returning to Christopher Fry's play, we hear Meadow say:

> Affairs are now soul size.
> The enterprise
> Is exploration into God.
> Where are you making for? It takes
> So many thousand years to wake,
> But will you wake for pity's sake?

A wise person once said that if you looked from space onto the dark Earth, you would see spots of light shining where individuals inwardly strive to overcome and transform evil forces emanating from the Earth, and that as long as this striving continues in a few places, humanity would be allowed to go on. When white magic triumphs, no more evil will remain on Earth.

Chapter 2

As Above, so Below — as Below, so Above

Dennis Klocek

THE ALCHEMICAL MANTRA "AS above so below, as below so above" comes from the Emerald Tablet of Hermes Trismegistus, the ancient alchemical adept. It refers to the penetration of the dense Earth with a cosmic principle and then the resurrection of the cosmos from the Earth in an ascending path of evolution. We can link this image to another, known in Christian literature as "the harrowing of Hell."

For St. John Chrysostom, the harrowing of Hell describes the most essential part of Christian faith: Hell took a body and discovered God; it took Earth, and encountered Heaven. It took what it saw and was overcome by what it did not see. "O death, where is thy sting? O Hell, where is thy victory?" (John Chrysostom's Paschal homily). The idea is that after the Crucifixion, Jesus Christ, who has come to Earth from the Cosmos, must go as far as possible from God into the very deepest layers of Hell. Even in Hell, the Cosmic Christ is still God, serving the Father by penetrating the depths of the dark Earth with the light of Heaven and transforming that darkness forever. The darkest center, then, has a core of gold that is the potential for the Earth to become a star. Whether it actually becomes a star in a moral and progressive way depends on human beings to repeat the harrowing of Hell in our own lives. Then the dark center will become entirely gold.

In these images, we find clues to the incredibly subtle Pythagorean and Rosicrucian teachings given by Rudolf Steiner early in his career regarding the subterranean spheres. The approach presented in this chapter aims to link the zones in the Earth's body, as penetrated by the descent of the Christ through the subterranean spheres, with the current divisions of the atmosphere as seen by natural science. The comparisons will be an aid to a broader conversation about these ideas.

The complexity, scarcity, and extreme subtlety of Steiner's descriptions of these phenomena provide the researcher with few concrete indications. This is a problem, on one hand, and, on the other, a prod for the researcher to move courageously into uncharted waters. These ideas move arguably into unknown areas and beg indulgence on the part of the perceptive reader, since they actually represent a series of questions rather than a definitive answer.

The fundamental form of this survey comes from an analysis of the upper atmosphere in the context of the concept of the elements and the ethers. It seemed that the layers of the atmosphere described in current science appear to be organized along the lines of divisions between the elements and the ethers as described by Rudolf Steiner.

Figure 1: Lucifer / Ahriman and the elements

As an introduction to these concepts, figure 1 shows a division of the elements suggested by Rudolf Steiner related to the areas of influence of Lucifer and Ahriman. The four elements of alchemical thought are earth, water, air, and fire. These are not the chemical elements of the periodic table. The terms refer instead to patterns of activity shared by many diverse phenomena. Earth refers to any form of precipitation out of a less-dense state. It could refer with equal ease to the precipitation of a concept in the mind of a thinker, to the formation of a fetus out of the waters of the womb, or to the deposition of a salt crystal out of a saturated solution. Fire, by contrast, is every process in which something formed moves from a dense state into a finer, more rarefied state and eventually moves so far that it cannot regain its former condition. Death, when the spirit leaves the body, is a fire process, as is the process of fruit and seed formation in a plant.

In the realm of consciousness, fire is the state wherein a thinker moves consciously into the realms of unknowing as an integral part of a meditative practice. It is the state in which the focus of the mind is complete, and the content of the focus is the activity of the focusing mind. This kind of self-awareness is the fire of the Kama Loca experience after death.

Earth and fire are polarities in the four-element theory. In Steiner's work, they are the precise realm of the work of Ahriman. In the diagram, we see that fire and earth are linked to Ahriman's influence. Symbolically, we could say that Ahriman presides over the processes whereby the celestial holy fire falls into an ash or corpse. This is his function as the Prince of the Earth. His kingdom is made of the ashes of what were once fiery celestial understandings in the minds of those beings who serve the creator as world creators who carry out the plan of the creation. It is useful to make such a distinction when trying to study Steiner's teachings about the subterranean spheres.

In the diagram, we see that Lucifer influences a whole other set of elemental forces: air and water. To an alchemist, and even to a chemist, air is rarefied water. According to electron shell theory, water is a compound of two very ephemeral elemental gasses. The shift from the denser state of water to the more rarefied state of gas involves the participation of the fire element, though it produces no ash. Water rarifies into air and condenses again into water, and there is no perceptible ash left over. The flow from air to water and back is the special domain of Lucifer. Steiner tells us that Lucifer separated from the other hierarchies (air and water), whereas Ahriman made the soul deed of Lucifer fall into the ash of matter (fire to earth). The polarity between the spheres of influence of these two beings provides a useful concept we will use later in this article, when we examine implications for the action of the subterranean spheres in relation to current soul dilemmas in the realm of the climate.

Our central idea of this article (as above so below; as below so above) is that the layering of the atmosphere above our heads is a polar reflection of the activity in the subterranean layers as described by Steiner. The purpose is to stimulate thinking in a way that will expand the possibilities for understanding these difficult but very important concepts. Comments are mostly in the form of comparing Steiner's statements on the subterranean layers and those of current science on the layers of the atmosphere.

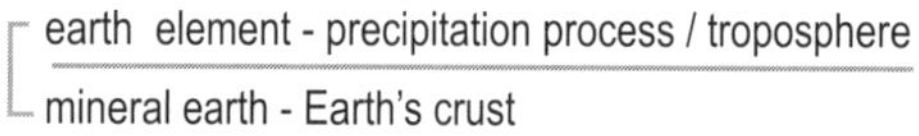

⌈ earth element - precipitation process / troposphere
⌊ mineral earth - Earth's crust

Figure 2: Mineral earth / troposphere

In this diagram, the earth element in the lowest layer of the atmosphere, the troposphere, is the precipitation process whereby gases and waves of energy interact to become the manifest phenomena of wind, rain, snow, and electrical discharge. Meteorologists know wind, rain, and snow as precipitation, a reference to the elemental earth patterns of force behind the alchemical term *earth*. Rain is a precipitate of air.

The mineral layer of the subterranean spheres is the actual mineral content of the Earth's crust. We could say that the mineral earth is the corpse that precipitated out of the living body of the Earth. We could liken the mineral earth to the enamel of our teeth or to bones, scars, or callus tissues in living bodies. The diagram links the first subterranean sphere of the mineral earth and the widespread activity of the appearance of water in the air through precipitation processes.

water element / tropopause, upper limiting surface of the weather sphere. Weather dies here.
earth element
mineral earth
liquid earth - soft rock below the surface, life dies in this layer, beyond oil-ingesting bacteria

Figure 3: Liquid earth / tropopause

In the first subterranean layer, the mineral layer, there is still a possibility of life. Anaerobic bacteria are in the deep rock of oil wells. When water is pumped down to lubricate drill heads, the bacteria return to life in that layer and gum up the drill. These are the bacteria linked to the formation of oil from prehistoric animal carcasses. There are no such bacteria in the layer below the crust. This deeper layer is devoid of life. Rudolf Steiner characterizes this second layer as the one in which life dies. Rock there is soft and pliable, hence the name fluid earth. This is not hard to visualize, since minerals such as mountain leather (chrysolite) and mica retain some of the flexible horn- or fingernail-like properties that make them flexible and soft, even though they are minerals. Steiner linked these forms of minerals to previous conditions of the Earth, when all minerals were in this condition. The second, or liquid, earth layer harks to a time when the whole Earth lived in this way. The mineral and plant beings did not manifest as separate kingdoms, but were instead in this living/lifeless form. In the liquid earth, the living qualities of the plants die.

The polarity to this death-of-life layer is the tropopause, the top, or pause, of the troposphere. *Tropopause* is the meteorological term for the atmospheric layer where weather ceases. Weather is the bringer of the life forces to the Earth's body through the life-enhancing properties of rain, snow, and other phenomena. In the tropopause, all water turns either to ice or to ionic forms of gas rather than water vapor. Water in the lower layers of the troposphere undergoes an archetypal transformation in the tropopause, where it begins to leave the Earth and become more of a cosmic entity. The tropopause, the threshold where weather-making forces stop, begins the upper reaches of the Earth's atmosphere. The tropopause is the top of the weather layer. Ninety-nine percent of the water in the atmosphere is below the tropopause. As a result, ninety-nine percent of the weather in the atmosphere is below the tropopause. At mid-latitudes, the 40,000-foot level marks the upper edge of the tropopause, where the last bit of water vapor encounters temperatures in the region of minus 50 to minus 70 degrees Fahrenheit. This extreme cold converts the remaining water vapor into microscopic ice crystals. This conversion further dries out the air until the only forms of water in a cloud at this height are ice crystals and the gases released as a part of the condensation process.

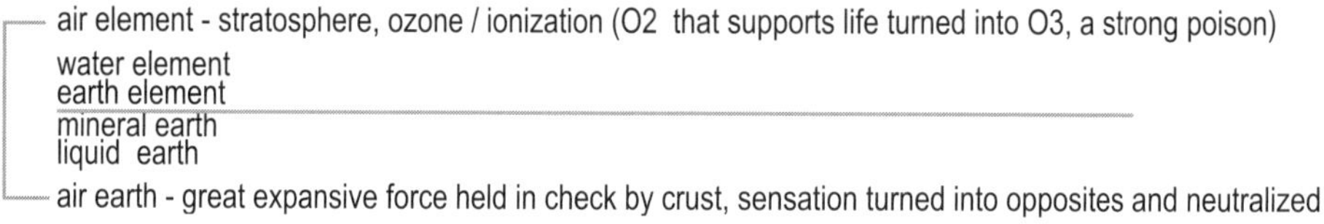

air element - stratosphere, ozone / ionization (O_2 that supports life turned into O_3, a strong poison)
water element
earth element
mineral earth
liquid earth
air earth - great expansive force held in check by crust, sensation turned into opposites and neutralized

Figure 4: Air earth / stratosphere

The air earth is, again, a representative of elemental forces. The first layer of the mineral earth, the second layer of the liquid earth, and now the vapor (or air) earth follow the progression of the classical or alchemical elemental sequences. According to Steiner's research, a great expansive force is present in the air earth. The resisting force of the mineral earth, which contains the expansiveness of the air earth, holds this expansive force in check and keeps it from moving out to the periphery. In chemistry, gas, or vapor, has the primary property of limitless expansion. In alchemical thought, air, or gas, is said to be seeking the periphery. This is the quality of the force in the vapor, or air, earth, the third subterranean layer. As an analog to soul forces, the air earth is where the sensations in the astral bodies of living entities are turned into their opposite and neutralized. It seems, as indicated in several of his lectures, that Steiner viewed the air earth as a neutralizing zone where the qualities of human passions are converted into their opposites. In this layer, Steiner begins to shift from descriptions of layers that have qualities that natural science can describe to descriptions of layers related increasingly to inner attitudes of human beings. The idea behind this is the eventual revelation of, or realization by, human beings that our consciousness has something to do with natural events. Alchemically, this shift is very appropriate for this layer. Air is a step further from the manifest realm of water and earth. It represents a kind of "plane of reversal" in which the laws that govern physical processes begin to shift from elemental relationships to what Rudolf Steiner would term etheric, or peripheral, cosmic processes. The laws governing these processes are very different from those of water and earth.

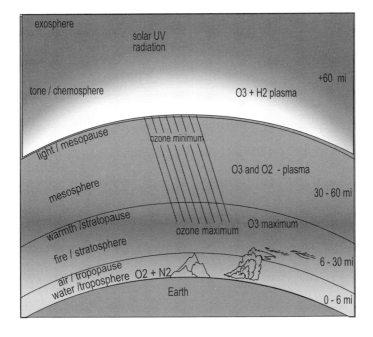

Figure 5: Ozone formation

Analogous to the vapor earth in the meteorological sphere, the stratosphere, is the next layer above the tropopause. The stratosphere is the domain of gases. In the lower layers of the atmosphere, water is present in its manifest form. In the stratosphere, water is present as its constituent gases. In this layer of the atmosphere, the moisture of the elements found in the lower layers transforms completely into rarefied gases and static electrical exchanges. The warmth in this layer, and in the layers above the stratosphere, depends mostly on chemical (ionic) reactions, as well as the energetic movements present in them caused by the rapid exchange of charges among oxygen and other compounds. The intense activity of solar rays and the constant bombardment of cosmic rays interacting with gas ions stimulate the charges. It is here, in the stratosphere, that the life-giving force of oxygen is torn apart and neutralized by cosmic rays and sunlight to form ozone.

Ozone itself is a curious anomaly. When high-energy rays in the stratosphere strike ionic oxygen, it breaks apart and quickly forms into a more unstable form of oxygen: ozone. The ozone interacts with the cosmic-ray bombardment coming from deep space, neutralizing the intense energies from space by breaking apart again and beginning the cycle anew. This exchange of energies protects the Earth by absorbing, neutralizing, and transforming the force of the cosmic rays that would otherwise destroy life on Earth. Those intense energies are converted into warmth through the production of ozone. This blanket of what would be a highly poisonous gas on Earth actually prevents life on Earth from succumbing to the hostile forces beyond the periphery of the weather sphere. In the subtle chemistry of the ozone layer, we can see the shadow, or double, of the sensation-neutralizing activity of the air earth.

The form earth is a curious level of the subterranean spheres. Rudolf Steiner describes it as a place where the physical substance of objects pours out into the surrounding space. The object would then be the negative of its form, which on Earth is filled with matter. Alchemical thinking has deep roots in the Platonic worldview.

fire element - stratopause, extreme limit of lower atmosphere; cosmos pours into upper layers

air element
water element
earth element
mineral earth
liquid earth
air earth

form earth - negative of mineral forms; physical contents of objects pour into surroundings

Figure 6: Form earth / stratopause

In its view of the world, the form of an object exists as the result of forces that pour into it from the periphery of space, where the archetypes behind the forms of nature are thought to exist as energetic prototypes of the movements that eventually come to rest in form. This is the source of the mantra "form is movement come to rest." We could say that the energetic, or potential, form forms the finished form.

This idea would be in line with the categories of the medieval scholastics, who designate the four levels of creation: being, revelation of being, ongoing work, and wrought work. In this model, the being, or archetypal being, reveals a creative idea, which inspires ongoing work toward an eventual manifestation of the image or form of the original idea. Of course, the image that forms as a result of this activity is not the idea itself. Nevertheless, the idea and the image are linked intimately through a kind of step-down transformation process.

In the level of form earth, manifestations pour out into the surrounding space in a reversal of divine creative acts. This activity of continuously hollowing out is a key gesture of the activity of the astral body as it acts in the human soul. With this layer, the stage is set for leaving the realms of the elements and going deep into the human soul forces, as they relate not so much to the elements but more to the ethers. We can think of the soul qualities exhibited by the form earth as a template for the realm of the sentient body. This is the lowest portion of the soul and a kind of reservoir of the inherited stimulus-response patterns that arise in the soul under the influence of sensory experience. The sentient body is not the soul proper but serves as a link, or buffer, between the life forces and the cognitional and feeling life of the soul. It is a kind of bridge between the realm of the beings and their revelations and the ongoing and wrought work of the natural forces behind the formation of the sense organs. As a soul analog, the form earth has strong parallels to the sentient body. Through the portals of the sense organs, the soul life pours out into the world. The sense organ activity is the focus of the sentient body.

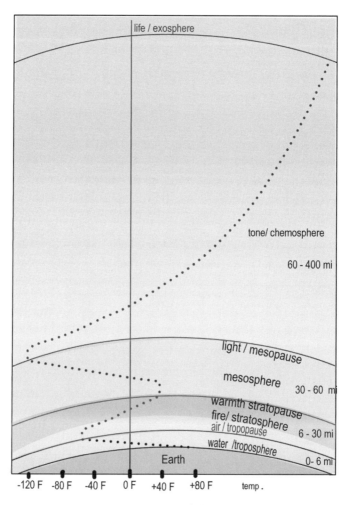

Figure 7: Diagram of thermal zones

In the atmosphere, the stratopause layer is the polarity to the form earth. This is where the warmth conditions created by the production of ozone reach their maximum. The diagram depicts the thermal divisions of the atmosphere according to current science. In it, we can see that the stratosphere is a warmth zone, with the stratopause at an altitude of about sixty miles acting as a kind of warmth lid that acts as a buffer to the intense radiation of outer space. The stratopause is the area with the greatest accumulation of ozone. In anthroposophic terms, ozone is the protective breath of the Christ being, who is now the Spirit of the Earth. In the language of science, the ozone layer protects humanity from destruction by extraterrestrial forces.

The stratosphere, with its ozone, is the last vestige of anything that resembles a form of the elemental patterns of the lower atmosphere. We could call it a doorway through which the fiercely spiritual nature of the cosmic forces in the periphery of space beyond the stratopause are softened and given an entry to the human realm. In this, we can see the stratopause as a polarity to the form earth, the fourth subterranean layer.

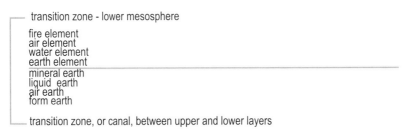

Figure 8: Transition zones above and below

Alchemically, a transition zone exists between the more material realm of the elements and the more cosmic realm of the ethers. We can understand this most easily by thinking of the distinction between a person's warmth of soul and the fire that consumes a burning stick. Human warmth heals and promotes intimacy; it is a blending force. In contrast, the consuming fire liberates warmth from the wood and renders the stick a corpse in the form of ash. The fire that consumes a stick is the manifestation, or "corpse," of the solar warmth that provided the forces to grow the stick. Those forces do not produce a corpse but promote growth and development. Whereas the physical stick contains the corpse of the sunlight that grew it in the form of energies locked into its combustible parts, the sunlight that grew it does not manifest in that corpse. The sunlight still exists to grow more sticks, because the sunlight is not the corpse of anything; it is pure, limitless potential. As a result, we could even say that sunlight is potential fire. It is warmth that has not yet died into fire. An alchemist would describe these ideas by saying that fire is the shadow of warmth.

In human life on Earth, fire and warmth have an intimate relationship; thus, this distinction is not easily apparent. A flame applied to a stick simply releases the warmth that died into the physical form of the stick. However, science recognizes the distinction between latent (potential) heat and sensible (measurable) heat. Rudolf Steiner, when speaking of the differences between an element and an etheric, uses such concepts. He describes living warmth (warmth ether) and dead warmth (fire), most notably in his Warmth Course and Agriculture Course.[1] This concept was seminal to Steiner's medical and agriculture work and underpins such profound works as the "Michael Letters."[2] In descriptions of the subterranean spheres, the concepts are slightly different yet very recognizable. The foregoing paragraphs are a lead-in to the thinking that Steiner uses to describe the void zone, or canal, between the form earth and the fruit earth.

The zone immediately below the fourth sphere of the form earth is the fruit earth. Between the form earth and the fruit earth, however, exists what Steiner calls a "canal." This canal is a hollow space, where the deeper layers (most notably the fruit earth) interact with the form earth in the processes that lead to volcanic eruptions. Between the form earth and the fruit earth is the hollow space where the restless movements of the fruit earth impinge upward upon the form earth, stimulating it to move outward with greater force. This image is very much in line with alchemical thinking, notably the Triumphal Chariot of Antimony by Basil Valentine and work on the generation of metals by the great physician Paracelsus. In this view, the metals in the Earth are part of a "great tree" that grows within the Earth and bears fruits, or embryonates, which are the metals themselves. They are a condensation of vapors that form in the branches of the great tree within the Earth. The tree's branches are hollow spaces in the Earth where vapors, waters, and metals shoot out and meet the "atmospheres" of the starry realms and the planets. According to Rudolf Steiner, the canal below the Earth serves as a transition between the more physical properties of the first four layers and the decidedly soul-imbued qualities of the lower layers. In general, the canal layer is the zone in which the intense activity of the fruit earth, during upheavals of tectonic masses, expands into the upper layer of the form earth.

In the atmosphere, there is also a kind of canal or void space between the lower elementally driven layers where weather and even "space weather" occur as a result of the more sensible interactions with remnants of gasses in ionic form that result in the heat of the stratosphere. The void space is the bottom of the mesosphere (see figure 5). In the mesosphere, this heating ceases and the temperature takes a radical dive. In the mesosphere, the ozone that has been left below in the stratosphere ceases to be a factor in the temperature regimes. The beginning of the mesosphere is at about thirty miles and the top of the mesosphere peaks at sixty miles. The void space that is the equivalent to the void in the subterranean spheres is the very bottom of the mesosphere. This space represents a kind of neutral space in between the lower layers, where weather takes place, and the higher layers where only electrical and chemical interactions take place. In the atmosphere the lower layers are designated as elementally significant, and the upper layers have the qualities of the ethers of the elements.

The relationship between the fire element and the warmth ether is very intimate. They are not separated by very much in the charts, with warmth ether residing directly above the fire element. At the next level, however, this will change, since we have crossed a boundary or void area. Now the air element and the light ether are separated from each other, with the fire element and the warmth ether between them.

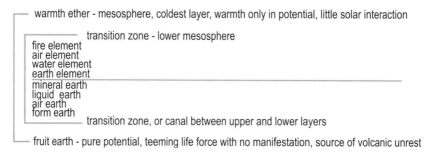

Figure 9: Fruit earth / mesosphere

The fruit earth marks a shift from the more elemental and sensible forces of the previous subterranean spheres. With the shift to a deeper layer, the soul forces of the human become more important. The characteristic of the fruit earth that is the most mentioned is the capacity for unchecked expansive growth. This, at first, may seem to be a positive quality. However, gardeners call unchecked growth rank growth. Doctors refer to rank growth as cancer. In plants, excessively vigorous growth occurs when too much water and fertilizer are available. Rank growth outstrips the ability of the plant organism to protect itself, with the result that parasites or fungi may invade the plant and feed on the hypertrophied cells. This process leads to decay of the plant's integrity as a whole. In cancer, a similar process takes place. Cancer cells establish an autonomous zone of rank, rampant growth that feeds on the integrity of the cells near the tumor, while the unchecked growth wreaks havoc on the integrity of the organism.

A similar process is present in the fruit earth. Rudolf Steiner likens the quality of this layer to a soul that yearns and struggles to attain a stable form. Instead, form after form arise and decay, while none of the soul qualities are actually able to form a soul. We might even venture an analogy to the human subconscious. In the language of Anthroposophy, we would call this layer the sentient, or sensitive, soul layer. The subconscious, with its impulses of sympathy and antipathy, is a repository of personality fragments that arise from half-recognized urges in the individual. These sub-personality fragments live a dark existence within the human soul, rising to the surface of the ordinary awareness only during moments of anger, fear, doubt, hatred, and similar emotions. Once these sub-personality fragments appear and exert themselves, they dive again into the darkness, leaving the individual in a state of feeling compromised. In the past, these kinds of reactions in the soul were called demons, a term that more accurately describes the moods of the lower subterranean levels as presented by Steiner.

The atmospheric counterpoint to the fruit earth is the mesosphere, which marks a shift from the more elemental and sensible forces of the previous layers of the atmosphere to a far more rarefied condition. With the shift to a higher and more rarefied layer, the etheric forces that are diametrically opposite to the elements become more important. In the diagram, the mesosphere represents the warmth ether. The mesosphere is nevertheless the coldest layer of the atmosphere. It may seem strange to link the coldest area to the warmth ether, but this offers a clear example of how scientists who study the upper air understand the most rarefied layers in the atmosphere. The intense ozone activity of the lower stratopause layer depletes ozone in the atmosphere, while carbon dioxide and an inert form of oxygen replace the highly reactive ozone in the mesosphere. The gasses in the mesosphere are so rarefied that they move into a condition called plasma.

Imagine a teaspoon of water in a room. If we heat the teaspoon, the water evaporates and expands into the room. Now, however, imagine that every molecule of water rises to an even more rarefied state, becoming increasingly attenuated. Meteorologists and atmospheric scientists know this process as aerosol formation. Most people call it cloud building. Now, however, we are far above the normal reach of earthly clouds. The water has separated into gases, and the gases have further separated and attenuated until a former drop of water now spreads out over hundreds of square miles. This is, roughly, the plasma state. It is the ether realm, in which substance disappears and the forces of the periphery dominate. Spiritually, these forces are the will activity of the beings who stand here at the portal of creation. The coldness of the mesosphere is the quality of fire that has lost its fire, or sensible heat, to the periphery, leaving only latent heat. To earthbound souls, the mesosphere would indeed be cold. However, as we shall see, the zone called the thermosphere begins above the mesosphere. The thermosphere extends to the Sun and is a zone of strong warming. Human beings in this zone would not find its warmth very comforting at all; its average temperature is many degrees below zero. The warmth in the upper atmospheric plasma zones is not the sort of dead, consuming warmth generated by one's fireplace fire. It is the living, or potential, warmth of the ether realm. This living warmth of the ether realm starkly contrasts the dead, all-consuming fire of an anomalously growing tumor.

The next subterranean layer in the sequence presented by Rudolf Steiner is the sixth, the fire earth. This layer takes us even deeper into the human soul. Here, we pass through the life forces of the fruit earth and find the deeper soul issues of sensory responses, as well as the inner life of urges and passions connected to sensory experience. Steiner indicates that pleasure and pain and the passions of sensory experience become the dramatic upheavals and catastrophes of earthquakes and volcanic eruptions. These events are examples of the way that the Earth's will forces manifest. They also exemplify the connection between the human will and the subterranean spheres.

```
┌── light ether - mesopause, extreme upper limit of gas mixing, Aurora Borealis
│
│   warmth ether
│   ┌──────────────── transition zone - lower mesosphere
│   │ fire element
│   │ air element
│   │ water element
│   │ earth element
│   │ mineral earth
│   │ liquid  earth
│   │ air earth
│   │ form earth
│   └──────── transition zone, or canal, between upper and lower layers
│
│     fruit earth
│
└── fire earth- pure will and passion, emotions amplified into catastrophic forces
```

Figure 10: Fire Earth / mesopause

In the soul life, the chaotic quality of this layer is diametrically opposed to the ordering and regulating force given to persons who work at the level of the mind soul. The biblical injunction toward metanoia (change your thinking) points to the need to overcome the darkened, impassioned lower soul forces with the light and clarity of organized thinking. This requires the transcendence of millennia of unrecognized sentient-soul experiences.

To understand this without simply repeating Steiner's indications about the fire earth is not easy. In other sources (notably the book *World of the Senses, World of the Spirit*), Steiner uses the term *ruling will* to describe ways that the residues of the cosmic creative beings' will constitute the world. Lucifer's task was to retreat from that progressive, or creative, will of the hierarchies and to grasp the ruling will for himself. Simultaneously, this luciferic tendency is behind both the light of human freedom in the thinking pole of the soul and the fall of the hierarchies' ruling will into a natural world that could support the view that individual human beings are somehow independent of the Creator's will. We could call that fall "the illusion of separate existence." This paradox of the illusory aspect of self and the reality of the individuality of each human being as an aspect of the Logos nature of Christ is at the heart of the work of Anthroposophy. It is central to the work on the mind soul and the core of the soul, or astral, body.

The fire earth is a layer in which the darkness of the creative will of the Creator and the hierarchies that served the creation has become sequestered in the hidden forces within each human being. The massive egotism that results from unrecognized sensory responses creates the will profiles of passion and desire. We can trace the current political, economic, and social strife rampant in the world to the hidden agendas lurking behind the ubiquitous unconscious consumption of mass media (sensory experience). In these simulated sensory experiences (for example, television broadcasts of human beings standing on the Moon), neither the creative (ruling) will of the hierarchies nor the individual will of the Logos-created human individual is present. The human being must participate vicariously without the capacity to understand truly what is being presented. This dulls the thinking and inflames the urge to act without thinking. It is a clear picture of passion.

Allegedly, we can see an example of how these unbridled passions can interact with the natural order in the weather patterns surrounding the assassination of Israeli Prime Minister Ishtak Rabin on November 4, 1995. On that day, a moderate low was moving eastward in the longitude and high latitude of St. Petersburg, Russia. On the next day after the assassination, that moderate low had streamed to the west (against the prevailing westerlies) and centered to the west of southern Italy. On November 6, the day Rabin was buried, the low had moved over the Aegean Sea and deepened considerably, forming what is known as an enclosed low. An enclosed low is a strong, focalized storm center. From November 7 to 9, the now intense low locked into position over western Turkey and the circulation from the intense low brought torrential rains to the whole of the eastern Mediterranean coast.

Contemporary science might consider a cycle like this to be simply a coincidence. To an esoteric scientist, events such as these begin to illuminate Rudolf Steiner's powerful indications about the interaction between the human (passionate) will and—owing to the mass production of unrecognized will forces on the part of human beings—the otherwise beneficial forces of the Earth being moved into catastrophic events in particular areas of the world.

In the atmosphere, the mesopause is the polar equivalent to the dark and passionate forces of the fruit earth. The mesopause is the area in the upper atmosphere that forms a lid for the radical forces of cooling in the mesosphere. This area is the site of some of the most intense current research in upper-air dynamics. Research shows that the superfluous amount of carbon produced in the atmosphere by fossil-fuel use actually makes the carbon dioxide content of the mesosphere, and the mesopause in particular, much more intense. Through complex aerosol chemistry, this in turn lowers the temperature of this delicate borderline area high above the Earth. This temperature and chemical differential creates a kind of energetic gradient membrane about fifty to sixty miles above the Earth. This layer thickens and thins each day in response to how the solar wind shifts the currents owing to the daily diurnal motion of the Earth. The light ether shows its true nature at this boundary layer between the much warmer plasmas of the higher layers and the cooler plasma of the mesosphere (keeping in mind that warmer and cooler are relative terms).

As an aside, the science of gravity-wave phenomena is making some of the best cases possible for one of the knottier problems in esoteric science: How does spirit interact with the natural world? Some scientists believe that gravity waves are gigantic sub-sound, or precursor sound waves, inaudible to the human ear. These waves propagate upward with successive waves of energy when strong currents of air pass across the tops of large mountains. The waves of energy propagate upward to astonishing heights and affect the cold regions of the mesosphere. Noctilucent (night-lighted) clouds are the tops of the gravity wave heights. It is similar to the way a whitecap forms on an ocean wave. These wondrous, light-filled ice clouds occur at the earth-side of the mesopause. They are so high that they appear magically illuminated by the Sun, while from Earth they appear many hours after sunset. Nevertheless, these beautiful,

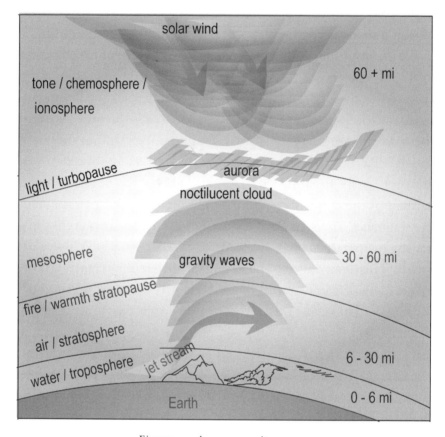

Figure 11: Aurora gravity waves

mysterious clouds are not actually luminous, but only reflect the sunlight. For a true manifestation of the properties of the earth-side of the mesopause, noctilucent clouds form under perturbations of gravity waves from terrestrial sources.

Noctilucent clouds form under the right conditions. These amazing cloud forms are massive layers of ice crystals at approximately sixty miles above Earth's surface. (By comparison, the highest weather clouds are over the equator at a maximum height of sixty thousand feet.) The high-altitude, noctilucent cloud forms are large strata of the light ether; the phenomena on the space-side of the mesopause are more significant. It is here that the sublime spectacle of the northern lights has a home. Long regarded by primitive peoples as the communications of deities, the appearance of the weaving veils of the aurora borealis always excites awe and wonder. The auroras are interactions between the terrestrially propagating gravity waves and the waves that move from deep space, generated by fluctuations of the solar wind. The two sources of energy, one terrestrial and one celestial, meet, and the space between suddenly springs into luminosity as the rarefied gasses provide inspiring evidence of the light ether and its luminosity.

The luminous phenomena of the mesopause are counter to the dark and threatening phenomena of the inflamed passions of the fire earth. These two layers in juxtaposition symbolize the polarity of inspired, enlightened thinking and self-centered willfulness.

In the seventh layer, the Earth reflector—deeper penetration into the Earth and into the human soul—takes a step inward. The movement has been from the sentient body in the form earth, through the sensitive, or sentient, soul in the fruit earth, and on into the mind soul in the fire earth. The plunge into the consciousness soul, that is the parallel of the Earth reflector, is based on the concept that the Earth reflector is the domain in which we find the negative aspects of human morality. This is the exact polar opposite of the task for the cultural period of the consciousness soul. The qualities bestowed upon the soul through the transformation of an esoteric student's base impulses into moral ones have their foundation in the consciousness soul. There, one transcends thought schemes provided through intellectual abstraction. By working to understand consciousness in the cosmos, spiritual researchers must begin to participate in direct esoteric work through the establishment of a meditative discipline. The consciousness soul, in other words, is about walking the talk and being authentic. This innate human quality is the force of transformation that occurs when a student realizes that all things in the cosmos are composed of various levels of consciousness. Once that happens, there is no longer any room for blame. However, there is still plenty of room for work.

tone ether - chemosphere; rarified gasses interact with UV solar energies; door to cosmos

light ether -
warmth ether

transition zone - lower mesosphere
fire element
air element
water element
earth element
mineral earth
liquid earth
air earth
form earth
transition zone, or canal between upper and lower layers
fruit earth

earth reflector- all that is moral and ordered (tone ether) is reflected into counter image

Figure 12: Earth reflector / chemosphere

The Earth reflector takes everything on Earth and produces an image counter to it. In a healthy soul, this is one's ability to stop the blaming, as just described. In the Earth reflector, this is the self-centered force of the lower ego, demanding that all things are simply a reflection of one's own sense of separateness from the world. In the consciousness of a person trying to transform the lower impulses, the most powerful healing vectors are from the creative periphery (the spiritual world) toward a relative center in the individual's consciousness. In the Earth reflector, the vector comes from a fixed center that reflects everything from that fixedness. The sole result is that cosmic wholeness, with its manifold complexity of relationships, can be experienced only as if in a mirror. The most fundamental quality of the mirrored consciousness is that it always shows an image of something but never the authentic thing itself. For the researcher who explores the dynamics of the consciousness soul, the task is to realize that there are always multiple ways of understanding things that appear fixed to the soul. The Earth reflector denies this by reflecting everything as its opposite. This keeps the opposites locked in a death struggle, while other possibilities are not allowed into the process. One could mention today's partisanship in the political realm and the general rise of fundamentalism as symptoms of how the Earth reflector has advanced in human consciousness, as well as the lack of will and understanding of the purpose of the consciousness soul.

In the atmosphere, we find the polarity to the ever-deepening forces of the Earth reflector in an escape from earthly conditions in the rarefied level of the atmosphere called the chemosphere. This layer extends from the mesopause upward to the edge of space and is entirely a plasma layer. Gases here exist in very fundamental ionic conditions. In the chemosphere, the Earth's atmosphere takes on a decidedly extreme attenuated form. Still, enough gas residues remain that their interaction with cosmic rays, gamma rays, solar wind, and solar-coronal fluxes are highly productive of warm plasma conditions.

To understand this, imagine a meteor traveling at a great speed and approaching Earth from the vacuum of deep space. The vacuum produces no friction on the meteor, but once the meteor enters the plasma layers, gas residues and ionic components make up part of the meteor's path. Those particles may be spaced at only a few molecules per square mile, but compared to a vacuum the plasma is dense. The meteor's extremely high rate of speed causes numerous collisions with the attenuated gases, which increase as the meteor comes lower into the Earth envelope. Finally, the plasma is dense enough to cause the meteor to burn up. Such an image can be useful when we try to form a picture of high-altitude plasma dynamics.

However, in the chemosphere, a speeding object such as a meteor moving into increasingly dense plasma does not generally cause the plasma dynamics. The chemosphere is extensive; it extends from sixty up to about four hundred miles above the Earth's surface. At such high levels, fierce solar and cosmic radiation affects the plasma envelope. The energetic interaction is composed of the fundamental ion formation of such gases as helium and hydrogen, as well as residues of non-ionized ozone that have escaped from below, having been chemically changed by the energy of the collisions. In the context of the energetic exchanges and bombardment of solar and cosmic energies, these chemical reactions are a perfect description of tone ether activity. The tone ether is the great cosmic chemistry laboratory that holds the potential for all things to combine or separate with all other things in ordered progressions. In contrast to the Earth reflector, the chemosphere is not a reflector of Earth forces, but the opposite. It is a spherical lens that draws in and focuses cosmic forces into a dance of fundamental chemistry through combination, dissociation, and subsequent recombination. Eventually, this rarefied chemistry becomes actual substances far below. Moreover, as we saw earlier, this chemistry becomes evermore fixed into the either/or properties of the Earth reflector.

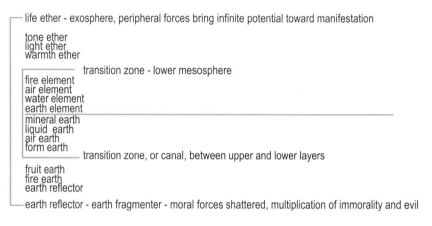

life ether - exosphere, peripheral forces bring infinite potential toward manifestation

tone ether
light ether
warmth ether

transition zone - lower mesosphere

fire element
air element
water element
earth element

mineral earth
liquid earth
air earth
form earth

transition zone, or canal, between upper and lower layers

fruit earth
fire earth
earth reflector

earth reflector - earth fragmenter - moral forces shattered, multiplication of immorality and evil

Figure 13: Earth Fragmenter / exosphere

With the next descent, into the Earth fragmenter, we leave behind any possible references to the life of the soul. With the previous level—that of the Earth reflector as a counter to the activity of consciousness soul in the life of the spiritual researcher—we reached the level at which the activity of the "I" within the soul created spiritual vehicles in spiritual realms beyond the soul itself. The first higher vehicle, in the language of Anthroposophy, is the manas sheath, the transformed soul, or astral body, with its four members: sentient body, sentient soul, mind soul, and consciousness soul. The second spirit vehicle is the budhi sheath, produced by the activity of the "I" in transforming the life forces that animate the physical body, especially in the realm of sensory perception. The third sheath is atma, the result of the action of the "I" upon the hidden urges and patterns in the physical body, which are the result of ahrimanic influences through the millennia.

In a banal way, we may think of this exalted process—the gradual transformation of the soul into spirit as a path toward the apotheosis of the human race—as a kind of cosmic, low-yield certificate of deposit. It grows very slowly and is not very liquid; the spiritual world could trust only initiates and saints to have the capacity to use the forces of these higher bodies to get along in this life. However, the dividends have a very good rate of return in the end, since any profit is rolled over immediately to the cosmic account. Eventually, at maturation, these vehicles will pay immense dividends. Although the analogy is a bit trite, the picture may be useful.

The "I" is a great force of unity in the human being, whereas the small ego is akin to the personality and is the great divider. The transition from great divider to great uniter is a cosmically ordained task of great importance that takes place over a very long time. In the Earth fragmenter, good and moral human actions are shattered and multiplied into immoral impulses of the dark will. Rudolf Steiner tells us that the immoral forces of evil and disharmony then radiate upward through the rest of the Earth's layers, causing disturbances in all of the layers above it. The Earth fragmenter is the source of much human conflict, disharmony, and consciously immoral activity. This level transcends the sympathy and antipathy of the unconscious realms of layers closer to the surface. It is the true descent into Hell, or what alchemists call gehenna. Here, acts of evil are not sins of omission and misunderstanding, but conscious and cunning. Such immorality contributes nothing to the gradual apotheosis of the human soul through the transformation of the soul members into spiritual sheathes. The Earth fragmenter is the doorway into the abyss of no return.

The polar image to this found in the atmosphere is the layer known as the exosphere. This is the space above four to five hundred miles, where remnants of the lower ionic atmosphere gradually give way to the gasless vacuum of space. This layer is in complete synch with the fluctuations of the solar atmosphere. Activities on the Sun that are produced by oscillations of planetary gravity waves pulling the Sun out of the center of the solar system's mass produce phenomena that, considered spiritually, are the creative deeds of high spiritual beings. Such beings interact with the rotation of time and the syzygies and occultations present among the planets in a local way. Farther out, the creative hierarchies, working through the medium of starlight, are active in the creation and destruction of whole worlds and universes. Their work comes to Earth in the form of solar flares, mass coronal ejections, solar wind oscillations, and fluxes in background cosmic radiation.

The exosphere is the last tenuous remnant of Earth's atmosphere. It is a doorway to the extraterrestrial spheres. The mysterious gifts of the hierarchies pour through it unceasingly to help offset the condensation of human consciousness caused by the pervading thought forms of materialism and reductionist abstraction, which prevent human thinking from penetrating cosmic realms of being and revelation. The exosphere is the doorway through which human beings can learn again to approach the mysteries of the creative cosmos through the sound application of thinking, coupled with a capacity for imaginative perception.

The final and most sinister layer of the subterranean spheres is the Earth core, the domain of consciously repeated immoral acts perpetrated upon others through the practice of magic. This is not stage magic or illusion, but definite, conscious activity intended to hurt others through the misapplication of human soul and spiritual capacities. The Earth core is the Faustian realm of proverbial pacts with the devil. Lust for power causes a fundamental estrangement from the progressive universe of the Trinity and the hierarchies. Instead, it places human soul and spiritual forces consciously at the

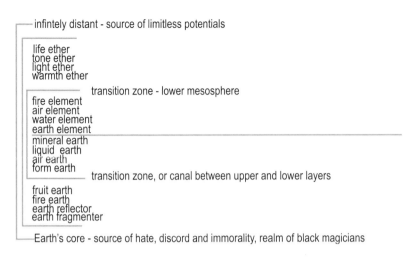

infinitely distant - source of limitless potentials

life ether
tone ether
light ether
warmth ether

transition zone - lower mesosphere

fire element
air element
water element
earth element

mineral earth
liquid earth
air earth
form earth

transition zone, or canal between upper and lower layers

fruit earth
fire earth
earth reflector
earth fragmenter

Earth's core - source of hate, discord and immorality, realm of black magicians

Figure 14: Earth core / infinitely distant

disposal of Ahriman for the purpose of helping the retarding beings create a parallel universe, where human beings worship Ahriman as a god, as though he were the Creator. The eventual reward for such souls is infinite power and complete loss of freedom.

At this point, we have long abandoned any remnant of physical atmosphere. We can now look to the qualities of the spiritual atmosphere beyond the influences of the solar system, in which our beautiful home planet shines as a sapphire jewel. We can even look beyond the influences of our galaxy. We can look out to the most remote galaxies, beyond the zodiac, and search for something that resembles the enlightened human being. There, we can turn our spiritual gaze back toward our shining home and see it from the perspective of the Cosmic Christ as he approached the Earth in the distant past on his mission to help humans take their rightful place among the hierarchies who wish to further the work of God.

CONCLUSION

Rudolf Steiner often locates the meteorological sphere as the central point between the terrestrial sphere and the cosmos. Most frequently, he characterizes it as chaotic and as a kind of wall that blocks the human capacity to perceive the true nature of how cosmic influences interact with matter in the terrestrial sphere.

After thirty years of research into the link between the ordered cosmic sphere and the chaotic terrestrial sphere, I can say truthfully that, in the middle meteorological realm where chaos apparently rules, it is possible to find the imprint of cosmic seed-like forces within the seeming chaos. A key to seeing this influence is to study the rhythmic syncopation between planetary motion and unfolding of climate patterns. Earth's climatic rhythms are slow enough that we can make sense of the seeming chaos of hurricanes, storms, droughts, and other catastrophic phenomena. The key is to view planetary motions as a kind of "musical" backdrop, from which a phenomenology of motion in arc events can be woven. Such work builds into the human rhythmic system and organs of cognition that are sensitive to the various qualities of motion in arc events. The study of rhythmic motion in arc events can also provide other ways to model the current climate crisis.

At a time when climate study is such an important aspect of our human future, the call is urgent to find approaches other than the ahrimanic, reductionistic approach to climate and weather study. It is possible to thwart the dire direction of current ineffectual research methods by learning to form research protocols based on the various qualities of rhythm instead of reductionistic concepts that tend to view climate patterns as physical and mechanical. Essentially, the climatic crisis is not a mechanical or physical problem, but a moral problem stemming from the contemporary inability of human beings to recognize the activity of higher forms of being that are active in what appears to be chaotic fluctuations of the climate and the general life of the Earth.

> Wherefore most diligently think on this; often bear in mind, observe, and understand that all Minerals and Metals together, in the same Time, and after the same manner, and of one and the same principal Matter, are

produced and genited. That Matter is no other, than a meer Vapour, which is extracted from the Elementary Earth by the Superior Stars, as by a Sidereal Distillation of the Macrocosm: which Sidereal hot infusion, with any Airy-Sulphureous Property descending upon Inferiors, so acts and operates, as in those Metals and Minerals is implanted spiritually and invisibly a certain Power and Virtue, which Fume afterward resolves itself in the Earth, into a certain Water, from which Mineral Water all Metals are thenceforth generated and ripened to their Perfection; and thence proceeds this or that Metal or Mineral, according as one of the three Principles acquires Dominion, and they have much or little of Sulphur and Salt, or an unequal Mixture of the weight of them, whence some Metals are fixed; that is, some constant and stable, some volatile and easily mutable. (BASIL VALENTINE, from the *Triumphal Chariot of Antimony;* from Levity.com)

Chapter 3

SUBNATURE AND THE SECOND COMING

ROBERT POWELL

IN MY BOOK *The Christ Mystery*, in the chapter "Star Wisdom and the Holy Grail," I refer to the significance of Jupiter's orbit around the sidereal zodiac[1] in connection with Christ's passage down from cosmic realms on his path of descent toward the Earth prior to the onset of his Second Coming. And in the chapter "Reflections on the Second Coming," I point to the importance of the thirty-three-and-one-third-year rhythm of Christ's earthly life for an understanding of the unfolding of the Second Coming.

In chapter 9 ("The Second Coming and the New Age") of my book *Hermetic Astrology: Astrological Biography*,[2] I expand upon this and juxtapose the two rhythms, giving exact dates. Summarizing the dates for the Jupiter rhythm (see table, following page). The dates given are those of Jupiter's heliocentric ingress (entrance) into sidereal Leo. These are the astronomically computed dates and, of course, the actual dates of Christ's descent may differ somewhat from the computed dates. Thus, it is evident that the commencement of Christ's passage through the realm of the Kyriotetes coincided with Rudolf Steiner's birth on February 25, 1861, which was five days after Jupiter's heliocentric ingress into sidereal Leo.

With the completion of Christ's descent through the planetary spheres, there took place his entrance into the human sphere, in

CHRIST'S DESCENT THROUGH THE SPIRITUAL HIERARCHIES		PLANETARY SPHERE	DATES
Kyriotetes:	spirits of wisdom	Sun	Feb.20, 1861– Jan.1, 1873
Dynamis:	spirits of motion	Sun	Jan.1,1873– Nov.11, 1884
Exusiai:	spirits of form	Sun	Nov.11, 1884– Sep.21, 1896
Archai:	spirits of personality	Venus	Sep.21, 1896– Aug.4, 1908
Archangeloi:	spirits of fire	Mercury	Aug.4, 1908– Jun.15, 1920
Angeloi:	spirits of twilight	Moon	Jun.15, 1920– Apr.25, 1932

the earthly realm. The computed date is April 25, 1932, close to Ascension Day (May 5) in 1932. It was on Ascension Day (May 14), 33 C.E., that Christ departed from the Earth to begin his ascension to the Father, when he took leave of the apostles and disciples on the Mount of Olives, to whom two angels then proclaimed: "Men of Galilee, why do you stand looking up into heaven? This Jesus, who was taken up from you into heaven, will come in the same way as you saw him go into heaven" (Acts 1:11). According to the foregoing and from one point of view, it seems that we can date the angelic proclamation of Christ's return, his Second Coming, approximately on Ascension Day 1932. This is the date attained by following the Jupiter rhythm. However, a slightly different date results if we follow the thirty-three-and-one-third-years rhythm of Christ's life. Let us now turn our attention to this second rhythm.

The span of time, from the moment of birth of Jesus of Nazareth to the resurrection at dawn on Easter Sunday morning, was exactly thirty-three-per-years (less one-and-a-half days).[3] As will emerge, this rhythm of thirty-three-and-one-third years is of immeasurable significance to the Earth and humankind, a rhythm that has repeated many times since the Mystery of Golgotha in 33 C.E.

For example, nine cycles of thirty-three-and-one-third years added to Easter Sunday (April 5) in C.E. 33 bring us to March 29, 333 C.E., and Rudolf Steiner referred to 333 C.E. as a critical turning point in human evolution:

> Before the year 333, the greater part of the astral body had been active essentially in the upper human being and its smaller part in the lower body of the human being.... In the year 333, the two parts became equal. This was the critical situation 333 years after the coming of Christ, and since then the upper part of the astral body has been continuously decreasing. That is the course taken by evolution.[4]

Another crucial date frequently spoken of by Rudolf Steiner is 1899, the end of Kali Yuga (the dark age), which began (according to Hindu chronology) five thousand years previously, on February 17/18, 3102 B.C.E. (3102 B.C.E. = -3101, and 3101 + 1899 = 5000). Adding fifty-six cycles of thirty-three-and-one-third years to the date of the resurrection on April 5, 33 C.E. brings us to September 10, 1899. This coincided with the end of Kali Yuga and the start of the New Age, Satya Yuga (the age of light). However, what is the deeper justification for referring to 1899/1900 as the start of the New Age?

As we shall see, through coming to an understanding of the significance of the thirty-three-and-one-third-year rhythm we shall be able to comprehend why it is justifiable to speak of the commencement of the New Age at that time. We shall also try to grasp the meaning of the twelve-year Jupiter rhythm in relation to the thirty-three-and-one-third-year rhythm. Before taking this step, however, it will be helpful to approach a deep and profound mystery concerning the relationship of Christ to human beings. This is an aspect of the Grail mystery, comprising the sublime mystery of the different modes of communion with Christ.

To approach this mystery, we need the "magic wand of analogy" (to use Novalis's expression). The hermetic principle of analogy offers us a key with which to grasp the relationship between Christ and human individuals. Just as the human being is fourfold (with a physical body, ether body, astral body, and "I"), likewise it is possible for the human being to enter a relationship with one of the members of Christ's being: his physical (resurrection) body, ether body, astral body, and "I" being. This leads to four kinds of communion with Christ. Let us consider these one by one.

The first mode of communion is that between the human self and Christ's "I." The words of St. Paul summarize this: "Not I, but Christ in me." This mode of communion is characterized by the fire of Christ's love burning in the human being as a heightened power of spirit and an intensified awareness of the relationship—through love—between oneself and the world.

When, through the activity of the Christianized human self upon the astral body, the latter becomes purified and transformed, the ennobled astral body becomes capable of entering communion with Christ's astral body. This second mode of communion is exemplified in St. Francis of Assisi who, through his purified astral body, entered ongoing communion with Christ's astral body. Mildness, gentleness, purity, and loving kindness are characteristic of this communion.

On the path of spiritual development, it is possible not only for the astral body but also for the ether body to become purified and transformed. This transformed ether body becomes capable of entering communion with Christ's ether body. St. Augustine provides an example of this third mode of communion. From a certain point in his life, he attained a more-or-less ongoing communion with Christ's ether body. This level of communion is characterized by creativity, inner strength, and a harmonious, flowing quality of life.

At a further stage of spiritual development, the physical body itself is transformed. It becomes possible for a person to enter communion with Christ's physical (resurrection) body. The apostles periodically experienced this level of communion during the forty days from the resurrection to the ascension; it filled them to the depths of their being and bestowed new spiritual powers.

Just as we find the fourth mode of communion in the forty days following the resurrection, we also find the other three modes of communion revealed in the life of Christ. During the period from the death on the cross to the resurrection, it was the "I" of Christ—alone, separated from the physical, ether, and astral bodies—that descended into the underworld and then ascended. In Christ's descent into the realm of the Mother, we find the archetype of the first kind of communion. Something of this search for the Divine Mother is found in the Grail legend of Parsifal, which depicts the development of courage in the Grail knights. Courage is needed for the descent into Hell and confrontation with the nine layers of evil in the subearthly realms interposed between humanity and Shambhala, the realm of the Divine Mother in the heart of the Earth. The descent to the Mother entails encountering, confronting, and overcoming evil. We find the first kind of communion—that of the "I" with Christ's "I"—as the central motif of the Grail legend of Parsifal.

We may think of Parsifal as a representative of the Jupiter human being, who will have realized St. Paul's words: "Not I, but Christ in me," and who has the courage to descend into the underworld and take up the battle against evil for the sake of humanity and Mother Earth. The Jupiter human being is of the future—Jupiter being the next stage of evolution after the Earth, and so named owing to its connection with spiritual wisdom. Jupiter has always been called the "planet of wisdom."[5] Thus, the planet Jupiter, with its twelve-year rhythm, is of particular significance for those consciously on the path toward becoming Jupiter human beings, as well as for the first mode of communion, between the human "I" and Christ's "I."

Let us now consider how the four kinds of communion are revealed in the life of Christ. We have found the archetype of the first mode of communion (that of the "I" with Christ's "I") in Christ's descent into the underworld between the crucifixion and the resurrection. Likewise, the archetype of the fourth mode of communion (that of the physical body with Christ's resurrection body) occurs in the forty days leading to the ascension. Where do we find the archetypes of the other two modes of communion?

Here it is a matter of communion with Christ's ether and astral bodies. When an individual separates from the physical body at the moment of death, leaving a corpse on Earth, one begins to live in the ether body. Inscribed into that body are all the experiences of one's earthly days of life. Here the word *days* is appropriate, since experiences during sleep are not inscribed into the ether body; rather, they are inscribed into the astral body, in which one lives during sleep, once the physical and etheric bodies have been left behind. At the moment of death, the human being, indwelling the ether body, witnesses a panorama of images of one's experiences between birth and death on Earth. Many who have "died" (or been at the brink of death) and returned to life describe the experience of seeing a panoramic vision of life's experiences.

For our consideration, it is important to note that, whereas the physical body belongs to the spatial realm (three-dimensional space), the ether body belongs to the temporal realm, being a time body into which the individual's biography is recorded. At the moment of death, one's entire life is vividly reexperienced, from the moment of birth to the moment of death. Death is actually one's birth into a higher realm. The moment of the resurrection on Easter Sunday morning was also a moment of birth, that of the Risen One. The biography of the Risen One extended from the birth in Bethlehem to the moment of resurrection. The ether body held all the experiences between Christ's birth in Bethlehem and the resurrection, a span of thirty-three-and-one-third years. When one dies, the ether body generally dissolves back into the cosmos, but Christ's ether body did not dissolve but was preserved. Moreover, ever since then, it has continued to unfold its activity rhythmically every thirty-three-and-one-third years. Since the Mystery of Golgotha, therefore, the thirty-three-and-one-third-year rhythm has played a role in the cosmic order, just as the planets have always done. It is a new cosmic rhythm, in addition to those of the planets such as Jupiter's twelve-year rhythm and Saturn's twenty-nine-and-a half–year rhythm. However, the thirty-three-and-one-third-year rhythm is a purely temporal rhythm, specified by the duration of the life of Jesus Christ, in contrast to the planetary rhythms, which are specified in terms of cosmic space (by their passage against the background of the zodiacal constellations, so that a planet's rhythm is determined by the time period that elapses between its conjunction with a given fixed star until its return to conjunction with the same fixed star).

Since the commencement of the New Age on September 10, 1899, the thirty-three-and-one-third-year rhythm has begun to play a much more significant role than it did previously. This fact is related to Christ's Second Coming. Whereas the first incarnation was an event on the physical plane, the Second Coming is occurring on the etheric plane of existence, in the realm of life forces. Thus, Christ's ether body is especially active.

Following the Mystery of Golgotha in 33 C.E., the etheric body of Christ expanded slowly out into cosmic realms, attaining its greatest expansion in 966 C.E,[6] a year that denoted a point of transition. Then began the slow path of Christ's ether body back toward the Earth. With the end of the fifty-sixth thirty-three-and-one-third-year cycle on September 10, 1899, and the close of Kali Yuga, Christ's ether body began to reenter the Earth's etheric aura, which attained a certain level of completion thirty-three-and-one-third years later, January 8, 1933. This was the birth of the New Age, Satya Yuga (the "Age of Light"), whereby 1899 can be likened to the dawn and 1933 to the sunrise of the New Age. It was precisely during that period, from 1900 to 1925, that Rudolf Steiner's teaching activity unfolded. According to Steiner, Anthroposophy (spiritual science) is preparing the way for the

Second Coming, the approaching advent of which he assigned the year 1933.[7] In his lectures (around 1910 and the following years), he proclaimed the advent of Christ's Second Coming as the greatest event of the twentieth century. Steiner acted as a kind of John the Baptist who proclaimed the approaching Second Coming, just as John the Baptist prepared the way for the first coming nineteen centuries earlier.

With the first coming, the life of Jesus Christ lasted thirty-three-and-one-third years, the most important of which were the last three-and-a-half years (the ministry, from the baptism to the Mystery of Golgotha). In contrast, the Second Coming is an event taking place primarily in the etheric world, which, in accordance with the thirty-three-and-one-third-year rhythm, will last for 2500 years, or seventy-five thirty-three-and-one-third-year cycles, from September 10, 1899, to May 22, 4399. During these 2500 years, the most important rhythm is the thirty-three-and-one-third-year cycle of Christ's ether body; through comprehension of this rhythm, we are given the possibility of attuning to that ether body. It is the renewed presence of this ether body in the Earth's etheric aura that gave birth to the New Age, thus opening up the possibility of a new, "third" communion with Christ (later, we shall focus mostly on the "first communion," related to the twelve-year, Jupiter rhythm of the "I" of Christ in relation to the descent into the underworld).

The "second communion" is that of the astral body with Christ's astral body. As indicated in in *The Christ Mystery* ("The Second Coming and the Approaching Trial of Humanity"), the "second communion" relates to the twenty-nine-and-a-half-year rhythm of the planet Saturn. This rhythm holds the key to the "Apocalypse code" of our time, in which each day lived by Christ during the three-and-a-half years of his ministry clearly prepared the work of the Christ impulse for one "Saturn day" (twenty-nine-and-a-half years) in history. Christ's judgment of each day was inscribed into his astral body, and since the Mystery of Golgotha in 33 C.E., this activity of the Christ impulse in history has been unfolding for humanity as a whole in parallel with Saturn's orbit of the sidereal zodiac.

In terms of the Apocalypse code, humanity is now living through (1988 to 2018) the thirty-ninth day in the wilderness. This means that humanity as a whole is living through what Christ experienced on the thirty-ninth day in the wilderness: his encounter with Satan (Ahriman in Persian tradition), who presented Christ with the third temptation, turning stones into bread.[8]

Thus far, we have focused on the communion with Christ's ether body in relation to the thirty-three-and-one-third-year rhythm. The yearly *Christian Star Calendar* indicates how to intensify communion with Christ by living with the daily events in the world of the stars as they correspond with events in the life of Christ.

In the case of the Second Coming, what is the relationship between the twelve-year Jupiter rhythm and the thirty-three-and-one-third-year rhythm? To understand this, we must distinguish among the members of Christ's being: his "I," astral body, ether body, and physical (resurrection) body. The central rhythm of the New Age is the thirty-three-and-one-third-year rhythm of Christ's life, and the presence of this ether body in the Earth's etheric aura gave birth to the New Age. If, however, we were to consider only the thirty-three-and-one-third-year rhythm, this would amount to looking at the renewed presence of Christ's ether body in isolation from the other members of Christ's being. While acknowledging that, as an event taking place in the etheric realm, Christ's ether body is of central importance for the Second Coming, we should not lose sight of the fact that all four members of Christ's being work together and are actively involved in the Second Coming. The twelve-year Jupiter rhythm may be seen especially in relation to the "I" of Christ.

As mentioned earlier, the twelve-year Jupiter rhythm is significant with respect to the first mode of communion—with the "I" of Christ. The archetype of this is the descent into the underworld by the "I" of Christ following the death on the cross. Just as at the first coming there was the descent and ascent of the Christ's "I," likewise with the Second Coming there is again a descent and ascent, but this time taking place over a considerable period of time, lasting approximately two hundred years.

At the start of this article, the descent of Christ through the spiritual hierarchies from the Sun sphere down to the Earth is dated in connection with the twelve-year Jupiter rhythm, from Rudolf Steiner's birth in 1861 up to Ascension Day in 1932 or shortly before. (The computed date is April 25, and Ascension Day was ten days later on May 5, 1932.) This gives us insight into the cosmic phase of the descent of Christ's "I" in his Second Coming. But this cosmic phase of descent was only the prelude to the next stage of descent, which again can be followed in connection with the twelve-year Jupiter rhythm.

The heliocentric ingress of Jupiter into sidereal Leo around Ascension Day 1932 saw the beginning of the passage of Christ's "I" through the earthly sphere, the human realm. Resistance to his Second Coming arose, with its central focus in the figure of the Führer, who tried to set up the Third Reich, a kingdom of evil opposed to the kingdom of heaven (Reich in German means kingdom). The ensuing struggle resulted in World War II (1939–1945). By Easter 1945, the allies had effectively won the war in Europe, and a decisive step in the war with Japan was the Hiroshima bomb on August 6, 1945. By that time, a new twelve-year Jupiter cycle had commenced, as well as Christ's descent into the underworld through the subearthly realms. However, to understand this new phase in Christ's descent, it is helpful to look back to the archetype of this event in the Mystery of Golgotha.

On Good Friday, April 3, 33 C.E., shortly after carrying the cross up Mt. Calvary (it was about midday that he arrived at the summit of Golgotha), Jesus was stripped of his clothes and nailed to the cross. At 12:30 p.m., just as the trumpets sounded from the temple to announce the slaying of the Passover lambs, the cross was raised, and the crucifixion began. At this moment, east of Jerusalem, the sidereal sign of Leo (the constellation of the Lion) started to rise across the horizon (1° Leo). Thus began the slaying of Christ, the Lion of Judah. The crucifixion lasted during the rising of Leo and culminated with the death on the cross as the sidereal sign of Virgo began to rise. At the moment of death, at 3 p.m., the Ascendant was 2½° Virgo (all degrees are in terms of the sidereal zodiac, as defined in my book *History of the Zodiac*).

Following this, a powerful earthquake took place, rending the earth in two at the foot of the cross, and the radiant Spirit of Christ—Christ's "I"—descended from the cross and into the bowels of the Earth. Thus commenced the fulfillment of the sign of Jonah that Christ prophesied: "Just as Jonah was in the belly of the whale three days and three nights, so will the Son of Man be in the heart of the Earth three days and three nights" (Matthew 12:40). These "three days and three nights" should not be taken literally (the descent and ascent lasted only thirty hours), but we may imagine thirty hours in the underworld ("hell") allegorically as "three days and three nights in the heart of the Earth."

For our purposes, it is significant that Christ's descent into the underworld began with the rise of Virgo. The deeper meaning of Christ's descent to the heart of the Earth was to reunite with the Mother prior to his ascent to the Father. The sign of Virgo corresponds to the womb in the female organism, and it was appropriate (in cosmic symbolism) that the descent of Christ into the womb of Mother Earth began as Virgo started to rise.

Knowledge of the profound significance of Christ's descent into Hell as a descent into the underworld to reunite with the Mother is related to the Grail mysteries. This mystery of the descent to the Mother is central to Christ's Second Coming. Just as the descent began with the rising of sidereal Virgo during the Mystery of Golgotha, likewise, with the Second Coming, the descent into the underworld began with Jupiter's heliocentric ingress into sidereal Virgo during Easter night (Saturday to Sunday), March 31 to April

1, 1945. At this time, there was intense preparation to produce the first atomic bomb at the Los Alamos laboratory in New Mexico. The world's first atomic bomb—named Trinity—was detonated at 5:30 a.m., July 16, 1945, one hundred feet above Jornada del Muerto ("Journey of the Dead Man") in the southern New Mexico desert. On seeing the fireball and mushroom cloud, J. Robert Oppenheimer recalled a passage from the Bhagavad Gita: "I am become death, the destroyer of worlds."[9] The next two atomic bombs (*Little Boy* and *Fat Boy*) were detonated at 9:15 a.m., August 6, in Hiroshima, Japan, and at noon, August 9, in Nagasaki, which ended World War II and began the nuclear age.

The earthquake at the foot of the cross was the outer sign of Christ's descent into Hell at the Mystery of Golgotha; similarly, the opening of the Earth's interior through the bomb in Hiroshima was an outer sign of Christ's descent at the Second Coming, albeit this time a sign made by human hands and inspired by an evil force of destruction working its way up from the underworld. By August 6, 1945, Jupiter had already reached, heliocentrically, 9½° Virgo; geocentrically, however, Jupiter was at 2½° Virgo, which coincided with the zodiacal degree rising at the time of Christ's death on the cross. The commencement (at Easter 1945) of Christ's spiritual descent into the underworld (indicated by Jupiter's heliocentric ingress into sidereal Virgo) was "proclaimed" to the world by the powers of evil through the explosion of an atomic bomb at Hiroshima, coinciding with Jupiter geocentrically reaching 2½° Virgo.[10] This explosion corresponded in our time—the time of Christ's Second Coming—to the earthquake on Golgotha two thousand years earlier, which denoted the commencement of Christ's descent at that time into the underworld.

To understand more deeply our own time, it is helpful to look more closely at the stages of the descent of Christ's "I" into the underworld, beginning in 1945. Again, here the twelve-year Jupiter rhythm is important. Whereas the stages of cosmic descent (1861–1932) through the realms of the spiritual hierarchies are connected with Jupiter's heliocentric ingress into sidereal Leo, the stages of the descent into the underworld are related to Jupiter's heliocentric ingress into sidereal Virgo, starting in 1945. Between Ascension Day 1932 and Easter 1945, Christ's "I" was present in the earthly sphere of humanity; it was a time of suffering on the part of Christ, comparable to his Passion of Good Friday in 33 C.E. Indeed, World War II was a kind of crucifixion of Christ (preceding his second descent into Hell), a crucifixion on the etheric plane of existence, within the Earth's etheric aura (see the postscript at the end of this article).

To comprehend Christ's descent into the underworld, we need to know something of the Earth's inner structure. According to Rudolf Steiner, we can distinguish nine subearthly spheres leading to the core of the Earth.[11] These nine subearthly spheres may be thought of as reflecting the nine cosmic spheres of the nine spiritual hierarchies. Each sphere of the spiritual hierarchies contains a particular kind of goodness (the love of the Seraphim, the harmony of the Cherubim, and so on), whereas each subearthly sphere is the source of a particular kind of evil. The evil of each subearthly sphere is the inverse of the goodness belonging to the corresponding cosmic sphere. For example, in contrast to the love of the Seraphim belonging to the highest cosmic sphere is the hatred directed against Christ that stems from the deepest subearthly sphere, the ninth subearthly sphere. Against the harmony of the Cherubim is the divisive influence of the eighth subearthly sphere, the source of all strife and disharmony.

The earthly human sphere, in which we normally spend our waking existence between birth and death, is placed between the nine cosmic spheres of the spiritual hierarchies above, extending up to the kingdom of the Father, and the nine subearthly spheres of the powers of evil below, which are situated within the Earth, between humankind and the realm at the heart of the Earth belonging to the Divine Mother, or Demeter, as she was known to the Greeks. Every human being incarnated on Earth is subject to the interplay of what streams from the heavens above and what arises from the depths below. Generally, what works its way up from below is subconscious. The forces of evil working up from the nine subearthly spheres into the human subconscious must be overcome; a first step is to become conscious of those evil forces. Not everything that works up from below is evil, however, because what belongs to the realm of the Divine Mother also works into human beings from below. How may we begin to understand the realm of the Mother?

As a start, let us consider Steiner's words from the night of the full moon, April 5 and 6, 1909, when he chose to lay the foundation stone of the Rosicrucian temple at Malsch, near Karlsruhe, Germany:

> We want to sink the foundation stone of this temple into the womb of our Mother Earth, beneath the rays of the full Moon shining down upon us here, surrounded by the greenness of nature enveloping the building. And just as the Moon reflects the bright light of the Sun, so we seek to mirror the light of the divine spiritual beings. Full of trust, we turn toward our great Mother Earth, who bears us and protects us so lovingly....In pain and suffering, our Mother Earth has become hardened. It is our mission to spiritualize her again, to redeem her, in that through the power of our hands we reshape her to become a spirit-filled work of art. May this stone be a first foundation stone for the redemption and transformation of our planet Earth, and may the power of this stone multiply itself a thousandfold.[12]

Here it is significant that the night of the full moon was chosen, as it was also full moon on the evening of Good Friday, 33 C.E., when Christ began his descent into the womb of the Earth, down to the Mother. Steiner also described the color seen clairvoyantly arising from the depths, from the realm of the Mother:

> The silver-sparkling blue below, arising from the depths of the Earth and connected with human weakness and error,

is gathered into a picture of the Earth Mother. Whether we call her Demeter or Mary, the picture is of the Earth Mother. Thus it is that, as we gaze downward, we must bring together in imagination all the secrets of the depths that make up the material Mother of all existence. While in all that is concentrated in the flowing form above, we feel and experience the Spirit Father of everything around us. Now we witness the result of cooperation between the Spirit Father with the Earth Mother, bearing so beautifully within itself the harmony of the earthly silver and the gold of the heights. Between the Father and the Mother, we behold the Son.[13]

Since the time of ancient Greece, following the rise of Christianity, knowledge of the Mother and the secrets of the depths has more or less disappeared from human consciousness. The cult of Demeter, celebrated in the Eleusinian mysteries at Eleusis, was suppressed by the emperor Theodosius at the end of the fourth century C.E. Now, however, through the Second Coming of Christ, new access to the Earth Mother and her mysteries is opening up. Summarizing briefly, a three-fold mystery is connected with the Mother:

> The name of the Mother (Demeter to the Greeks);
> Her realm (Shambhala in the East);
> Her will (eternal faithfulness to the Father, despite the
>   withdrawal, since the Fall, of the Mother into the
>   depths of the underworld, the heart of the Earth).

Concerning the lost realm of the Mother, Shambhala, it is interesting to consider Rudolf Steiner's words to Countess Johanna von Keyserlingk at the end of his *Agricultural Course* (Pentecost 1924), at which he laid the foundations for a new and conscious relationship to the Earth Mother, Demeter, through the spiritually based form of agriculture known as the biodynamic method:

> Rudolf Steiner had the kindness to come up to my room, where
> he spoke to me about the kingdom in the interior of the Earth.
> We know that, at the moment when Christ's blood flowed
> down onto the earth at Golgotha, a new sun-globe was born

in the Earth's interior. My search had always been directed toward studying the Earth's depths, because I had seen within the Earth a golden kernel light up, named by Ptolemy the primeval Sun. I could connect those golden depths only with the land that Steiner said was hidden from human sight, and that Christ would open the gates to lead those who seek it to the submerged fairy-tale land of Shambhala, of which the Indians dream.... I asked Rudolf Steiner, "Is the interior of the Earth made of the gold that comes from the hollow cavity in the Sun and is destined to return there?" He replied, "Yes, the interior of the Earth is of gold."... I continued to question him for my assurance: "Doctor, when I am standing here on Earth...the golden land is beneath me, deep within the interior of the Earth; if I now attain sinlessness and remain in the depths, will the demons be able to harm me, and will I be able to penetrate beyond them and reach the golden land?" He replied, "If you pass through them accompanied by Christ, the demons will be unable to harm you—but otherwise they would indeed be able to destroy you." He added emphatically, "They can, nevertheless, become our helpers. Yes, this is true; the path is a true one, but very difficult."[14]

Here, therefore, we see that, owing to the nine spheres of evil inserted between humanity and the realm of the Mother, the path to the Mother is beset with difficulty; however, this path is possible with Christ. Indeed, Steiner emphasized that opening the way to Shambhala is the central meaning of Christ's Second Coming.[15] As mentioned earlier, this path has opened up to humanity at large since 1945.[16] Previously, it was accessible only to the highest initiates. At the same time, with the opening of the gates of Hell, humanity is increasingly exposed to the demonic influences of subearthly spheres.

Against this background, we may view certain developments in the twentieth and twenty-first centuries. As outlined, the only safe way we can begin to look at these developments is together with Christ. In connection with the descent of Christ himself, his Second Coming, we shall briefly review the course of the twentieth century and the first years of the twenty-first. Before taking this step, however, it is useful to be aware that Christ's nine Beatitudes in the Sermon on the Mount contain the Christian impulses to counteract the demonic influences from each of the nine subearthly spheres. The sixth Beatitude, for example, says, "Blessed are the pure in heart, for they shall see God." Purity of heart counteracts the demonic influence of the sixth subearthly sphere, which is the source of evil passions that, when they take hold, render a person oblivious to the spiritual world, leaving awareness only of the lower impulses that lead to depravity. The qualities of the other eight Beatitudes likewise relate to the evil of the other subearthly spheres. The nine Beatitudes are therefore of key significance on the path that accompanies Christ on his descent into the underworld. Moreover, since the human being is a microcosm that reflects the macrocosm, we should keep in mind that the nine subearthly spheres are also within each human being, and that the descent into the underworld is at the same time a descent into our own being. In fact, each of the nine Beatitudes refers to a particular member of the human being, and, in similar fashion, the nine subearthly spheres are the source of counter-impulses to the nine members of the human being.

Supplementing the table at the beginning of this article, we can add to the passage of Christ through the spheres of the spiritual hierarchies, culminating in his passage through the sphere of the archangels (1908–1920) and through that of the angels (1920–1932), with the passage through the realm of humanity between Ascension Day 1932 and Easter 1945. Following this is Christ's descent into the underworld, indicating the relationship underlying the counter-impulses to the nine members of the human being, as shown in the table on the following page.

The given dates are those of Jupiter's heliocentric ingress into sidereal Virgo (these astronomically computed dates may differ somewhat from the actual dates of Christ's descent). On this path of descent, each sphere involves confrontation with a particular

CHRIST'S DESCENT THROUGH THE SUBEARTHLY SPHERES:	COUNTER-IMPULSES TO:	DATES:
1. Mineral earth:	physical body	May 25, 1933– Apr. 1, 1945
2. Fluid earth:	ether body	Apr. 1, 1945– Feb. 10, 1957
3. Air earth:	astral body	Feb. 10, 1957– Dec. 21, 1968
4. Form earth:	sentient soul	Dec. 21, 1968– Nov. 1, 1980
5. Fruit earth:	intellectual soul	Nov. 1, 1980– Sept. 11, 1992
6. Fire earth:	consciousness soul	Sept. 11, 1992– July 24, 2004
7. Earth mirror:	spirit self (manas)	July 24, 2004– June 5, 2016
8. Earth serverer*:	life spirit (budhi)	June 5, 2016– Apr. 14, 2028
9. Earth core:	spirit body (atma)	Apr. 14, 2028– Feb. 24, 2040

*The eighth subearthly sphere is also known as the "divisive layer."

kind of evil. We can begin to understand this struggle through an analogy with the confrontation in the human realm on Earth between 1932 and 1945. The powers of evil working from the subearthly spheres found a vehicle in the human kingdom (the Führer Adolf Hitler) to act as a focus of their opposition to the Second Coming. A full-scale attack was launched through this vehicle as a counter to the impulse brought by Christ. This counter-impulse can be followed down to the last detail. For example, instead of

"Hallowed be thy name," the chant arose on Earth to hallow (heil) the name of the Führer. And instead of "Thy kingdom come" the Führer sought to establish an evil kingdom (the Third Reich) in place of the kingdom of God.

A titanic struggle ensued, culminating in World War II; as mentioned earlier, this can be regarded as a second crucifixion. However, the conflict did not end with the triumph over evil in 1945. Although that year saw the end of conflict in the earthly human realm, the confrontation continued in the subearthly spheres, into which Christ descended, signifying the opening of the gates of the underworld. The explosion of the atomic bombs at Hiroshima and Nagasaki were a human-made sign that the gates of Hell have opened, shattering the Earth's surface, which, like an eggshell, encloses the Earth's interior: the subearthly spheres and the realm of the Mother. Through the Hiroshima and Nagasaki bombs, the first major cracks appeared in the shell that separates the Earth's surface from the underworld, or Hell. It should be noted that on July 16, 1945, the first test explosion of an atomic bomb at Los Alamos, New Mexico, took place one hundred feet above the ground and thus had a somewhat different relationship to the Earth's surface than did the atomic bombs dropped on Japan, which affected the Earth itself at those locations.

Strictly speaking, this "eggshell" is the first subearthly sphere, or mineral earth. As such, it is not like the other eight subearthly spheres; rather, it is a layer that separates the human realm from the underworld. Even during the period before 1945, especially during World War II, the influence of the mineral earth was exerting an ever-stronger hold on human consciousness. In 1939 to 1940, the search began in Britain and the U.S. for a military application of nuclear fission. Under the direction of Enrico Fermi, this led to the first self-sustaining nuclear chain reaction, which took place in Chicago on December 2, 1942, and was known as the Manhattan Project. This whole line of scientific research was symptomatic of the increasing influence of the mineral earth on humankind.

How should we describe the influence of this first realm of subnature? Here, we find an approach to the subearthly spheres in the Beatitudes, which contain the counter-impulses to the subearthly spheres. For the first subearthly sphere, the mineral earth, the first Beatitude is relevant: "Blessed are the seekers of the spirit, for theirs is the kingdom of heaven." The influence of the mineral earth is the opposite of this and leads to turning away from the spirit and toward the earthly kingdom: the mineral, material, mechanical realm and its laws. The scientific research that led to the explosion of bombs at Los Alamos, Hiroshima, and Nagasaki is an example of this, starting with the disintegration of the nuclei of lithium through bombardment by artificially generated protons, first accomplished by John Cockcroft and Ernest Walton at the Cavendish Laboratory, Cambridge, on April 13, 1932. This was shortly before April 25, 1932, the date in the table at the beginning of this article for the onset of the Second Coming in the human kingdom. On September 12, 1933 (less than four months after the first date in the previous table), Leo Szilard conceived the idea of a nuclear chain reaction, subsequently realized in 1942 as part of the Manhattan Project in Chicago, involving the collaboration of Leo Szilard, Enrico Fermi, and others.[17]

This whole direction of scientific research, under the spirit-denying influence of the mineral earth, was characteristic of the first Jupiter period (preceding 1945) of the age of the Second Coming. During that period, a counter-impulse to that connected with the physical body held sway. Indeed, the titanic struggle during World War II was for dominion of the kingdom (*Reich*) on the physical plane of existence and for the very existence—physically—of countless human beings. This means that, during the first Jupiter period of the age of the Second Coming, instead of the impulse of seeking for the spirit, for the kingdom of heaven, there lived the counter-impulse of turning away from the spirit toward the earthly kingdom, especially matter.

During the second Jupiter period (1945–1957), which coincided with the descent of Christ through the second subearthly sphere (fluid earth), a new counter-impulse began to play into human life on Earth. How may this be characterized? The relevant Beatitude is "Blessed are those who bear suffering, for they shall be comforted." The counter-impulse of the fluid earth is that of caring only for oneself and avoiding suffering according to the principle of "survival of the fittest." In the wake of devastation and the pain and suffering of World War II, ample opportunity existed for the awakening of a new worldwide human consciousness: caring and sharing, give and take, and comfort for the mourning ones. But with the crack in the "eggshell," the rupture in the mineral earth caused by the emerging atomic age, something new entered and assumed a role in human life on Earth.

Here an impulse arose that was counter to the ether body, the subtle body of life forces that interpenetrates the physical body. When the ether body separates from the physical body at death, the true nature of the physical body is revealed as a corpse. The ether body bears the principle of life, the counter-impulse of which is anti-life. This is the substance of the fluid earth, the second subearthly sphere. When the mineral earth cracked because of the atomic bomb, massive quantities of this anti-life substance were released on Earth as radioactive fallout. Radioactivity has the quality of being destructive to life. As soon as it comes into contact with anything alive, it destroys that life.

Against the background of Christ's passage through the second subearthly sphere, we can see the development from 1945 onward. Confrontation with the evil at work in each subearthly sphere takes place within that sphere; such a confrontation relies primarily on becoming aware of the nature of the evil principle arising from that sphere. Many people were inspired after World War II to take up the challenge offered by this confrontation. For example, Leo Szilard, as a leading atomic scientist, took up a crusade of raising awareness of the fearful implications of atomic war. In 1947, with

Albert Einstein as the chair, he formed the Emergency Committee of Atomic Scientists. He also initiated the movement for the civilian control of atomic energy. Later, in Washington, DC, he organized the Council for a Livable World.[18]

Nevertheless, the governments of the U.S. and the Soviet Union continued to support the type of research that led to developing the atomic bomb. Consequently, on March 1, 1954, the U.S. exploded a hydrogen bomb on Eniwetak-Atoll, Marshall Islands, in the Pacific, reckoned to be six hundred times more powerful than the Hiroshima bomb. In the wake of that explosion, 287 people within 160 miles of Eniwetak-Atoll suffered the effects of radioactive fallout. The radioactive fallout was measured as far away as Heidelberg, Germany. Following suit, on November 22, 1955, the Soviet Union exploded an even more powerful hydrogen bomb in the atmosphere above Siberia. With these two hydrogen bomb explosions, the arms race took a sinister turn, allowing the anti-life substance of the fluid earth to find its way in large quantities onto the Earth's surface via radioactive fallout.

Following the attack on the level of the physical body during the first Jupiter period (1933–1945) of the Second Coming, which culminated with World War II, and during the second Jupiter period (1945–1957), the attack on the ether body began—radioactive fallout being the principle bearer of the anti-life principle belonging to the second subearthly sphere. The attack on the ether body also started to make itself noticeable in other ways. The main indication of this is the interpenetration of the ether body with electrical effects through increased use of electrical household devices and the spread of television during the post-war years. Another potent means of electrification in the ether body was the advent of rock and electrically amplified music, which surfaced around 1950. This prepared for a new onslaught from the third subearthly sphere, the air earth.

During Christ's descent into the underworld, passage through the air earth occurred from 1957 to 1968. We find the active Christ principle during that time in the third Beatitude: "Blessed are the meek, for they shall inherit the Earth." This relates to the human astral body and to its becoming Christianized through meekness or, expressed more actively, through loving kindness, goodness, and peace. The counter-impulse from the air earth works to paralyze the astral body and cut it off from cosmic astrality, whereby the suffocating atmosphere of the third subearthly sphere annuls feeling.

Just as the Hiroshima and Nagasaki bombs were human-made indications of the mineral earth cracking and opening up contact with the fluid earth, so there was a human-made sign of opening up a connection with the air earth. This sign was the Soviet launching of the first *Sputnik* on October 4, 1957, the first artificial satellite to circle the globe above Earth's atmosphere. This step began the space age. The deeper significance of this step was that it began to cut humanity off from cosmic spiritual realms of existence by inserting human constructions (satellites, rockets, and space stations) between the cosmos and earthly humankind. On a macrocosmic level, this corresponds to the microcosmic effect of the air earth cutting off the human astral body from cosmic astrality.

Following the example of the Soviets, on February 1, 1958, the U.S. also successfully launched a satellite into space above the Earth's atmosphere. Then, on April 12, 1961, Uri Gagarin orbited around the Earth in a spaceship. This feat was matched shortly after when, on February 20, 1962, John Glenn circled the Earth in a space capsule. The U.S. emerged triumphant in the space race on July 21, 1969, with the remarkable feat of landing men on the Moon.

During adolescence, the astral body becomes prominent in the development of a human being; it is the time of one's awakening sexuality and feeling life, as well as a time of turbulent emotions. During the period from 1957 to 1968, the third Jupiter period of the Second Coming, owing to the confrontation that arose in the third subearthly sphere on account of Christ's passage through this realm, an onslaught of evil was directed at the astral body, the third member of the human being (after the physical and ether bodies). During that time, toward the end of the previous Jupiter period, we see many signs of "cultural adolescence," one of which was the rise and spread of rock music around 1956, which had a negative effect on the ether body. Moreover, it also has a detrimental effect upon human emotions and thus upon the astral body in the sense of the counter-impulse of the air earth. Rock music, on the whole, works on the level of the adolescent feeling life. When rock music first surfaced in 1950, one of the first rock musicians, Bill Haley, said that a new kind of music had been discovered through which the souls of young people could be captured (away from the influence of their parents). In the meantime, numerous studies have shown that rock music can encourage not only rebellion against parents, but also rape and other violent behavior, sadism, masochism, and all manner of sexual perversion, criminal behavior, anarchy, and even black magic.[19] The phenomenal spread of rock music during the period under consideration points to the onslaught of evil coming from the third subearthly sphere and directed toward the astral body. Whereas genuine music (Bach, Mozart, Beethoven, and other composers)—being a reflection of the harmonies of the spheres—is capable of elevating the astral body toward cosmic spiritual realms, the effect of rock music, generally speaking, is to set up a connection between the astral body and the third subearthly sphere, thus dragging the astral body down.

The astral body was formed in the preceding cosmic eon, the Moon period of existence, and thus the astral body has a strong relationship to the Moon. The U.S. space mission, which initially had the goal of landing human beings on the Moon, unfolded by and large during the Jupiter period under consideration (1957–1968), motivated in part by the subconscious relationship to the Moon. In fact, at the completion of this Jupiter period, December 21, 1968, the U.S. National Aeronautics and Space Administration (NASA) launched *Apollo VIII*, which orbited the Moon ten times. This was followed on July 16, 1969, shortly after the start of the next Jupiter period, by the launch of *Apollo XI,* which carried Neil Armstrong and Edwin Aldrin to the Moon, an event that denotes (inversely) a kind of coming of age for humanity following the period of cultural adolescence. We shall return to this after considering other aspects of the Jupiter period from 1957 to 1968.

The Moon forces in the human being are expressed most directly through sexuality, the awakening of which generally takes place during adolescence. During the period of cultural adolescence, from 1957 to 1968, this awakening was expressed in the sexual revolution of the late 1960s. At the same time, with the introduction and subsequent widespread use of the contraceptive pill, another step was taken in cutting off humanity from its divine origins. This can be understood quite simply in the fact that conception is—and always has been—the door through which incarnating souls enter the path of incarnation into a physical body on Earth. The deliberate and systematic prevention of conception closes this door to the realm of souls.

At the same time, by way of books, films, and magazines, an onslaught was launched to corrupt and pervert every aspect of sexuality and desecrate its holy and sacramental character. In this connection, the words of Hermes addressed to Asclepius (Greek text written prior to the end of the third century c.e.) are relevant:

> In the conjunction of the two sexes, or, to speak more truly, that fusion of them into one, which may be rightly named Eros, or Aphrodite, or both at once, there is a deeper meaning than human beings can comprehend. It is a truth to be accepted as sure and evident above all other truths, that by God, the Master of all generative power, has been devised and bestowed upon all creatures this sacrament of eternal reproduction, with all the affection, all the joy and gladness, all the yearning and the heavenly love that are inherent in its being. And there were need that I should tell you of the compelling force with which this sacrament binds man and woman together, were it not that each one of us, if he directs

his thought upon himself, can learn it from his innermost feeling. For if you note that supreme moment when, through interaction without pause, we come at last to this: that either sex infuses itself into the other, the one giving forth its issue, and the other eagerly taking hold of it and laying it up within. You will find that at that moment, through the intermingling of the two natures, the female acquires masculine vigor, and the male is relaxed in feminine languor. And so this sacramental act, sweet as it is, if it were done openly, the ignorant should mock, and thereby the deity manifested in either sex through the mingling of male and female should be put to blush—and the more so, if the act is exposed to the eyes of impious men.[20]

Through exposure, therefore, as effected by way of the media, the divine aspect of sexuality is driven out. Beyond this, the rise and spread of pornography has served not only to debase sexuality, but also to pervert and corrupt it. This, too, is connected with the counter-impulse upon the astral body working from the third subearthly sphere, the air earth.

Yet another aspect of this counter-impulse manifested and spread during the period from 1957 to 1968 as a drug epidemic, including especially the widespread use of hallucinogenic drugs such as marijuana, hashish, mescaline, and LSD. Above all, this counter-impulse corrupted the true impulse of the third Beatitude, "Blessed are the meek, for they shall inherit the Earth," which was seeking to emerge at that time. The impulse of love, peace, and goodwill ("flower power") that arose was a genuine inspiration of the Christ impulse at work in the transformation of the astral body. However, through the drug prophets such as Timothy Leary, whose experiments with LSD date from 1960, a powerful counter-impulse was directed at the astral body. The mind-altering properties of LSD had been discovered in 1943, but it was not until 1957 that the term "psychedelic" was introduced by Dr. Humphrey Osmond, who used "psychedelic therapy" to treat alcoholics. During this time, too, the CIA experimented with LSD with the aim of creating an "exploitable alteration of personality" in selected personalities.[21] As I described in *The Christ Mystery,* it was in 1958 that the trial of casting oneself down from the pinnacle of the temple began for humanity as a whole. In promoting LSD, Timothy Leary used to say, "Turn on, tune in, drop out," which is an exact modern-day rendering of casting oneself down from the pinnacle of the temple. This signifies abandonment of the temple pinnacle (the highest in the human being: reason and conscience) in favor of abandoning the "I" by plunging into the experience of subconscious forces, achieved through the intoxicating influence of drugs (and other means), LSD having proved well-suited to attaining this goal.

Christ responded to this temptation—the second of the three in the wilderness—by saying, "You shall not tempt the Lord your God" (Matthew 4:7). In other words, the Divine in the human being (the "I") should not be tempted by what is lower, the astral body. The activity of the Christ impulse in transforming the astral body leads to the development of conscious clairvoyance (Imagination), which is a metamorphosis of the dream consciousness of the astral body. On the other hand, the use of hallucinogenic drugs serves to evoke an artificially induced, atavistic clairvoyance in which astral dream consciousness is activated without the conscious participation of the human "I," which leads to hallucinations instead of Imaginations. In this sense, we can view hallucinogenic drugs in direct relation to the counter-impulse of the third subearthly sphere upon the astral body.

These are just some of the phenomena that can be seen in connection with the confrontation between the Christ impulse and the counter-impulse of the air earth from 1957 to 1968. There are other phenomena as well, but here the following two phenomena may be mentioned:

1) The fight against racial discrimination from the days of Little Rock, Arkansas, in September 1957 to the shooting on April 4, 1968, of Dr. Martin Luther King Jr., whose martyrdom did much to help establish racial equality. Just one week later, April 11,

1968, the Civil Rights Law was passed under President Lyndon B. Johnson, which (from a legal standpoint) largely ended racial discrimination in the U.S.

2) Student rebellion, which reached a climax in Europe, particularly in France, in May 1968 in the mass demonstrations and ensuing clashes with the police, resulting in the closure of the Sorbonne.

After this, a cultural coming of age took place. The student rebellion, which reached a climax in 1968, was the last phase of the period of cultural adolescence that ended December 1968. The human sign of the new phase that opened up in 1969 was the landing of human beings on the Moon. This extraordinary feat symbolized the birth of human beings as citizens of the cosmos, albeit as a caricature of what these words mean in a spiritual sense. Here again, a counter-impulse was at work. True human destiny is to become spiritual citizens of the cosmos through an awakening of consciousness to include the cosmic dimension of existence. The physical landing on the Moon worked to counter this awakening by influencing human consciousness toward an awareness directed solely toward the physical-material dimension of the cosmos.

Following the Moon landing, the U.S. space program began to explore the solar system, sending rockets to Mars and Jupiter. *Mariner 9* encircled Mars on November 13, 1971, and *Pioneer 10* passed close by Jupiter on December 4, 1973. The space exploration program has accomplished many remarkable feats since then, including the spectacular "zapping" of Comet Temple on July 4, 2005. However, these achievements generally serve to intensify a physical-material view of the cosmos, leading to a completely false impression of humanity's relationship to the cosmic spiritual world. This can be seen in relation to the counter-impulse of the fourth subearthly sphere, the form earth. In this sphere forms become inverted and caricatures. The space program has helped to build a kind of negative image of the solar system. This negative image is devoid of all spirituality and excludes the human being, except as an astronaut. However, the human being viewed as an astronaut, encapsulated in a space suit, is a negative image of the spiritual human being, who is connected with the whole cosmos. The entry to the era of space travel was opened up by the Moon landing in 1969 and may be viewed in direct connection with the counter-impulse of the fourth subearthly sphere.

In terms of the opening of the gates of Hell, occasioned by Christ's descent through the subearthly spheres, the period from 1969 to 1980, the fourth Jupiter period of Christ's Second Coming, was that of confrontation with the evil of the fourth subearthly sphere, directed against the human sentient soul. The true impulse for this period—connected with the fourth stage of unfolding the new Christ impulse in the age of the Second Coming—is conveyed by the fourth Beatitude: "Blessed are those who hunger and thirst after righteousness, for they shall be filled." Something of this impulse inspired those who demonstrated for peace, especially for peace in Vietnam, and who hungered and thirsted for a righteous solution to the unjust situation in that country. On November 13 and 14, 1969, some 250,000 demonstrators for peace gathered in Washington, the largest demonstration of its kind ever to have taken place there.

The influence of the fourth subearthly sphere is to turn everything into its negative. The "hunger and thirst for righteousness" in its negative form can give rise to terrorism. Against this background, we saw the escalation of violence in Northern Ireland, which began with the wave of unrest in August 1969 and resulted in the British sending troops to Ulster. The relationship between the Catholics and Protestants of Northern Ireland is something on the level of the sentient soul, beneath the reasoning level of the intellectual soul; it thus seems to defy the rational intellect. Here, the counter-impulse directed against the sentient soul began to work in 1969. The influence of this counter-impulse is to render human beings insensitive to the just claims of other human beings. The flames of terrorism are fanned by infatuation with one's own claims for justice while viewing the claims of everyone else as wrong and unjust. This continues as the terrorism of the Islamic Jihadists, but now with the new and sinister twist of suicide bombing, representing the inverse of "No one has greater love than this, to lay down one's life for one's friends" (John 15:13).

During this period, terrorism raised its ugly head not just in Northern Ireland, but elsewhere as well. In February 1970, Arabs and Palestinians (again, people living mainly on the level of the sentient soul) launched several terrorist attacks. On September 5, 1972, at the Olympic Games in Munich Arab terrorists killed two Israeli athletes and took nine hostages, all of whom were killed when police tried to free them. Earlier that year, the Baader-Meinhof terrorist gang in Germany had carried out attacks in May, prior to the capture of Andreas Baader on June 2, 1972. Terrorist activity—murder, kidnapping, and bombing—became widespread, with one of the worst examples taking place August 2, 1980 (toward the close of this Jupiter period), when a right-wing terrorist group bombed a railroad station in Bologna, killing eighty-three people.

On the positive side, there was increase in the movement for human rights during the 1970s, with the efforts of Amnesty International being the best-known examples. In January 1977, "Charter '77"—signed by more than 250 prominent people and issued in Prague—called for liberalization in that country. Twelve years later, one of the signatories, the playwright Vaclav Havel, who had been persecuted and imprisoned for his calls for democracy, became president of Czechoslovakia. Here we see the triumph of the hunger and thirst for righteousness. Another positive manifestation of the Christ impulse during this period was the work of Mother Teresa in caring for the sick and needy people of Calcutta. In recognition of her work, on December 10, 1979, Mother Teresa received the Nobel Peace Prize.

On the whole, however, it was the counter-impulse that came to the fore from 1969 to 1980. This was the Brezhnev era in the Soviet Union, when the cold war intensified, characterized by General

Secretary Leonid Brezhnev's inverted sense of justice: "When forces hostile to socialism seek to reverse the development of any socialist country whatsoever...this becomes the concern of all socialist countries." What this Brezhnev doctrine really signified was the Soviet Union's claim to the right to provide "military aid [read "invade"] to a fraternal country" whenever there is a "threat to the common interest of the camp of socialism" (meaning any challenge to Soviet dominance). Reading between the lines, we clearly see the inverting influence of the form earth, which produces a negative image of true righteousness, which would mean allowing the people of each land to determine the future of their own country.

In the United States, a negative image of righteousness emerged with the Watergate scandal, which involved the break-in and attempted illegal electronic surveillance of the Democratic headquarters in Washington, DC, by five members of Richard Nixon's Committee for the Re-election of the President. As a result of the Watergate affair and in the face of persistent investigations and public revelations, Nixon was eventually obliged to resign as president.

In the cultural realm, alongside the increase in violence and terrorism, a more positive development was the opening up on a widespread scale in relation to esoteric and spiritual matters. The New Age movement quickly gained momentum, a key step of which was the publication of David Spangler's *Revelation: The Birth of a New Age* (1971). Spangler, a major prophet of the New Age movement, is essentially Christian-oriented, whereas many New Age impulses have been more influenced by Eastern impulses, including Yoga, Tai Chi, breathing and meditation practices, as well as various forms of healing, many of which work mainly on the sentient soul and demand little intellectual effort or deeper consciousness, though there are notable exceptions.

One disturbing phenomenon of this period was the massive increase in drug addiction, especially to heroin. As mentioned earlier, hallucinogenic drugs, which enjoyed widespread popularity during the 1960s, affect the astral body and the dreamlike picture consciousness connected with it. Heroin, which is injected into the blood, the bearer of the "I," attacks directly on the level of the soul, the sentient soul. It overwhelms human feeling and works in the sense of the fourth subearthly sphere by making the user insensitive to everything outside of one's immediate sense of wellbeing.

On November 1, 1980, a new Jupiter period began and lasted until 1992. Just three days into this period, on November 4, 1980, Ronald Reagan became the U.S. President, beginning the "Reagan era." At the same time a new phase in Christ's descent into the underworld commenced, this confrontation being with the evil belonging to the fifth subearthly sphere, the fruit earth. A sign of this new stage of confrontation with evil emerged in the form of the AIDS virus, which attacks the life-support system of the human being. Those most susceptible to this virus are people who seek the exuberant energy of egotistically directed life forces.

Exuberant energy is the characteristic of the substance of the fruit earth, and the drug most closely related to this quality of the fruit earth, the fifth subearthly sphere, is cocaine. The fifth subearthly sphere bears the counter-impulse to the intellectual soul, and similarly, cocaine is directed against the intellectual soul, just as heroin is directed against the sentient soul. Both heroin and cocaine work into the blood, the bearer of the "I," which they attack. However, heroin overwhelms the feeling nature (sentient soul), whereas cocaine overwhelms the mental nature (intellectual soul). In the confrontation with the counter-impulse to the intellectual soul, which began in 1980, it is not surprising that addiction to cocaine has assumed epidemic proportions.

Because cocaine is able to stimulate a relationship with the exuberant energy of the fruit earth, cocaine addicts establish an inner connection with the fifth subearthly sphere, just as heroin addicts connect with the fourth subearthly sphere, and hallucinogenic drug users connect with the third subearthly sphere. Seen in this light, drugs can become the instruments of underworld demonic beings to gain access to the human soul and astral body. The war against drugs is actually a war against demonic forces and beings that take possession of human beings and drag them downward in the direction of the subearthly spheres.

The redeeming impulse to these demonic forces is the Christ impulse. The fifth Beatitude indicates the nature of the relevant Christ impulse as a positive counter to the evil of the fifth subearthly sphere: "Blessed are the merciful, for they shall receive mercy." It is a matter of compassion and forgiveness, not intellectual judgments. When Ronald Reagan branded the Soviet Union as the "evil empire," he passed judgment on a whole people. Unfortunately, he allowed his overly hasty judgment to become the basis of his arms policy, which led to the massive build-up of nuclear arms and commitment to Strategic Defense Initiative (SDI), or "Star Wars," a fantastically expensive defense project to defend the U.S. against the "evil empire." This is very different from the merciful attitude implicit in the fifth Beatitude. In fact, if it had been realized, SDI would represent another step along the path of cutting off the Earth and humankind from the spiritual cosmos.

When Mikhail Gorbachev became General Secretary of the Communist Party on March 11, 1985, he had every reason to reciprocate Reagan's hostile attitude, in which case the Cold War would have continued to escalate. However, President Gorbachev appears to have been imbued with some of the quality of mercy expressed by the fifth Beatitude. He did not judge but met with President Reagan in a spirit of openness. Similarly, he later met open-mindedly with President George Herbert Walker Bush. Astonishingly for the head of an officially atheistic state, in November 1989, he also met with Pope John Paul II. On the day prior to his meeting the pope in Rome, Gorbachev said, "We need a revolution of the mind." This is evidently an impulse on the mental level (intellectual soul) that characterizes Gorbachev's reforms, the key words of which were *glasnost* (openness) and *perestroika* (restructuring).

The spectacular achievement of Gorbachev's reforming impulse was to open up the possibility of democracy in the East European countries that had been satellites of the Soviet Union since 1945. If we recall that democracy was born in ancient Greece with the development of the intellectual soul, it is easy to see the level on which Gorbachev's reforming impulse worked and to see—at least, in its positive side—that it worked in conjunction with the Christ impulse. The deeper background to this is the preparation of the ground in Eastern Europe for the development of a new culture there, in which the Christ impulse can emerge on a new level during the future Age of Aquarius.

The counter-impulse to the fifth Beatitude is cruelty and lack of mercy, the source of which is in the fifth subearthly sphere. This impulse took the upper hand among those in power in China, whose orders led to the massacre of hundreds of peacefully demonstrating students in the Tiananmen Square during the early morning hours of June 4, 1989.[22]

Seven years earlier, cruelty underlay the massacre of over one thousand Palestinian refugees on September 18, 1982, at the hands of Christian militia who entered a refugee camp in Beirut, while the occupying Israeli troops stood by and watched. It was mainly women, children, and the elderly who died in the hail of bullets. We may also think of the assassination attempt on Ronald Reagan on March 30, 1981, and on Pope John Paul II May 13, 1981, as symptoms of the same counter-impulse. The violence to which cocaine addicts are prone may also be connected with this impulse.

This counter-impulse is active in the thousands of murders and acts of violence each year around the world. It is also expressed in more subtle ways, without necessarily being lived out. Just consider the violence depicted in films and on television. More sinister, however, are the "video nasties" that depict savage and sadistic acts of violence and brutality, establishing a link between human consciousness and the fifth subearthly sphere, just as rock music helps facilitate a link with the third subearthly sphere.

In writing this, I am aware of the danger of over-generalization, since there are examples of rock groups who are endeavoring to raise consciousness through their music. The point is, though, that electrified music as a medium actually invokes subearthly forces from the third subearthly realm, which was evident in an extraordinary phenomenon of mass hysteria at concerts of the Beatles, the Rolling Stones, and other leading rock groups. Similarly, there are many films made with good intentions. Yet, according to Rudolf Steiner in 1917, the medium of film itself has a detrimental effect on human beings:

> While people are sitting at the cinema, what they see there does not make its way into the ordinary faculty of perception; it enters a deeper, more material stratum than we usually employ for our perception. A person becomes etherically goggle-eyed at the cinema and develops eyes like those of a seal, only much larger, I mean larger etherically. This works in a materializing way, not only upon what the person has in consciousness, but upon their deepest subconsciousness.[23]

During a later conversation with the musician Jan Stuten (1890–1948) in the fall of 1918, Steiner added these comments about movies:

> They meet an elementary need in human beings in a clever and cunning way—this is the hunger for the world of pictures, images, and the forces connected therewith [this was the period of silent movies]. However, film is not an artistic medium....It corrupts the human being's relationship to space and time, kills fantasy, harms the ether body, and works against human freedom....It leads to compulsive thoughts and destroys the faculty for Imagination."[24] [The latter term refers to conscious clairvoyance.]

Another modern phenomenon, which sometimes tends to form an alliance between human consciousness and the counter-impulse directed against the intellectual soul, is the computer, the spread of which has been especially remarkable in recent years. While we cannot deny the beneficial aspect of computers when rightly applied, an excessive preoccupation with them tends to exaggerate and overemphasize the intellect in the direction of a mechanical mode of thinking. This mechanical element of the intellect forms a link with the subearthly spheres, particularly the fifth subearthly sphere, which bears the counter-impulse to the intellectual soul. The true nature of the intellectual soul, as seen during the Greco-Roman period (the age of the developing intellectual soul), exemplified by the Greek philosophers, is organic thinking, which is comfortable pondering the relationships among God, humanity, and nature. Organic thinking may be trained by contemplation of the living, organic realm of nature. In the case of an excessive preoccupation with computers, thinking is trained by the machine and its rigid, inorganic logic; thinking becomes mechanized. This simple consideration shows that the mechanization of thought—an inherent danger for those obliged to deal extensively with computers in daily life—may be safeguarded against by deliberately cultivating living (organic) thinking.

Here we can point to the major role of computers in the arms race. Indeed, a project such as SDI would be unthinkable without computers. In 2007, a metamorphosis of SDI emerged in the form of the Missile Defence System (MDS), which, like SDI, employs the idea of tracking and destroying incoming ballistic missiles using a network of satellites, ground-based radars, high-velocity intercepting missiles and airborne lasers. Military satellites with infrared sensors are designed to spot the trail of heat given off by a ballistic missile during its launch phase. Mid-course sensors then track their trajectory and feed data to a network of ground-based radars, which monitor the missiles when they come over the horizon. When the trajectories are tracked, long-range interceptors are supposed to destroy the missiles by direct hits. Any that get through are then mopped up by shorter-range interceptors. The U.S. began plans in 2007 to establish MDS in various European countries. Sergei Ivanov, Russia's defense minister, described plans for a U.S. missile shield as "a new, virtual Berlin wall." Moreover, Russian analysts see effort to install MDS close to Russia's borders as a revival of the Cold War.

As mentioned earlier, the arms race is built on a principle opposite to that expressed in the fifth Beatitude: "Blessed are the merciful." The "Star Wars" project, conceived of in the fall of 1979, shortly before the start of the fifth Jupiter period on November 1, 1980, epitomized the lack of mercy. That project was a significant stage in the human-made signs of the new alliance between humanity and subnature and the subearthly spheres. The stages in this development in relation to the twelve-year Jupiter rhythm are: the Hiroshima and Nagasaki bombs (1945); the *Sputnik* (1957); the Moon landing (1969); and SDI, which was publicly proposed by Ronald Reagan March 23, 1983, but conceived three-and-a-half years earlier. Apart from *Sputnik* (the U.S. did not launch its own version, the Explorer satellite, until 1958), each of these stages was an initiative of the U.S. Thus, the most powerful links between humanity and subnature are evident in the United States of America. Moreover, this applies not only to the technological side of humanity's alliance with the subearthly spheres, but also to the cultural side.

The impulse living in the souls of the American people may be characterized by what is termed the descent into the underworld. This, however, signifies confrontation with the evil of the subearthly spheres. In addition, it is only with Christ that this descent may be accomplished safely. This is the path to the Mother, Demeter, and to her realm, Shambhala, which existed in antiquity in a somewhat different form, for example, in the mysteries of Eleusis. To take this path means to begin awaking to Mother Earth as a living being. The worldwide growing awareness of environmental problems—the Green Movement—indicates the growing consciousness of Mother Earth. In 1983, the Green Party was voted into the German parliament on a platform of protecting the environment, disarmament, and rejection of atomic energy. There are signs that in the U.S., too, politicians are beginning to take environmental issues seriously. What a step it would be if, instead of spending hundreds of billions of dollars on SDI or on its successor, MDS, or on other military projects, this money could be channeled into solving social and environmental problems. Seeing that the Star Wars project—on account of the National Missile Defense Act (1999)—has been superseded by the Missile Defense System (MDS), it is evident that the United States and other national governments still have a distance to travel in awakening to the virtue of mercy rather than exercising the raw might of military power. Shakespeare wrote of both mercy and earthly power:

> The quality of mercy is not strain'd,
> It droppeth as the gentle rain from heaven
> Upon the place beneath: it is twice bless'd;
> It blesses him that gives and him that takes:
> 'Tis mightiest in the mightiest; it becomes
> The throned monarch better than his crown;
> His sceptre shows the force of temporal power,
> The attribute to awe and majesty,
> Wherein doth sit the dread and fear of kings!
> But mercy is above the sceptred sway,
> It is enthroned in the hearts of kings,
> It is an attribute to God himself,
> And earthly power doth then show likest God's
> When mercy seasons justice.[25]

Just as the quality of mercy was central to unfolding the Christ impulse during the Jupiter period from 1980 to 1992, likewise in the following Jupiter period from 1992 to 2004, it was the quality of purity: "Blessed are the pure in heart, for they shall see God." The sixth Beatitude relates to a different level of unfolding the Christ impulse in confronting the evil of the sixth subearthly sphere, the fire earth, in which the counter-impulse to the consciousness soul is active. Instead of awaking human consciousness to the spirit (consciousness soul), the fire earth is a sphere of passion that fans the flames of human passions, causing one to follow the lower nature and forget one's higher nature. Whoever becomes subject to the influence of the sixth subearthly sphere receives the impulses of evil passions from below, and may eventually become utterly depraved. This is the counter-impulse to purity. Consider Steiner's comments on the link between human passions and the fire earth:

> There are occasions when the very substance of the passions of the fire earth begins to rebel. Aroused by human passions, it penetrates through the fruit earth, forces its way through the channels in the upper layers and even flows up into and violently shakes the solid earth. The result is an earthquake. If this passion from the fire earth thrusts up some of the Earth's substance, a volcano erupts... There is still this connection between human passions and the passion layer in the interior of the Earth; and it is still to an accumulation of evil passions and forces that earthquakes and volcanic eruptions are due.[26]

Here it suffices to say that, with the level of working of the Christ impulse in confronting the evil of the sixth subearthly realm in the Jupiter period from 1992 to 2004, the possibility arose of attaining a new and conscious relationship to the Christ impulse and to Christ's descent into the underworld. With the opening of the gates of Hell along Christ's path of descent, at each stage a new level of the Christ impulse begins to unfold, and at the same time a new evil counter-impulse has to be met. The question could be raised: What is the point of it all? Do we have to be confronted with the evil of the subearthly spheres?

The answer is quite simple: by confronting and overcoming evil, human beings are able to advance on the path of spiritual development—not just as individuals, but also for humanity and the entire Earth. The forces of evil in the subearthly spheres exist whether we like it or not, and they work into us continuously on a subconscious level. The task is to raise them to consciousness, to recognize them for what they are, and to overcome them—or rather to transform them—through the Christ impulse. The Christ impulse of purity (the "pure in heart" of the sixth Beatitude) helps those who open themselves to it in the struggle against the bestial and depraved passions that arise through the influence of the sixth subearthly realm. In overcoming, human evolution advances a step. In Steiner's words:

> You will see that human beings are related to all the layers [of the subearthly spheres], for they are continually radiating out their forces. Humanity lives under the influence of these layers and has to overcome their powers. When human beings have learned to radiate life on Earth and have trained their breathing so that it promotes life, they will have overcome the fire earth. When they overcome pain spiritually through serenity, they overcome the air earth. When concord reigns, the "divisive layer" is conquered. When white magic triumphs, no evil remains on Earth. Human evolution thus implies a transformation of the Earth's interior.[27]

From this point of view, the period since the onset of the Second Coming in 1932/1933 offers an unprecedented possibility for human evolution, through the confrontation with the evil of the subearthly spheres—a confrontation led by Christ, with Christ at our side. At the same time, it is a period fraught with terrible danger, for never before in human history have the gates of the underworld been opened. Positive advances seem small and frail compared to the onslaught of evil arising from the underworld through the opened gates of Hell.

Positive manifestations of the activity of the Christ impulse in the twentieth century include: the popular uprising for freedom in Hungary (1956); the emergence in Czechoslovakia of "Socialism with a human face" (1968); the rise of the Solidarity movement in Poland, calling for liberalization (1979 to 1980); and the dissolution of the Soviet Union (1991). These events at twelve-year intervals took place in connection with Jupiter's heliocentric passage through sidereal Leo. Seen in relation to the unfolding Jupiter rhythm against the background of Christ's descent through the subearthly spheres, the passage through sidereal Leo always denotes the last phase of descent through a particular subearthly sphere. In other words, when Jupiter is passing through sidereal Leo, the Christ impulse has, from one perspective, "triumphed" in the confrontation with evil in this sphere. The heliocentric passage of Jupiter through sidereal Leo (from August 25, 1991, to September 11, 1992) was the time of the "triumph" of the Christ impulse in confronting the evil of the fifth subearthly sphere, which manifested historically with the "peaceful revolution" leading to the liberation of the Soviet Union from the yoke of Communism. The role (wittingly or otherwise) of Gorbachev in dissolving the Soviet Union was completed December 25, 1991, when he announced his resignation as President. The most significant phase in the dissolution process began on August 23, 1991, when Boris Yeltsin decreed the suspension of the Russian Communist Party on the grounds that it had lent its support to the three-day coup by Moscow hardliners, which lasted from August 18 to August 21, 1991. As noted, around this time heliocentric Jupiter entered sidereal Leo on August 25, 1991.

When heliocentric Jupiter entered Virgo on September 11, 1992, a new twelve-year period began—that of Christ's descent through the sixth subearthly sphere, lasting until July 24, 2004. The Beatitude, "Blessed are the pure in heart, for they shall see God," expresses the nature of Christ's activity during this period in relation to the corrupting influence of the sixth subearthly realm, the fire earth. Here, in this sixth region of the Earth's interior, lies the primary source of opposition to the development of the sixth member of the human being, the consciousness soul.

The development of the consciousness soul is aided by the extension of one's cognitive faculties beyond oneself to embrace the different realms of existence: the kingdoms of nature and the cosmic spheres of the spiritual hierarchies, as well as the whole of earthly humanity's life on planet Earth. The awakening of conscience enables one's awareness to expand beyond the narrow, personal sphere of interest. To be pure in heart means that our conscience is awake to the suffering of others, that we are genuinely interested in the well-being of one another, in contrast to one's exclusive focus on selfish desires. Ideally, every medical doctor has some of this quality, which entails looking therapeutically at human beings and the world and asking: What is lacking here? What ails thee?[28]

Three-quarters of the way through this period, the terrorist attacks on the World Trade Center occurred on September 11, 2001. In the wake of this horrific event, the U.S. had the sympathy of the entire world. It was a unique opportunity for the political leadership of the U.S. to usher in a new world for the new millennium, making peace, not war, the priority. Instead of asking "What ails thee?" in relation to what motivated the terrorists, the response was to take revenge, giving birth to the "war on terror." Who can say how different things would be if, at that moment, the voice of conscience had made itself heard?

A significant feature of the period from 1992 to 2004 was the surfacing, supported by the Internet, of sheer depravity in the form of pornography and perverse sexuality (sadomasochism, child sexual abuse, child prostitution, sexual slavery, bestiality). In the Book of Revelation, this is called fornication with "Babylon, the great whore, the mother of harlots and of Earth's abominations" (Rev. 17:4).

The onslaught upon humanity through the corrupting influence of the great whore of Babylon (an expression of forces from the sixth subearthly sphere) emerged in full force during this period. In the words of Rudolf Steiner: "The fall of Babylon...will come upon us in a particular form after the time when Christ appears on the Earth for the first time in the ether body—in other words, actually after Christ's second appearance on the Earth."[29] With the surfacing of sexual depravity a powerful force of opposition to the development of the consciousness soul is present. The awaking of conscience, the hallmark of the Christ impulse in the consciousness soul, is blocked by sexual depravity as an expression of the forces of passion residing in the sixth subearthly sphere. Instead of the heart forces of selfless love, sun-like, ruling the human soul, subconscious instinctual drives take control, and depravity replaces the "purity of heart" of the sixth Beatitude. The subconscious then asserts itself against the consciousness soul.

The culmination of the sixth Jupiter period of Christ's Second Coming was with Jupiter's passage heliocentrically through Leo between June 30, 2003, and July 24, 2004. After the U.S.-led invasion of Iraq in March 2003, this period was a time during which British and American troops became increasingly embroiled in the process leading to the creation of the Hell on Earth manifesting in modern Iraq. Although U.S. political leadership had received clear warnings from numerous experts that toppling Saddam Hussein would unleash an uncontrollable cauldron of destabilizing forces in the Middle East, they went ahead with the war anyway. This blatant lack of consciousness, despite the warnings of experts, was a dramatic blow to humanity's task of unfolding the consciousness soul.

Another more subtle blow came with the publication in April 2003 of Dan Brown's book *The Da Vinci Code,* which during the heliocentric passage of Jupiter through Leo became one of the bestselling books of all time. The task of the consciousness soul is to learn to distinguish between good and evil; since Christ is the Good, this means learning to see Christ, who is God, or, as the Son of God, an expression of God. ("Blessed are the pure in heart, for they shall see God.") Distinguishing between good and evil is not easy, because evil often clothes itself as something good. A mixture of truth and falsehood is generally the result. The kernel of truth in Dan Brown's novel is that the Divine Feminine has been suppressed and needs to reawaken and be reestablished. Mixed in with this core truth is a fantastic web of lies concerning Mary

Magdalene (see my book *The Mystery, Biography & Destiny of Mary Magdalene: Sister of Lazarus John and Spiritual Sister of Jesus*).

The real significance of Mary Magdalene is that two thousand years ago she was the first to behold the Risen Christ. Her significance in our time is that she points the way for humanity to behold Christ in his spiritual form at this time of his Second Coming. Mary Magdalene herself, in her younger years, lived through the temptation of the whore of Babylon and triumphed, coming to behold the Risen Christ. Her message, central to humanity today, has unfortunately become twisted and distorted in the minds of millions through the false message concerning the "Mary Magdalene" presented in the book and the film *The Da Vinci Code*.

False thoughts and images act like viruses in the human soul. Just as a computer infected by a virus cannot function properly, viruses in the human mind (as thoughts) and in the human soul (as images) work to distort human perception. The human being is then no longer pure (in heart) but infected. One of today's tasks, therefore, is to uproot and render impotent all such viruses through conscious activity. Mary Magdalene shows that this is possible, even if we fall. It is possible to triumph over the corrupting influences from the sixth subearthly realm working against the development of the consciousness soul.

On the positive side, a modern Mary Magdalene appeared during this culminating time of the sixth Jupiter period in the anthroposophist Judith von Halle, who received the stigmata on Good Friday, April 9, 2004, at 1:47 p.m. in Berlin. She was thirty-two years old at the time. Since receiving the stigmata, she has not eaten or drunk anything except water, and that only occasionally and in small quantities. She lives from the word of God, as in Jesus' reply to Satan's temptation: "One does not live by bread alone, but by every word that comes forth from the mouth of God" (Matt. 4:4). Like Anne Catherine Emmerich (1774–1824), the Augustinian nun who received the stigmata at the age of thirty-eight, and who neither ate nor drank thereafter except for the daily sacrament of the host and drinking small quantities of water, Judith von Halle lives in visions of the life of Christ, particularly the Mystery of Golgotha, beholding his death and resurrection. In her books, she describes what she witnesses from the time of Christ. There is a remarkable agreement between her descriptions and those of Anne Catherine Emmerich, whose works Judith von Halle reports she deliberately avoided.[30] As a young woman bearing witness to Christ, she is a kind of modern-day Mary Magdalene, testifying to the reality of Christ's resurrection and his love for humanity. Like St. Francis of Assisi (1182–1226), who received the stigmata at the age of forty-two, Judith von Halle can be thought of as a standard-bearer of Christ in the modern world, as in the words attributed to St. Francis in the "Considerations on the Glorious Stigmata of St. Francis":

> When I was on Mount Alverna, all rapt in the contempla-tion of the Passion of Christ, in this Seraphic vision I was by Christ thus stigmatized in my body; and then Christ said to me, "Knowest thou what I have done to thee? I have given thee the marks of my Passion in order that thou mayst be My standard bearer."[31]

The descent of Christ through the seventh subearthly sphere began July 24, 2004, signifying the confrontation (not only for Christ, but also for all humanity) with the forces of the earth mir-ror. The relevant aspect of the Christ impulse here is expressed in the words: "Blessed are the peacemakers, for they shall be called children of God." The corrupting influence of the mirror earth works to turn everything into its opposite. The seventh Beatitude expresses the quality of peace connected with attaining the next level beyond the consciousness soul, the spirit self, the purified astral body, known in the East as *manas*. The spirit self, the sev-enth level, involves a new, spiritual birth, and becoming children of God through the "second birth": "Truly, truly, I say to you, unless one is born anew...unless one is born of water and the spirit, one cannot enter the kingdom of God" (John 3: 3–5). The inverse of this means becoming children of the evil one, or to be possessed. This is the danger that Rudolf Steiner indicated in the wake of the fall of Babylon, as mentioned here in connection with the surfacing of the forces of the sixth subearthly sphere during the period 1992 to 2004.

> The first stage is the fall of Babylon....The second stage is the fall of the Beast and his associate, the False Prophet, who spreads the teachings of the Beast....The city of Babylon is to be found among all of earthly humankind. It exists wherever human beings have fallen victim to the Babylonian temptation....The first downfall, the fall of Babylon, is the fall of errors that human beings have themselves brought about....The second downfall is one in which not only human beings alone participate. Those actually affected by the fall of Babylon are human beings; it happens because of human error. In the fall of the Beast and of the False Prophet, who represents the teachings of the Beast, something supra-human and spiritual falls, not something human. Something falls that is not within the human kingdom. The Beast, who breaks in on human communities, falls, and the one who proclaims the teachings of the Beast, the False Prophet, falls. What falls is something that can make human beings possessed...that their human "I" is not in them, so that one cannot address them as human beings, because they are possessed by the Beast and by the False Prophet. This will come about after the fall of Babylon. After the fall of Babylon there will be people on the earth who will be like wandering demons.[32]

This is the challenge facing humanity during the present Jupiter period (2004–2016), the seventh following the onset of Christ's Second Coming. This is the counterpart to "Blessed are the peacemakers, for they shall be called children of God." It can be formulated: "Woe to the war-makers, for they shall be children of the evil one." As indicated in my book *The Christ Mystery*, this current Jupiter period is the one in which humanity's encounter with the Beast (also know as the Antichrist) and the False Prophet is taking place. There would be enough material on this topic to fill several volumes, but here it suffices to draw attention to chapter 13 of the Book of Revelation, which describes the emergence on the world stage of the Beast and the False Prophet, representing a historical counterpoint to the emergence two thousand years ago of Christ and his Prophet, John the Baptist. A key date in the confrontation with the Antichrist (the incarnated Ahriman) and the False Prophet is the year 2012. In particular, the winter solstice December 21, 2012, is the date signifying the end of the Mayan calendar in its present cycle.[33] It is too simplistic to speak of a simple linear sequence—first, the fall of Babylon, then the coming of the Antichrist and the False Prophet—since the fall of Babylon is an ongoing event.

One of the signs for humanity of entering into this new period, perhaps the most dramatic period in all of human history, was the tsunami on December 26, 2004, when more than 283,000 people lost their lives. This event, in the words of Judith von Halle, was a manifestation of "Ahriman rattling his chains."[34] Eight months later, the devastation of Hurricane Katrina occurred on August 30, 2005. Regarding "Ahriman rattling his chains," Rudolf Steiner stated:

> Upheavals in nature—earthquakes, volcanic eruptions, great floods and the like—are not an integral part of the ongoing evolution of the Earth.... The ordinary natural laws of the earth are not operating, but the Old Moon is beginning to stir, to rumble in the Earth.... And it is here ... in respect of many events of an elemental nature [that] initiation science ... must ask: When and where was this event set in motion? And the answer is that it derives from the horrors and atrocities of enmity and warfare.[35]

This is a clear indication by Steiner. It might be interpreted that the tsunami and the trio of powerful hurricanes that struck the U.S. Gulf Coast—Katrina on August 30, Rita on September

24, Wilma on October 24, 2005—as well as the devastating great Kashmir earthquake (7.6 on the Richter scale), which claimed the lives of more than 87,000 people on October 8, 2005, could perhaps all be seen in relation to the horrors and atrocities of the Iraq War, which, although the "end of major combat" was declared by President Bush on May 1, 2003, is still ongoing (as of this writing, Palm Sunday, April 1, 2007).

In keeping with the seventh Beatitude ("Blessed are the peacemakers, for they shall be called children of God"), instead of war, "Peace on Earth to all beings of good will" (Luke 2:14) is the hallmark of the Christ impulse during the seventh Jupiter period (2004–2016) of Christ's Second Coming. On the positive side, there is an event that has been prophesied and is expected to take place toward the end of this Jupiter period. This is the coming of the Kalki Avatar. This appearance is connected with the beginning of Satya-yuga, or "Age of Light":

> When the Supreme Lord has appeared on Earth as Kalki, the maintainer of religion, Satya-yuga will begin, and human society will bring forth progeny in the mode of goodness.... When the Moon, the Sun, and Brhaspati (Jupiter) are together in the constellation Karkata (Cancer), and all three enter simultaneously into the lunar mansion Pushya—at that exact moment the age of Satya, or Kritta, will begin. (Bhagavatam, 12.2.22, 24)

Thus, when the Sun, Moon, and Jupiter are in conjunction in the Hindu lunar asterism Pushya (4°–17° Cancer), the emergence of the Kalki Avatar, the "bearer of goodness," is expected. It is in this lunar mansion that the beautiful star cluster Praesepe, Jupiter's place of exaltation in the zodiac, is to be found. Evidently the Hindus attributed something special to Jupiter's location in this part of the zodiac: a special impulse of the Good comes to expression here.

The prophesied conjunction of the Sun, Moon, and Jupiter in Pushya will take place July 27, 2014, possibly signifying the emergence of the Kalki Avatar as the bearer of a new and mighty spiritual impulse for the evolution of humanity, for the redemption of Mother Earth, and to inaugurate a new spiritual era. Let us consider the following words to better understand the work of the Kalki Avatar in our time as the transmitter of a power of goodness that our modern world so desperately needs:

> By the time the age of Kali ends...religious principles will be ruined...so-called religion will be mostly atheistic...the occupations of human beings will be stealing, lying, and needless violence, and all the social classes will be reduced to the lowest level....Family ties will extend no further than the immediate bonds of marriage...homes will be devoid of piety, and all human beings will have become like asses. At that time, the Supreme personality of the Godhead will appear on the Earth. Acting with the power of pure spiritual goodness, he will rescue eternal religion....
>
> Lord Kalki will appear in...the great soul of Vishnuyasha [the human being who will be the bearer of the Kalki Avatar].... When the Supreme Lord has appeared on Earth as Kalki, the maintainer of religion, Satya-yuga, will begin, and human society will bring forth progeny in the mode of goodness. (Srimad Bhagavatam, 12; 2; 16–23)[36]

The date of this event (2014) coincides with an indication by Rudolf Steiner in connection with the six-hundred-year rhythm of culture. This rhythm (as I discussed in *Hermetic Astrology*, volume I) is actually a half-rhythm of the 1199-year Venus rhythm, the time it takes for the Venus pentagram to rotate once (moving retrograde) through all twelve signs of the sidereal zodiac.[37] This period of almost exactly twelve hundred years is the length of time that elapses between the start of a new zodiacal age and the beginning of the new cultural epoch corresponding to that age. For example, the Age of Pisces, which began when the vernal point shifted—moving in a retrograde direction—from Aries into Pisces, started in 215 C.E., reckoned to be the birth year of the Prophet Mani. In 1414 C.E. (1199 years later), the corresponding Piscean cultural epoch commenced, and it is striking that Joan of Arc was born in 1412 C.E., immediately preceding this date. Looking at the half-period, going back six hundred years from 1414, we arrive at 814 C.E., the year of Charlemagne's death,[38] and the beginning of a new era in Europe, when the monastic schools started to flourish. Going forward six hundred years from 1414, we reach 2014. Concerning this date, Rudolf Steiner indicated, "We are living today at the beginning of a period of transition before the onset of the next six-hundred-year wave of culture, when something entirely new is pressing in upon us, when the Christ impulse is to be enriched by something new."[39]

Here it is clear that six hundred years is the half period of the 1199-year rhythm of the Venus pentagram. Steiner describes the six-hundred-year period as a "cultural wave." Evidently, two six-hundred-year cultural waves elapse between the beginning of a zodiacal age and the start of the corresponding cultural epoch. Applied to the Piscean Age, the first cultural wave of six hundred years was from 215 to 814, the year of the death of Charlemagne (Carolingian Renaissance), and the second cultural wave of six hundred years lasted from 814 to 1414 (early Renaissance). Adding another six hundred years, we arrive at 2014 as the start of a new cultural wave.

Given that 2014 begins a new six-hundred-year cultural rhythm, it is possible that a spiritual leader (such as the Kalki Avatar) could emerge at that time as a bearer of the impulse for the new wave of culture as a seed impulse for the next six hundred years. It is a matter of a new culture being seeded after the toppling of the reign of the Antichrist and his False Prophet, which Steiner calls "the fall of the Beast and of the False Prophet."

Then a new Jupiter period will begin on June 5, 2016, when Jupiter enters Virgo heliocentrically—denoting the start of the eighth twelve-year period since the onset of Christ's Second Coming in 1932/1933. This eighth period will be the time of Christ's descent through the eighth subearthly sphere, the divisive layer and source of all strife and conflict. During this time, confrontation with the forces of the human double will be the primary focus. The eighth Beatitude, "Blessed are those who are persecuted for righteousness sake, for theirs is the kingdom of heaven," refers to this approaching conflict with the separating forces of the divisive layer. A historical prototype of how to deal with this conflict is given by Moses, as I described in my book *The Most Holy Trinosophia*.[40] Moses battled the forces of the double that manifested as the golden calf, as indicated in the following meditation by Rudolf Steiner:

> Imagine to yourselves Moses as your teacher and master, the whole as a vision: Moses, to whom you direct your question as to why you do not make more rapid progress, seeing as you have such a great longing to penetrate to the spiritual world. One should then quietly await the answer, which very often will come quite unexpectedly. Usually, then, the form of the golden calf appears next to the figure of Moses—the whole as an image before the soul. Then, through Moses, fire breaks forth from the Earth, which burns up the calf, and the ashes are dissolved by Moses in water and given to the meditant to drink.[41]

This meditation indicates how the modern human being can begin to combat the double, which appears in this vision as the golden calf. Since the beginning of the appearance of the etheric Christ in 1932/1933, human beings have been confronted increasingly by the activity of the double, which is evident in the dramatic increase in the crime rate. Many crimes are committed at the instigation of the double working in the human being as a vehicle for the forces streaming up from the subearthly realms of the underworld.

I am not the only person who is aware that the gates of Hell have been opening since 1933. In his book *The Healing of Europe*, Harrie Salman writes, "Since 1933, Europe has begun a descent into Hell, which can only be withstood if certain soul qualities and spiritual forces are developed."[42] As Rudolf Steiner predicted in his lectures on the Book of Revelation in 1924, "Before the etheric Christ can be comprehended by human beings in the right way, humanity must first cope with encountering the Beast, who will arise in 1933."[43] Who can doubt that this prophecy was fulfilled when Hitler rose to power that year?

Another author who looks at the spiritual background behind the tragic turn of events in 1933 is Jesaiah ben Aharon. In his book *The Spiritual Event of the Twentieth Century,* he focuses on the first Jupiter period from 1933 to 1945. This book was published in 1993; two years earlier, I published the original version of this article "Subnature and the Second Coming,"[44] outlining the sequence of twelve-year periods beginning in 1933. The first period lasted from 1933 to 1945, which ben Aharon also discussed in his book. As he described in relation to what took place then, "Through the evil enacted on the Earth, a situation was created in which a real hell…came into being."[45] In the last chapter of the book, he discusses the special relationship between the suprasensory aspect of the Christ's Second Coming and the main world events from 1933 to 1945.[46] He refers to the evil nature of the atom bomb, which was created at the end of this period. Ben Aharon stops at that point. The present study goes further, investigating the esoteric significance of the Christ event (his descent into the underworld in accordance with the twelve-year rhythm of Jupiter) in relation to significant world events in the twentieth and twenty-first centuries.

Without going into too much detail about Christ's descent into the underworld, it is appropriate to look briefly into the future. Christ's descent through the eighth subearthly sphere lasts from June 5, 2016, to April 14, 2028, the culminating year (Jupiter in Leo) of the period lasting from March 21, 2027, to April 14, 2028, when the descent through the ninth subearthly sphere begins, lasting until 2040. As indicated earlier in this article, the deepest point on this path of descent will be at the end of Christ's descent through the ninth subearthly sphere in 2040, with the heliocentric passage of Jupiter through sidereal Leo from January 31, 2039, to February 24, 2040.

To summarize the stages of Christ's descent through the last three subearthly spheres, let us consider the following table:

SUBEARTHLY SPHERE:	COUNTER- IMPULSE TO:	CORRESPONDING BEATITUDE	SPIRITUAL BEING TO CALL UPON
7. Mirror earth July 24, 2004 to June 5, 2016	Spirit self (manas)	Blessed are the peacemakers...	Sophia (Fifth Seal)
8. Divisive layer June 5, 2016 to April 14, 2028	Life spirit (budhi)	Blessed are those who are persecuted...	Michael (Sixth Seal)
9. Earth core April 14, 2028 to Feb. 24, 2040	Spirit body (atma)	Blessed are you when they revile you...	Christ (Seventh Seal) Holy Grail

During these last three Jupiter periods, as the attack upon the members of the human being goes beyond the present level of humanity's development, they can be met only with the help of higher spiritual beings. The beneficial forces for humankind are depicted in the last three Apocalyptic Seals: Sophia, Michael, and Christ.[47] The forces of the seventh subearthly realm, which influence humanity subconsciously today, are mainly those of Sophia, who shepherds the development of spirit self (manas) and who may be called upon in the spirit of the seventh Beatitude as the Queen of Peace. Close to the beginning of the period under consideration (2004–2012), there was an influx of the Sophia impulse at the transit of Venus across the face of the Sun on June 8, 2004, which will occur again during this period on June 6, 2012. As described in my article "Sophia and Venus" in the *Christian Star Calendar 2004*, a special relationship exists between Sophia and the planet Venus.[48] The influx of Sophia's grace through the two cosmic events of the Venus transits during this period are intended to help humanity in the conflict with the anti-manas forces from the

*The fifth, sixth, and seventh Apocalyptic Seals (painted by Clara Rettich,
Stuttgart, 1911, based on designs by Rudolf Steiner)*

seventh subearthly sphere, focused especially through the Beast
(Antichrist) and the False Prophet.

As already mentioned in connection with the forces of the
eighth subearthly sphere, this is the confrontation with the human
double. In fact, the forces of all the subearthly spheres work into
the double. In the case of the eighth subearthly sphere, it is a matter of confronting and taming the double consciously, as indicated
in the sixth Apocalyptic seal, in which Michael holds the Dragon
under his feet in chains. The Dragon represents an image of the collective forces (for all humanity) of the double, and Michael, as the
Lesser Guardian of the Threshold, shepherds humanity through
this encounter with the double.

Regarding the confrontation with the forces of black magic
emanating from the ninth subearthly sphere, Christ, as the
Greater Guardian of the Threshold, enables humanity to develop
the white magic needed to counter the challenge of the ninth subearthly realm. The seventh Apocalyptic Seal, depicting the Grail
Mystery, symbolizes the manifestation of the Heavenly Jerusalem
through Christ's transformation and spiritualization of the Earth
into the New Earth and Sophia's descent from above, bringing
down the New Heaven.

When Christ's "I" reaches the Earth Core in 2040, it will fulfill the purpose of the Mysteries of Eleusis: to unite with Demeter,
the Earth Mother, whose realm, Shambhala, is in the heart of the
Earth. Christ, as the new High Priest of the new Demeter Mysteries,

is reopening her Mysteries to humanity through his descent, opening the path to Shambhala, which will be complete in 2040.

At that point, Christ's ascent through the subearthly spheres will begin, which may be followed again in relation to the twelve-year Jupiter rhythm. The descent, the passage through the "eggshell" of the Mineral Earth, began with the first Jupiter period of the age of the Second Coming and was completed around Easter 1945. The return through this "eggshell" will occur around the time of the completion of Jupiter's passage through sidereal Leo on January 20, 2135. This date falls just two years after the commencement of a new thirty-three-and-one-third-year period on January 2, 2133. Here is a juxtaposition of the twelve-year rhythm (Jupiter) of Christ's "I" with the thirty-three-and-one-third-year rhythm.

The thirty-three-and-one-third-year rhythm is that of Christ's ether body; it is the key rhythm underlying the Second Coming. Thus, around 2133 to 2135, Christ's "I" will reunite with his ether body, an event analogous in importance to the resurrection on Easter Sunday morning in 33 C.E. This will begin a period that I described in appendix 2 of *Hermetic Astrology I* as the core period of the age of the Second Coming.[49] I dated this core period from 2133 to 4233, comprising three seven-hundred-year periods. This core period is analogous to the forty-day period in 33 C.E., following the resurrection and culminating with the ascension.

Thus, the two-hundred-year period from 1933 to 2133 leading up to the core period (when Christ's underworld descent and ascent are taking place) is preparing for a new resurrection event around 2133 to 2135, this time on the etheric level. This etheric resurrection will have profound significance for the following epoch, from 2133 onward, just as the resurrection in 33 C.E. has until now. By Christ's uniting with the impulse of the resurrection, evil will be overcome ultimately, and the interior of the Earth will be transformed.

In conclusion, therefore, during the present period (through Christ, working in conjunction with human beings), the possibility is opened up for the transformation, in successive stages, of the Earth's interior. This transformation entails confrontation with the evil of subearthly spheres, which is being released in successive stages. Once a particular kind of evil gains entry to civilization (for example, via a negative technological development or through a perverted cultural impulse), it continues to work further until it is overcome. A prime example of this, as a perverted cultural impulse, is drug addiction. Humanity is called to awaken morally and spiritually and deal with such problems. Matters will improve only as we clearly recognize these challenges as the struggle with evil in which Christ (as well as Michael and Sophia) must be called upon for deliverance from the evil. Underlying this call are the words of St. Paul, "Not I, but Christ in me," which indicates the communion between the human "I" and Christ's "I," the archetypal background of which is the descent into Hell described here.

Here, it has not been possible to go into the other modes of communion with Christ. We have directed our attention primarily toward communion with the Christ "I" in relation to the twelve-year Jupiter rhythm. In my book *Christian Hermetic Astrology: The Star of the Magi and the Life of Christ*, I outlined some aspects of communion with the astral body of Christ in connection with the twenty-nine-and-a-half–year Saturn rhythm, but the main content is concerned with communion with Christ's ether body in relation to the thirty-three-and-one-third-year rhythm. The *Christian Star Calendar* offers indications about how to intensify communion with Christ by living with the daily events in the world of stars as they correspond to events in the life of Christ.

To conclude, I am aware that this article allows only a cursory overview of a vast topic and that many important aspects relevant to the theme have had to be omitted or mentioned only briefly. Nevertheless, it is my hope that this article will stimulate further research and investigation into the Mystery of Christ's Second Coming and the confrontation with evil in our time—the major keynote of the modern world.

FURTHER READING

For the relationship of the Beatitudes to the members of the human being, see Rudolf Steiner, *According to Matthew,* lecture 9. See also Valentin Tomberg, *Christ and Sophia,* part 2, chapters 3 to 5.

Concerning dating of the Second Coming, see Robert Powell, *Hermetic Astrology I: Astrology and Reincarnation,* appendix II ("The Second Coming"); *Hermetic Astrology II: Astrological Biography,* chapter 9 ("The New Age and the Second Coming"); and *Chronicle of the Living Christ,* the afterword.

Further aspects of the Second Coming are outlined in *Christian Hermetic Astrology: The Star of the Magi and the Life of Christ,* where also the twenty-nine-and-one-half-year rhythm in relation to communion with Christ's astral body is discussed.

For a detailed account of the life of Christ in its historical, biographical aspect, see *Chronicle of the Living Christ,* in which the exact length of Christ's life, from the birth in Bethlehem to the moment of resurrection, is shown to be thirty-three-and-one-third years minus one-and-one-half days. The yearly *Christian Star Calendar* is based on a precise chronology of the life of Christ and offers the possibility of following the daily events in the world of stars in relation to the stellar events that accompanied the major events in Christ's life.

POSTSCRIPT

The article "Subnature and the Second Coming," to which this postscript is written, is the third revised and expanded version of the article first published in *Shoreline* in 1991 and then republished in my book *The Christ Mystery* in 1999. The German edition of *The Christ Mystery* was published in 1999 and again in a second edition in the year 2000. The second German edition included an afterword, and the following text is based on the afterword.

The purpose of the presentation of the research in the foregoing article is, on the one hand, to stimulate a deepening into the mystery of Christ's second coming and, on the other hand, to extend the foundation of cosmic Christianity provided in my book *Chronicle of the Living Christ*. It was Willi Sucher (1902–1985) who encouraged me to research into the foundation of cosmic Christianity, to develop astrosophy as a *science of cosmic Christianity*, and a small group of astrosophers meets yearly in Boulder, Colorado, to explore this and other astrosophical themes.[1] Elisabeth Vreede (1879–1943), a coworker of Rudolf Steiner, supported Willi Sucher in his astrosophical research. She was the first leader of the Mathematical-Astronomical Section at the Goetheanum University, near Basel, Switzerland. I mention this line in order to indicate the context of the research work presented here. It has to be emphasized—in relation to this line—that it is a matter, first, of the coming into being and development of a new wisdom of the stars (astrosophy) on the basis of serious research. There are numerous individuals who are researching and working on the development of astrosophy, and it is quite natural that there are differences of opinion and a variety of approaches and ways of working. It is in a spirit of research, coupled with tolerance and respect for various perspectives, that the foregoing article is written as a contribution to spiritual-scientific research on the basis of astrosophy.

Many readers have expressed their positive response to the content of my research into the Christ Mystery, and I am particularly grateful to one reader who pointed to the following words by Rudolf Steiner:

> Through that which since the sixteenth century had become necessary for the evolution of the Earth, namely the triumph of science at higher and higher levels, something that has significance also for the invisible worlds entered the whole evolution of humanity. With the triumph of science, materialistic and agnostic sentiments of greater intensity than hitherto

arose in humankind. In earlier times, too, there had been materialistic tendencies, but not the intense materialism that has prevailed since the sixteenth century. More and more, as human beings passed into the spiritual worlds through the gate of death, they bore with them the outcome of their materialistic ideas on the Earth. After the sixteenth century, more and more seeds of earthly materialism were carried over, and these seeds effected more and more darkness, forming a "black sphere of materialism." This black sphere was taken by Christ into his being in order to transform it.... The angelic being, who since then has been the outer form assumed by Christ, suffered an extinction of consciousness as a result of the opposing materialistic forces that had been brought into the spiritual worlds by materialistic human souls who had passed through the gate of death. A "spiritually suffocating death" was brought about in the angelic being in whom the Christ being has revealed himself since the Mystery of Golgotha. This sacrifice of Christ in the nineteenth century is comparable to the sacrifice on the physical plane in the Mystery of Golgotha and can be designated as the second crucifixion of Christ—a crucifixion in the etheric world. This spiritually suffocating death, which led to the extinction of consciousness of this angelic being, is a repetition of the Mystery of Golgotha in the worlds which lie directly beyond ours. This extinction of consciousness in the spiritual worlds will lead to the resurrection of Christ consciousness in the souls of human beings on Earth in the twentieth century. In a certain sense, it may be said that, from the twentieth century onward, Christ consciousness will arise again for clairvoyant vision. At first only a few, and then an ever-increasing number of human beings in the twentieth century will be capable of perceiving the manifestation of the Etheric Christ—that is to say, Christ in the form of an angel. It was for the sake of humanity that there was what may be called an extinction of consciousness in the worlds immediately above our earthly world.... Thus Christ consciousness may be united with the earthly consciousness of human beings from our time on into the future. For the dying of Christ consciousness in the sphere of the angels in the nineteenth century signifies the resurrection of the direct consciousness of Christ; that is, Christ's life will be felt in the souls of human beings more and more as a direct personal experience from the twentieth century onward.[2]

In my previously published research into the Christ Mystery, it was an omission on my part not to have mentioned or discussed this reference by Rudolf Steiner to *"the second crucifixion of Christ"*—a crucifixion in the etheric world in the nineteenth century. In the following I would like to elaborate on my approach and then return to this reference by Rudolf Steiner in relation to the research that I have presented.

As a mathematician and astronomer, I have been trained in the methods of the exact sciences and have studied the history of astronomy.[3] In the context of spiritual research, as far as possible, I apply the same principles underlying the scientific method of research. One obvious principle is not simply to believe or disbelieve something before having investigated it thoroughly. In this connection, the principle of making hypotheses, which is central to the scientific method, can be helpful. For example, the reader could take what has been presented in the foregoing article as a hypothesis (or series of hypotheses) to be tested.

However, there is a fine distinction between two different attitudes: 1) to consider something as a hypothesis, and 2) to believe in it. In true scientific research, one always observes the boundary between these two attitudes. The moment one steps across the boundary and starts to believe in something without really knowing if it is true, one enters the realm of superstition. A true scientist guards against this as far as possible, so as not to fall prey to superstition.

For a true scientist there are three possibilities with respect to testing a hypothesis: 1) to reach certainty that the hypothesis is true; 2) to reach certainty that the hypothesis is not true; and 3) not being certain in either direction, it remains a hypothesis. Regarding the third, this requires patience in order not to make the mistake of making a "leap of faith"—in the course of time, often without noticing, to come to believe in a hypothesis without really knowing if it is true or not.

The reason for considering this is that as a matter of principle I would not want any reader simply to believe in the content of the research I have presented on the Christ Mystery. The method of formulating hypotheses offers the possibility for the reader to remain objective in relation to the content. Everyone who is able to think logically is able to critically test the content for themselves, to decide whether the ideas and the results of research presented, regarded purely hypothetically, hold water or not.

Let us return to the omission in my previously published work on the Christ Mystery of a reference to *"the second crucifixion of Christ"*—a crucifixion in the etheric world in the nineteenth century. First, this reference might be interpreted as a contradiction to what I have described in the foregoing article as *"a kind of crucifixion of Christ"* at the time of World War II. That it is not a real contradiction will be evident, I hope, after considering the following words of Rudolf Steiner:

> Since the Mystery of Golgotha, many human beings have been able to proclaim the name of Christ, and from this twentieth century onward, an ever-increasing number will be able to make known the knowledge of the Christ that is given in spiritual science. Out of their own experience, they will be able to proclaim him. Twice already, Christ has been crucified: once physically, in the physical world at the beginning of our era, and a second time, spiritually, in the nineteenth century, in the way described above. It could be said that humankind experienced the resurrection of his body in that former time and will experience the resurrection of his consciousness from the twentieth century onward.... This is what may be said today about the relation of the Mystery of Golgotha, which took place at the beginning of our era, and the Mystery of Golgotha as it can now be understood. From

time to time, other revelations will be given and for these
our minds must be kept open.[4]

Here Rudolf Steiner clearly says that other revelations will come,
and we can assume that he had in mind further revelations of Christ
in the etheric realm. For example, he himself had proclaimed such
a Christ event for the end of the twentieth century:

> Just as on the physical plane in Palestine, at the beginning of
> our era, an event occurred in which the most important part
> was taken by Christ himself—an event that has significance
> for the whole of humanity—so in the course of the twentieth
> century, toward the end of the twentieth century, a signifi-
> cant event will again take place, not in the physical world,
> but in the world we usually call the world of the etheric.[5]

The central purpose of my research into the Christ Mystery
is to penetrate through to the true significance of these words.
In earlier publications, I present research showing fairly conclu-
sively that the event prophesied by Rudolf Steiner evidently took
place in 1999, sometime around September 3 to 5, 1999, referring to this event as "a repetition of the Mystery of Golgotha in
the etheric in September 1999." This event was heralded by the
great European eclipse of August 11, 1999. The question naturally
arises: What led me to understand the Christ event prophesied by
Rudolf Steiner as a "repetition of the Mystery of Golgotha in the
etheric in September 1999"?

As it is a matter of the return of Christ in his etheric body, it is
possible to approach this question by way of considering the rhythm
of Christ's etheric body. What is the rhythm of Christ's etheric
body? As indicated already, it was thirty-three-and-a-third years,
because the life of Jesus Christ lasted exactly thirty-three-and-a-
third years, from the birth shortly before midnight on December 6,
2 B.C.E. [-1], to the resurrection at sunrise on April 5, 33 C.E. One
can rightly ask: How is it possible to know with certainty that this
birth date is accurate?

I was able to determine the birth date from Anne Catherine Emmerich's visions, as I described in my book *Chronicle of the Living Christ*. She communicated the day of the week and the date in the Hebrew calendar of various events in the life of Christ. Mathematically, through probability theory, I and two other mathematicians investigated the dates she communicated. We discovered—independently of one another—that the probability of these weekdays coinciding by chance with the right dates in the Hebrew calendar is 1:435 billion.[6] One does not need to be a mathematician to see that it would have been impossible for Anne Catherine Emmerich to have simply made up the dates. In other words, her dates are authentic.

When she says that Jesus was born on the twelfth day of the Hebrew month of Kislev at around midnight on the evening after the Sabbath, then this date is in all probability accurate; in other words, Jesus was born at midnight Saturday/Sunday, the twelfth day of Kislev. This date in the Hebrew calendar corresponds to Saturday/Sunday, December 6/7, 2 B.C.E. [-1]. From this point in time until the resurrection on April 5, 33 C.E. is exactly thirty-three-and-a-third years (minus one-and-a-half days).

This communication by Rudolf Steiner confirms this period of thirty-three-and-a-third years:

> In the historical process, everything arises after thirty-three years in a transformed state—arises from the grave through a power that has to do with the most holy redemption that humanity has received....[7]
>
> Then, when such a seed that has been laid ripens, it works further. A "thought seed" ripens through one generation of thirty-three years to become a "deed seed." Once ripened, it works further in the unfolding of history through sixty-six years. One can recognize the intensity of an impulse that someone implants into the historical process also in its effect through three generations, through a whole century.[8]

A whole century of one hundred years equals three times thirty-three-and-a-third years. Here Rudolf Steiner's indication of thirty-three-and-a-third years is confirmed. In the lecture, for the sake of simplicity, he says simply "thirty-three" years—that this rhythm works further in the unfolding of history.

The reader can imagine how encouraging it was to discover that the statement by the clairvoyant Anne Catherine Emmerich regarding Jesus' birth date was confirmed in this (indirect) way by Rudolf Steiner. In this way, I arrived at certainty with respect to the truth of this thirty-three-and-a-third-year rhythm and the fact that one can follow the rhythm of thirty-three-and-a-third years through history. This is all the more exciting, since Rudolf Steiner speaks of a *"new astrology"* in this connection: "This is an introduction, my dear friends, in order to read the new astrology—the astrology that leads our attention to the stars that shine in the history of human evolution."[9]

It was a special joy to be able to confirm the discovery of the thirty-three-and-a-third-year rhythm as the basis for a new star wisdom—emerging as the "crown" of astrosophical research. The next step was then to follow this rhythm through history.[10] In this way, the dates September 3 to 5, 1999, emerge as the sixtieth return of the dates April 3 to 5, 33 C.E., of the Mystery of Golgotha. For $60 \times 33\frac{1}{3} = 2000$, added on to December 6, 2 B.C.E. [-1], corresponds to December 6, 1999. However, since the exact rhythm is one-and-a-half days less than thirty-three-and-a-third years, $60 \times 1\frac{1}{2} = 90$ days (the exact number is ninety-two) have to be subtracted from December 6/7, 1999. This leads to September 5/6, 1999, as the completion of the sixtieth cycle of thirty-three-and-a-third years, the rhythm of Christ's life (taking account of the change in 1582 from the ancient Julian to the modern Gregorian calendar).

A sceptical reader might say: This is simply a computed date. This is true, of course, and yet the research that led to this result concurs with Rudolf Steiner's statements concerning the rhythm of thirty-three-and-a-third years and with his statement about a significant event having to do with Christ in the etheric world that would take place "toward the end of the twentieth century."

Let us return to consider the question whether a contradiction exists between the astrosophical research presented here and Rudolf Steiner's communication concerning "the second crucifixion of Christ"—a crucifixion in the etheric world in the nineteenth century. First, let us consider the date September 3 to 5, 1999, which can be considered as a cosmic memory of the Mystery of Golgotha (April 3–5, 33 C.E.). How may this be understood?

Like all the events in the life of Jesus Christ, the Mystery of Golgotha was inscribed into Christ's ether body as the crowning of this life. This ether body is a *time body*, whose rhythm is thirty-three-and-a-third years. Every time this rhythm is completed, the Mystery of Golgotha lights up as a cosmic memory in Christ's ether body—for example, at the completion of the fifty-seventh cycle in the year 1899. Around this time Rudolf Steiner inwardly experienced the Mystery of Golgotha:

> It was during this time...that the true substance of Christianity began germinally to unfold within me as an inner phenomenon of knowledge. About the turn of the century, the seed unfolded more and more... I stood in spirit before the Mystery of Golgotha in most inward, most earnest solemnity of knowledge.[11]

Through his Christ experience, Rudolf Steiner became an "apostle of the Etheric Christ." The New Age, which began in 1899, began with Rudolf Steiner's experience of the Mystery of Golgotha. Of course, one could think that Rudolf Steiner perhaps arrived at the start of the New Age simply by way of computation ($57 \times 33\frac{1}{3}$ = 1900). However, according to his own account he had a genuine spiritual experience of the Mystery of Golgotha. One could, therefore, have the hypothesis that Rudolf Steiner's experience of the Mystery of Golgotha was a "cosmic memory" of the Mystery of Golgotha, which was bestowed upon him through a connection with Christ's etheric body—i.e. that the Mystery of Golgotha shone forth in Christ's ether body at that time (1899) with the completion of a cycle of the thirty-three-and-a-third-year rhythm. In this case, one could put the question: Was this spiritual experience of the cosmic memory of the Mystery of Golgotha in contradiction to his description of "the second crucifixion of Christ"—a crucifixion in the etheric world in the nineteenth century? By the same token, the events connected with World War II could be viewed also as "a kind of crucifixion" for the Etheric Christ, and this perspective in no way contradicts that there was a "second crucifixion of Christ" in the nineteenth century.

Rudolf Steiner spoke about this second crucifixion on May 2, 1913, in London. Three months earlier, he had communicated about this in the Esoteric School in Berlin on February 8, 1913:

> What is new and what will now gradually be revealed to humanity is a recollection, or repetition, of what St. Paul experienced at Damascus. He saw the ether body of Christ. The reason this will now become visible to us derives from the fact that a new Mystery of Golgotha has, as it were, taken place in the etheric world. What took place here in the physical world at the crucifixion as a result of the hatred of uncomprehending humanity has now been repeated on the etheric level, owing to the hatred of human beings who have entered the etheric world after death as materialists. Let us visualize once more how, at the Mystery of Golgotha, a cross of dead wood was erected, on which the body of Christ hung. Then let us visualize the wood of that cross in the etheric world as green, sprouting, and living wood that has been turned to charcoal by the flames of hatred, and on which seven blossoming roses appear, representing Christ's sevenfold nature. There we have the picture of the second Mystery of Golgotha, which has now taken place in the etheric world. Moreover, through Christ's dying this second death, we gained the possibility of seeing the ether body of Christ. The densification, the dead part of Christ's ether body, will be seen by human beings.... The Rose Cross is a symbol for the second death of

Christ in the nineteenth century, the death of the ether body, owing to the army of materialists. The result is that Christ can now be seen in the twentieth century, as I have often described to you, namely in the ether body.[12]

Here Rudolf Steiner communicates that the Rose Cross is the real sign of the Mystery of Golgotha in the etheric world, just as the Cross (without roses) was the real symbol of the Mystery of Golgotha two thousand years ago. It is clearly evident that Rudolf Steiner's spiritual science stood under the sign of the Rose Cross. Is this not a confirmation that in 1899 Rudolf Steiner became an apostle of the etheric Christ?

In my research into the Christ Mystery, I have described the incarnation, stage by stage, of Christ in his etheric body. The years 1899, 1933, 1966, and 1999 are the main stages—the culminating points—of this gradual incarnation since the onset of the New Age in 1899. Could it not be, in the same way as we have considered Rudolf Steiner's experience in 1899 under the hypothesis formulated earlier, that at each of the culminating points the Mystery of Golgotha shone forth as a cosmic memory from Christ's etheric body? Would this be in accordance with Rudolf Steiner's prophecy of a continually progressing revelation of Christ in the etheric world? If this is correct, it signifies the following in relation to the series of dates coinciding with the start/end of each thirty-three-and-a-third-year cycle:

1899: the initiation of Rudolf Steiner through the cosmic memory of the Mystery of Golgotha, through the entrance of the Etheric Christ into the Earth's etheric aura, coming from the Moon sphere, whereby Rudolf Steiner became an apostle of the Etheric Christ (comparable to St. Paul who became an apostle through his experience of the Risen Christ).

1933: the completion of the first cycle of the activity of Christ in the Earth's etheric aura—a time, above all, of Christ's activity on the level of thinking (the birth of Anthroposophy, or spiritual science, through Rudolf Steiner). Here it is interesting to consider that if Steiner had lived longer, he would have been seventy-two years old in 1933, corresponding to the cosmic archetype of seventy-two years for human life indicated by the retrograde movement of the vernal point through one degree of the zodiac.

1966: the completion of the second cycle of the activity of Christ in the Earth's etheric aura—a time, above all, of Christ's activity on the level of feeling (birth of the worldwide impulse of community).

1999: the completion of the third cycle of the activity of Christ in the Earth's etheric aura—a time, above all, of Christ's activity on the level of the will (birth of the worldwide impulse to protect and care for the environment and also to penetrate the mystery of destiny expressed in human biography).

2033: the completion of the fourth cycle of the activity of Christ in the Earth's etheric aura—a time, above all, of Christ's activity on the level of the human "I." This is expressed in St. Paul's words "*Not I, but Christ in me,*" which are the answer to the forces of the Antichrist manifesting in the world particularly strongly since September 11, 2001.

With respect to the period from 1966 to 1999, there are two sides to the will. First, our destiny unfolds on the level of the will:

> When we begin to think along these lines, we become aware of the immense intricacy and deep significance in the workings of our destiny or karma. Moreover, this all goes on in the domain of the human kingdom. All that thus happens to us is deep in the unconscious life. Until the moment when a decisive event approaches us, it lies in the unconscious. All this takes place as though it were subject to laws of nature.... Only with awareness of this does one learn to put the question of freedom in the true way. Read my *Philosophy of Spiritual Activity* and see how much importance I attach to the point that one should not ask about the freedom of the

will. The will lies deep down in the unconscious, and it is nonsense to ask about freedom of the will. We can speak only about freedom of thoughts. I drew the line very clearly in my *Philosophy of Spiritual Activity.* One must become free in one's thoughts, and the free thoughts must give the impulse to the will—there one is free.[13]

The will is "deep down in the unconscious," and it is here that our destiny impulse plays itself out. This is the one side of the will. Now, before we consider the other side of the will, let us look once again at Steiner's words concerning the significant Christ event in the etheric world "toward the end of the twentieth century." Rudolf Steiner characterizes this event as that of Christ becoming the Lord of Karma:

Just as on the physical plane in Palestine, at the beginning of our era, an event occurred in which the most important part was taken by Christ himself—an event that has significance for the whole of humanity—so in the course of the twentieth century, toward the end of the twentieth century, a significant event will again take place, not in the physical world, but in the world we usually call the world of the etheric. And this event will have as fundamental a significance for the evolution of humanity as the event of Palestine had at the beginning of our era. Just as we must say that for Christ himself the event of Golgotha had the significance that with this very event a God died, a God overcame death—we will speak later concerning the way this is to be understood; the deed had not happened before and it is an accomplished fact which will not happen again—so an event of profound significance will take place in the etheric world. And the occurrence of this event, an event connected with the Christ himself, will make it possible for human beings to learn to see the Christ, to look upon him. What is this event? It consists in the fact that a certain office in the cosmos, connected with the evolution of humanity in the twentieth century, passes over in a heightened form to the Christ. Esoteric, clairvoyant research tells us that in our epoch, Christ becomes the Lord of Karma for human evolution. This event marks the beginning of something that we find intimated also in the New Testament: He will come again to separate or to bring about the crisis for the living and the dead. Only, according to esoteric research, this is not to be understood as though it were a single event for all time that takes place on the physical plane. It is connected with the whole future evolution of humanity. Moreover, whereas Christianity and Christian evolution were thus far a kind of preparation, we now have the significant fact that Christ becomes the Lord of Karma, so that in the future it will rest with him to decide what our karmic account is, how our credit and debit in life are related.[14]

In the context of the preceding description of the incarnation, stage by stage, of Christ in his etheric body—taking this as a hypothesis—would not 1999 as the culmination since 1899 of the third cycle of thirty-three-and-a-third years be on the level of the *will*? Is it conceivable that at this point in time Christ assumed the office of Lord of Karma? In other words, could 1999 have been the beginning of this Christ event in the etheric that "is connected with the whole future evolution of humanity"—the event of Christ becoming the Lord of Karma?

How is it with regard to the other side of this Christ event? The other side of this Christ event is related to the side of the human will connected with nature. It is a fact that, through the will, human beings stand in a direct relationship with nature. We breathe in the air, we drink water, we take our food from the world of nature, and it is transformed in our digestive system, which is connected with our will. The "inner side" of the will is the bearer of our destiny. The "outer side" of the will is related directly to nature. Therefore, the other side of the Christ event in the etheric world at the end of the twentieth century has to do with nature. In Rudolf Steiner's words:

> When one understands the Mystery of Golgotha, that is the only thing that enables us to experience the whole of nature

morally. If one then gazes up at the clouds and sees lightning flashing from them, one will then be able to behold Christ in his etheric form—with the "clouds," that is to say, with the elements. He will appear in spirit form. This vision will one day appear to every human being, whether it is sooner or later, only the Father knows the day and the hour—as it says in the Gospel.[15]

Here Rudolf Steiner quotes the words from the Gospel: "Of that day and hour no one knows, not even the angels in Heaven, nor the Son, but only the Father" (Matt. 24:36). Related to the individual: "The day and the hour are known to the Father alone, for every individual, but for each the time will arrive."[16] Related to the Earth and the whole of humanity, the words from the Gospel applied at the time when Christ spoke these words. Now, however, since Steiner became an apostle of the etheric Christ, for the first time in history something of this mystery—the "greatest mystery of our time," to use Steiner's words—has been revealed. For example, Steiner clearly indicated the year 1933 in connection with Christ's return in the etheric world.[17] In addition, he often referred to the year 1899 as the start of the New Age, which we see in connection with the onset of the new activity of Christ in the etheric realm.

What exactly is the relationship between the dates 1899 and 1933? The year 1933 (thirty-three-and-a-third years after 1899) marked the end of the first period of Christ's activity in his etheric body in the Earth's etheric aura. The thirty-three-and-a-third-year rhythm of Christ's etheric body proceeds further, culminating in 1966 and again in 1999. There are also other rhythms having to do with Christ's renewed activity in our time: the rhythm of Christ's astral body of twenty-nine-and-a-half years (the rhythm of Saturn) and the twelve-year rhythm of Christ's "I" (the rhythm of Jupiter). The latter rhythm is the focus of attention in the foregoing article on subnature and the second coming.

In this postscript to the article, it is a matter of correcting the omission of not having mentioning Rudolf Steiner's reference to "the second crucifixion of Christ," a crucifixion in the etheric world in the nineteenth century.

To conclude, I would like to draw attention to the second crucifixion in the light of Christ's descent through the planetary spheres. This descent is at the same time a descent through the ranks of the spiritual hierarchies.[18] According to this descent, Christ in his etheric body was in the Moon sphere during the nineteenth century. As Steiner indicated, this is the sphere of the angels. He speaks of "the dying of Christ consciousness in the sphere of the angels in the nineteenth century." In this sense, one could understand Steiner's words about the "second crucifixion," related to the "black sphere of materialism," as applying primarily to the Moon sphere. The reason for this is that the seeds of earthly materialism, which are carried across the threshold of death into the spiritual world by departing souls, are causing increasing darkness.

The Moon sphere is the first planetary sphere that the soul enters after passing across the threshold of death. It is here in this realm where negative impulses are left behind, when the soul ascends on the journey through the planetary spheres. We can understand how Christ, in his ether body during the nineteenth century, passed through the Moon sphere at the last stage of his descent from cosmic realms to the Earth. We can perhaps grasp how Christ, on his path of descent in his ether body, passed through the Moon sphere, meeting there the "black sphere of materialism." We can imagine that he took up much of the "black sphere of materialism" into his own being in the spirit of transforming evil into good.

One important thing clearly emerges here, if one asks: Why did the second crucifixion not occur until the nineteenth century, as—since the sixteenth century—the black sphere of materialism was beginning to be formed *at that time* through the seeds of earthly materialism? Why did the second crucifixion not take place in the sixteenth, seventeenth, and eighteenth centuries? The simple reason is that the black sphere of materialism formed primarily in the *Moon sphere*, and Christ on his path of descent through the planetary spheres in his etheric body did not enter this sphere until the nineteenth century, whereas in the sixteenth, seventeenth, and eighteenth centuries Christ descended through the Sun, Venus, and Mercury spheres.[19]

A deeper understanding of the second crucifixion is possible by cognizing, in the light of astrosophy, the descending path of Christ though the spheres of the planets—in other words, through the ranks of the spiritual hierarchies, passing through the sphere of the angels, the Moon sphere, during the nineteenth century as the last stage of descent prior to entering the Earth's etheric aura in 1899, denoting the onset of the New Age. Thus, astrosophy sheds light on cosmic Christianity.

By grasping the connection here of Christ's descent through the Moon sphere with the rise in materialism during the nineteenth century, new insight arises into the second crucifixion in the etheric world. Here it is a matter of showing that the seeming contradiction with Rudolf Steiner's statement concerning "the second crucifixion of Christ" in the etheric world during the nineteenth century is only of an apparent nature. The real purpose of this work is to penetrate deeper into the significance of Steiner's words by exploring the "greatest mystery of our time," the mystery of Christ's return in the etheric, the Christ Mystery in the twentieth and twenty-first centuries.

It is my hope that the reader will sense the activity of conscience—the working together of head and heart—as the underlying orientation of the research into the Christ Mystery presented in the article "Subnature and the Second Coming" and also in this postscript to the article.

Chapter 4

PORTALS TO THE INNER EARTH

MARKO POGAČNIK

BEFORE SAYING ANYTHING ABOUT the inner dimensions of the Earth, I have to confess that I do not believe the Earth to be a rounded ball rotating around the Sun. I believe in an autonomous Earth Cosmos. Of course, it is impossible to deny the multitude of convincing proofs that the Earth is round and that it is a sphere of matter rotating within the solar system. Yet, considering all those seemingly unshakable truths, one needs to be aware that we are dealing with a specific language, not with reality itself. We are dealing with a language that the rational layer of our consciousness has developed to understand the universal creation, including the Earth, according to its own logic. Moreover, we need to understand that the Earth, which has lost its identity as a complete cosmos centered within its divine core, may be nothing more than a mirror image of the human self confined to its rational way of viewing life, a stranger to its own soul purpose.

What we are interested in here is another type of language, one of wholeness and connectedness, a language that does not exclude rational logic, yet honors equally our intuitive insights. Shall we call the language we are aiming for "holistic language"?

Other clarifications must also be offered before diving into the inner layers of the Earth Cosmos. If we are going to deal with the so-called invisible dimensions of the Earth, we are, in effect, going to practice geomancy. This term, meaning "to dedicate one's attention to the spiritual dimensions of the Earth," will be the right word for our purpose: *Gea* is the Greek word for Earth Soul, and *mantein* is the Greek for divination. *Divination* can be understood as a mode of perception that reaches beyond the confines of linear time and physical space.

There is a reason why the ancient knowledge of geomancy was replaced by its sister science, geography, during the rise of natural science in the eighteenth century. The Greek word *graphein* means to describe. *Geography* describes what is seen on the outside, on the Earth's surface, as landscape.

To discover a holistic language and to talk about all the existing dimensions of the Earth, visible and invisible, requires overcoming the dualistic split between the spiritual and materialistic way of interpreting our planetary home. Work has to be done on both sides. It should be possible to extend the knowledge of classical geography so that it encompasses some of the more spiritual realms. This means introducing symbolic, psychological, and even religious interpretations of places and landscapes. On the other side, the ancient science of geomancy is often too esoteric in its way of interpreting the invisible dimensions of reality. It needs to be attuned to today's ecological attitude of approaching natural environments.

To be ready to tread the path leading to the inner dimensions of the Earth, we must understand another term that I forged a few years ago: Earth Cosmos. It sprang, after a fashion, from my emotional resentment toward the way Earth is treated as an object among objects by our modern logical consciousness.

I love the Earth. I continue to have the profound experience of meeting the Earth Soul, this terrible angel, too powerful to withstand its gaze. There is an urgent need to transcend the image of the Earth that is wrapped in a rationalistic network of mental gravel and confined to the sphere of its material body. Thus, I began to speak of the Earth as a complete "cosmos," as a self-contained "holon," to put it in the language of modern geomancy.

There are many different kinds of phenomena in the universe, some even capable of manifesting an objective form, such as plants, planets, animals, and human beings. Just as every human being is a complete, self-contained cosmos, with a divine core, a soul essence, and bodily dimensions, there are other phenomena in the universe, the Earth included, that are also complete in themselves. This self-contained completeness knows its source and purpose and gives each the quality of being a "cosmos."

In order to meet the Earth as a holistic being with its inner and outer worlds, I generally avoid the geographical term Earth, and substitute a term that underlines its autonomy and multidimensionality. I propose the expression Earth Cosmos.

WORLD OF DEPARTURE

We perceive ourselves as walking on the surface of a planet only when we speak the language of the rational mind. The planetary body extends below our feet, the wide universe expands above our heads, and both beyond our reach. The planetary body seems too dense and hot for us to experience its inner structure. The stars and planets are too distant for travel. They are not listed as destinations on the pages of our travel catalogs. We need to develop another kind of language, a different mode of perception, before we can experience the possible inner worlds of the Earth and communicate freely with the spiritual worlds symbolized by stars and planets. We do not need to drill into the Earth, nor do we need to launch rockets.

First, we need to abandon the fragmented consciousness of separation, perceiving Heaven above and the Earth beneath as two separate planes of reality. What is above is also below; what is below exists above. This is a fact, not just some poetic fancy. If the Earth represents a fractal, or holographic unit complete in itself, likewise the universe is part of its holon, as are the inner layers of the planet. When walking through a beautiful spring or winter landscape, we walk and breathe right at the center of the Earth Cosmos. Imagine it as a spherical mandala. Together with plants, animals, surrounding landscape, and other beings incarnated in matter, we exist right at the center of the universe. We do not need to go anywhere else to know the angelic realm, the world of our ancestors and descendants, or civilizations of the inner Earth. They are all positioned within our reach and permeate us, but of course, each holds to its own dimension of existence.

The incredible distances that seem to separate us are nothing but a translation of the embarrassment in rational consciousness of not kowing the code through which to move within the integrated Earth Cosmos. Shall we try to reconstruct that code?

It is not as simple as it seems. The material dimension of reality we live within is also a distinct holographic unit, autonomous in itself. I do not mean the world of illusion (maya), but the material dimension of reality as a place where spirit, soul purpose, and cosmic consciousness incarnate. Its destiny is not merely to serve as a body container in which more highly evolved beings can incarnate. Following the law of a holographic universe, all the diverse dimensions of the Earth holon, from the most subtle to the most spiritual, must be present within the material layer of reality. This is why ancients were able to read divine messages in the rustling of oak leaves at Dodona, or in the shapes of kidney channels, as the Etruscans did.

After leaving our mother's womb, we incarnate in the material dimension. We take part in a world that does not allow us to move freely through the vital spiritual and soul dimensions of the Earth Cosmos. We must learn how to interact with, and create in collaboration with, the invisible world by using the language of the visible world, almost exclusively. The one exception to this is during an epoch of major planetary change.

When preparing for an epoch of major transformations within the Earth Cosmos, the Earth consciousness starts to manifest a system of interdimensional portals. A geomantic system is revealed that is composed of diverse etheric organs, capable of translating the material dimension into other, presently invisible extensions of the Earth Cosmos (pulsing behind the scene) and vice versa. Yet in the case of the interdimensional portals, translating means not just enabling information to flow between different dimensions of reality, but also the possibility of transmuting the structure of information flow, so that it can be transmitted from one level of existence to another.

INTERDIMENSIONAL PORTALS

According to my experience, there are several systems of inter-dimensional portals. Some are constantly in use, such as those employed by human souls incarnating or those leaving the material realm behind while entering the death process. The descending and ascending paths of death and of birth should not be compared with merely changing a suit. To incarnate means to translate the individual soul dimensions into a three-dimensional, spatial and temporal framework. Moreover, it means accepting a bodily structure developed by natural evolution, combined with the elemental consciousness, as one's temporary dimension of existence. To make possible a mutual exchange of experiences between the Earth consciousness and the individual human soul during a period of incarnation, the human soul has to translate its mode of existence into the language of the materially manifested Earth.

Many landscapes are found on the Earth's surface that provide spaces for the different stages of the incarnation and excarnation processes to take place. Ancient cultures recognized these as sacred landscapes. These places, which represent different stages in the process of a soul's descent or ascent, were used as places of communication with the spiritual world, the world of ancestors and descendants. They can be compared to a system of portals that allow the transition from one level of existence to another.

To offer a different example, as incarnated human beings we can use our chakras and acceleration channels and connect them as a system of interdimensional portals. Using them consciously or subconsciously, we are instantly able to translate our state of consciousness into other dimensions of existence, whether through meditation or during the process of extrasensory perception.

Yet there exists another system of interdimensional portals that interests us here: the complex geomantic system that sleeps during periods when evolution and civilizations unfold on their proper plane of existence. During these eras of quiescence, these portals seem not to exist. However, when major planetary changes approach, when revolutionary (re-evolutionary) counter-streams start to prevail and shake the existing plane of reality down to its core, the previously dormant system of interdimensional portals begins to awake and activate its potential. A building's emergency "fire exit" system is a fair comparison.

THE REVELATION OF ST. JOHN AS A KEY

I would not know that such a "fire exit" system exists if I hadn't followed indications in the Apocalypse of St. John. As I explained in my book *Earth Changes, Human Destiny: Coping and Attuning with the Help of the Revelation of St. John,* I experience the Apocalypse as one of the most important keys given to the human race by Divine Providence. It was given to us early enough that we could use it as a compass during the approaching Earth trans-figuration process. This compass, if properly decoded, can help us understand what is going on as we see the space of reality around us breaking down through unusual storms, the dangerous heating of the planet's atmosphere, unexpected world events, and so forth.

When I compare my geomantic observations and dream mes-sages received by my soul to the images found in the Apocalypse, I find astonishing parallels between the changes observed at the etheric and consciousness levels of the Earth organism since the late autumn of 1997 and various statements of the Apocalypse. Yet I was unable then to see that not only is a deeper understanding of Earth changes offered by that ancient book, but also practical instructions on how to act in such conditions, so that the stream of life is not broken.

Only after I visited the ruins of the famous Seven Churches (or cities) of the Apocalypse did I discover the key statements about interdimensional portals. The seven messages in the Apocalypse, chapters 2 and 3, are addressed to the seven early Christian churches in Asia Minor: Ephesus, Smyrna, Pergamos, Thyatira, Sardis, Philadelphia, and Laodicea. After observing their locations on a map, one can perceive that they form a kind of necklace around a mountainous region that extends from Ephesus to Laodicea, the first and last city mentioned in the Apocalypse. The ancient Greeks called this region the Lakmos Mountains.

Geomantic research shows that this entire mountainous region has the quality of an interdimensional portal. This means that, within the ether body of that sparsely inhabited landscape, two distinct levels exist, one above the other. The lower level shows a geomantic structure that is typical for such a landscape. Above it is another level having a distinct vibration comparable to the quality of the fairy world.

When the portal is in a dormant phase, the two levels are separate from each other. The portal allows entry to the realms of the Earth's interior only when the two levels touch each other. The "opening of the gate" requires a double pyramidal, etheric structure that encompasses the entire region of the interdimensional portal. It is comprised of two four-sided pyramids, whose peaks are turned in opposite directions: one toward the center of the Earth, the other toward the stars. To provide a sense of a scale, the sides of these pyramids, in terms of the materialized landscape, would stretch approximately one hundred miles.

The geomantic workshop I led to explore the interdimensional portal in the region of the Seven Cities took place in September

2005. After that, I began to discover interdimensional portals in other countries, usually much "smaller" (if physical size has any meaning at this level of discourse). They differ widely in their shape and function. Some are described in my book *Sacred Geography*.

THE ARCHETYPAL LAYER OF THE INNER EARTH

My knowledge of the inner realm of the Earth does not depend entirely on the latest discovery of interdimensional portals in the landscape. While geomantically exploring the Earth's surface in prior years, I encountered places that displayed a distinct relationship to a layer within the Earth, which I call the "archetypal layer." When I use my chakra system as an interdimensional portal to dive into the archetypal layer of the inner Earth, I find myself in a world of archetypal landscapes, which my consciousness translates into images of "Paradise." Archetypes of beings and configurations seem to be stored there, which one finds on the surface of the Earth as different forms of manifested reality.

After observing the elemental world and trying repeatedly to understand how it works, I began to believe that the archetypal layer of the interior of the Earth has decisive importance for elemental beings by enabling them to perform their role within the creation process. The term elemental beings, or environmental spirits, is used to pinpoint that aspect of the Earth consciousness that works continuously to manifest invisible vibrations and qualities as forms of tangible reality. In effect, the task of elemental beings, as holographic consciousness units of the Earth Soul, is to translate its impulses, expressed through the archetypal images, into manifested forms.

In this sense, the archetypal layer of the interior of the Earth can be seen as a subelemental world. It provides elemental beings and environmental spirits with archetypal patterns—a kind of a chart or plan to guide the process of manifesting time-and-space reality on the Earth's surface. To say it in the language of the fairy tale, the elemental beings return repeatedly to the treasury of the Earth's archetypal layer to gain the tools needed to sustain the manifestation of spatial reality.

INTERMEZZO

To approach the interior dimensions of the Earth, we first create a mandala, or rosette-like image, of the Earth Cosmos. The manifested and materialized space of reality at the center of the Earth's universe is surrounded by several layers of invisible worlds that we perceive as belonging partly to the interior of the Earth, partly to the atmospheric space above. In effect, each forms an uninterrupted spherical layer that binds heavenly and earthly aspects into an interconnected unity.

We already explored two such uninterrupted spherical layers rotating around the manifested world that represents the center of rotation. First, we mentioned the so-called spiritual world: the world of ancestors and descendants. The spiritual landscapes and laboratories of the world of souls are positioned all around manifested reality (so above as below), even partially permeating spaces that we consider to be mere material nature.

The second spherical layer, which rotates beyond the sphere of ancestors and descendants, is the world of the archetypes. The archetypal layer can be perceived as belonging in part to the inner Earth and in part to the heavenly hemisphere, where it is angelic in character. The two aspects mirror each other as two halves of a whole. Only in our minds are they separated, with one belonging to Heaven above and the other to the Earth below.

Rotating between these two spherical layers, I sense the existence of another set of dimensions associated with the so-called sunken civilizations. The interdimensional portals mentioned here represent doors to approach that mysterious layer. In effect, it seems that the veil of mystery covering that aspect of the Earth Cosmos disintegrates after the interdimensional portals have started to open.

TRANSFORMED CIVILIZATIONS

Western mythological tradition, as well as the experiences of many highly sensitive individuals of different times and epochs, tell the story of at least two great civilizations that disappeared beneath the waves of the oceans. We generally consider the civilization of the fire element, called Lemuria, as having sunk into the depths of the Pacific Ocean. The civilization of the water element, Atlantis, lies beneath the surface of the Atlantic Ocean. According to my experience, the sinking of a continent into the depths of the ocean represents a logical interpretation of an interdimensional transformation that a complete civilization experiences after its mission upon the surface of the planet has been accomplished.

Let me explain. Each global civilization has a specific role in developing the core of the planetary space that we presently know as materialized reality. This core of the planetary rosette is the precious "child" of the Earth Soul; it is the dimension of her body in which the development takes place. There, at the center of the Earth Cosmos, a laboratory was created by the Earth Soul in which methods are developed so that spirit can incarnate gradually into the physical-material dimension of the universe.

Each of the two previous global civilizations mastered one essential step toward this goal. The civilization of the fire element (Lemuria) was able to incarnate within the ether body of the Earth space. The water element civilization (Atlantis) was able to incarnate within the emotional (astral) body. Only our present civilization (the development from the Palaeolithic epoch up to the present day) has been able to step into the densest dimension of matter: the earth element.

After discovering interdimensional portals throughout the world, I gained the possibility of immediate experiences of the previous civilizations as two autonomous layers of the inner Earth. By decoding the image of the sunken continents, I learned that our antecedent civilizations were transformed at the point of their "destruction" into another dimension of reality, a dimension the following civilization was unable to perceive. Seen from the outside, they simply disappeared. Yet in the context of the Earth Cosmos, they changed their mode of existence and position within the world rosette; they were transformed into inner layers of the Earth. In this context, the ancient civilizations that disappeared long ago from the Earth's surface exist today as memory layers within the Earth's interior. Their precious experiences and their knowledge are stored there to be used today as inspiration for the further development of the Earth Cosmos. They represent one of the sources of wisdom associated with the Earth Soul.

Fairy Worlds

The question may arise, however: Where are the souls who acted as the driving force of evolution in those "sunken" civilizations? Are they now active in the inner layers of the Earth? Certainly not. We, the people of the present age, are those same souls. We left behind experiences of the fire and water civilizations and have incarnated within the civilization of the earth element.

But who are those people, etheric in appearance, whom I meet when I dive through my consciousness into the inner layers of the Earth and touch the realm of the past civilizations? They are neither human souls nor elemental beings—that is, holographic units of the Earth consciousness, familiar to me from the Earth's landscape. When I met them for the first time, fourteen years ago at Craigan's Mill in the north of Donegal, Ireland, the beings of the subterranean civilizations appeared to me as normal human beings, with bodies that had the form expected of any human being, but without the corresponding substance. I simply asked them who they were. In response, one of them appeared to me in a light-and-color form that resembled the ceremonial dress of the Maya or Inca peoples, signifying that he belongs to the past civilizations.

For many years I was somewhat confused about these experiences—which were repeated several times in different parts of the world—until I discovered the system of interdimensional portals just discussed. Only then was the path of communication with the civilizations of the inner Earth lifted to a relatively firm and logical basis, allowing such experiences to be translated and communicated properly into the language of the rational mind.

It turned out that beings of the inner Earth belong to the world of Gaia's consciousness. Yet, they are not simply elemental beings or nature spirits as we know them from the Earth's surface, but are much closer to the Earth Soul and to its cosmic aspect. In effect, they are guardians of the cosmic aspect of the Earth Soul; thus, they could justifiably be called "cosmic elemental beings." Some traditions know them as fairy beings of the inner Earth.

During the transformation process that leads the Earth body through its evolution from one elemental epoch to another (fire, water, earth), all beings on the Earth's surface had to go through profound transmutations to attune to the frequencies of the new element. This was the concern not only of human beings but also for elemental beings. (More details on this kind of transition can be found in chapter 5 of my book *Nature Spirits and Elemental Beings*.)

However, a large part of the elemental beings, those who did not follow an evolutionary path on the Earth's surface, remained with the "sunken" civilizations to become their "ensouling" spirits as those civilizations were transformed into layers in the Earth's memory. They previously served as the personal elemental beings of the human souls incarnating on the Earth's surface. As they were representing the cosmic archetype of the individual human being for the period between their "birth" and "death," they collected immense experiences, which they now embody within the Earth's memory layers.

One may speak of different layers of memory that past civilizations form within the realms of the inner Earth. These layers do not represent a mere treasury of valuable experiences from the past civilizations; rather, they are alive in their own way, and they are relevant to the present moment. These cosmic elemental beings are agents that enliven the realm of the past civilizations, even if they sank long ago into the inner space of the Earth Cosmos. In relation to this layer of cosmic elemental beings, we may speak of the fairy world of the Earth's interior universe.

WHAT DOES IT MEAN IN A PRACTICAL SENSE?

At first glance, these descriptions of the layers of the universe within the Earth seem interesting yet abstract. Yet this evaluation quickly changes, especially once it is realized that the Earth changes we see gradually increasing within our environment are so far-reaching that they cannot be dealt with exclusively on the physical plane of existence.

I have observed an alternative that has been developing during the last ten years, which can best be described as a possibility to resolve ecological and social crises spreading over the Earth surface through collaboration with the inner layers of the Earth, their powers, and their intelligence. It seems that the challenges of the approaching Earth changes can be solved in peace and harmony only by reconnecting the fragile life organism of the Earth's surface to its basic strata, represented by the subterranean layers of the Earth Cosmos.

First, it is necessary to find ways to reconnect individually and collectively with the Earth Soul and its archetypal wisdom. The Earth Soul knows the path of evolution that the Earth Cosmos is about to take. It knows the possibilities of transition and transformation that must be taken to protect life on the Earth's surface.

Second, it is equally important to strengthen communication and initiate ways of collaboration with the world of ancestors and descendants. Knowledge of the cosmic transformations, of which they are guardians, can represent a fountain of inspiration to us, their brothers and sisters presently incarnated on the Earth. Such knowledge may guide us toward optimum solutions to world affairs.

Third, I wish to stress the importance of the emerging inter-dimensional portals and, with them, the possibility of overcoming the exclusivity of the present Earth's space of reality, which is bound to a single dimension of existence—the material one. The interdimensional portals make possible the flow between different dimensions of reality. They allow the emergence of new, unanticipated solutions to the ecological problems threatening the life of the Earth. They also allow interaction with the fairy worlds of the Earth's interior.

Global warming and other signs of profound Earth changes can no longer be ignored. Humanity is becoming aware that far-reaching decisions have to be taken to meet the arising challenges. Why should we bind ourselves exclusively to the material plane of existence while searching for solutions? It is time to open our consciousness to the wider dimensions of existence. Why desperately search for new possibilities to appear within the framework of the outer universe? Stop sending rockets to the Moon; solutions to these problems are much closer at hand. Let us begin to listen to the inner voice of our soul essence, which knows the path of life. Let us be open to the message sounding from the inner worlds of the Earth. There is where our home is. There our strength pulsates, which can be reached in our hour of need.

Chapter 5

TRANSFORMING SUBEARTHLY
ENERGIES THROUGH EURYTHMY

RACHEL C. ROSS

RUDOLF STEINER CREATED EURYTHMY in 1912 as a performance art having both visual and auditory expression in speech and music, thereby making the elements of speech and music visible.[1] Eurythmy is a profound art of movement that is only beginning to reveal its underlying mysteries. As with all forms of movement and dance, it is a challenging task to describe the real nature of the movements without performing and experiencing them oneself. Through proper training and practice, the healing powers of eurythmy may be revealed in human beings. In an introduction to one of the earliest performances of eurythmy, Rudolf Steiner spoke of the unique relationship between the creative forces of nature and those of the artist:

> Just as the creative forces of nature draw upon the inexhaustible source of the infinite, so that it is always possible to perceive in something that has come to fruition much more than was originally implanted in it, the same is true when artistic impulses unite with the powerful creative forces of nature. In such a case the artist does not merely develop some more or less limited impulse, but reaches the point of becoming an instrument for the creative powers of the universe, so that much more grows from this activity than one could originally have intended or foreseen.[2]

Through the artistic, pedagogical, and therapeutic practice of eurythmy, one may become an active conduit or bridge between Heaven and Earth.[3] By doing so, one is able to transform one's own fallen nature and soul. Eurythmy is a discipline of body, soul, and spirit that will gradually evolve and transform as we evolve and transform ourselves through our path of self-development.

Eurythmy embodies the whole of the path Rudolf Steiner called Anthroposophy, or spiritual science. It makes spiritual experience and the reality of higher spiritual truths accessible for students of spiritual science through artistic movement, in contrast to relying solely upon the disciplines of concentration and meditation.[4] One can study spiritual science devotedly and diligently, but the danger always exists that such studies will remain intellectual, abstract, and detached from the rest of one's human nature. When one undertakes eurythmy in the proper fashion, a living, imaginative thinking is engaged, stimulating higher organs of perception. As the actual language of the Sophia being, eurythmy has the potential to transform the relationship of the suprasensory human bodies, as well as the physical. By damming up what is so essentially human (the creative power of speech, which is connected to the zodiac and our archetypal human form), we are able to enter the forces that create our organs, bones, and muscles. This enables us to be the true bridge between the spiritual and the physical. We create something that never existed before, something new, each time we perform it. Eurythmy provides a healing element when practiced individually or in a group, as it activates the life-giving powers of the etheric beyond the personal by stimulating the integration of one's "I" into the astral, ether, and physical bodies. Eurythmy helps overcome the mechanical qualities that permeate our life in movement, breathing, digestion, and thinking. It fosters consciousness of one's body and, when working with others, enhances awareness of objective social connections. The individual, when participating as a member of a group, may raise personal experience to a higher vibration or level. Group work challenges us to overcome egotism and subjective judgments and to be more open to others.

Therapeutic eurythmy originated from the practical work of eurythmists and doctors who, while working with the students of the first Waldorf school in Stuttgart, observed the healing effects of tone and speech eurythmy lessons on the students. They saw that there must be something more behind artistic eurythmy that would offer opportunities for a new form of therapy. They wished to connect eurythmy with medicine in a more conscious and direct way. This initiative resulted in a course of six lectures on therapeutic eurythmy given by Rudolf Steiner to doctors and eurythmists in April 1921, and two more to doctors and medical students in April 1921 and October 1922.[5]

Therapeutic eurythmy is a complimentary therapy with anthroposophically extended and homeopathic medicine, enabling the body to be more receptive to the dynamic activity of the remedies. It can be effective in treating many illnesses and disorders on various levels. This movement therapy can mitigate, or even cure, a condition as severe as scoliosis—without ever touching the person physically—by strengthening and realigning the body's energies into the skeletal system of the physical body.

As architecture may be considered the art of the physical body, sculpture that of the etheric body, painting that of the astral body, and music the art of the "I," eurythmy is the art of the spirit self (manas), the first spiritual member of the higher nature of the human being, which will be fully developed in the future. In our age, the consciousness soul and the spirit self form a unity,[6] and, in advance, we may undertake to develop the spirit self.

Conscious confrontation with the forces of death and evil is required to give birth to the consciousness soul and spirit self. The connection of evil with illness is indirect but clear. Before the Fall (or the luciferic intervention), human beings had no physical body or individual "I" and were incapable of error. Owing to the Fall, both humanity and the Earth acquired a physical form. The process of individuation began with the onset of selfishness, along with the possibilities of error, illness, and death.[7] "Illness is the embodiment of a deformation that otherwise might inhibit human evolution."[8] Therapeutic eurythmy can help people transform and overcome illness and the type of evil that expresses it.

Therapeutic eurythmy exercises predominantly involve the limb system, yet these exercises permeate one's entire body and soul. Movement of the legs engages the will organization, which lives both in the limbs and the metabolic system. Each eurythmy movement must be grounded and connected with the forces coming from both the Earth and the heavens, and then transformed and directed through conscious "I"-experience into the body.

THE VOWELS

The eurythmy movements of the vowel sounds reveal the deep connection of the vowels with the human soul's response to inner and outer events. We naturally say "ah" when expressing wonder and awe. The outer gesture of *A* ("ah") is opening the arms to receive the forces we stand in awe of into our souls. Young children make this gesture often and express wonder in their souls with each new inspiring event or experience. We would all be healthier today and would strengthen our immune systems if we could experience wonder more often as adults. *A* (ah) also strengthens the inhalation process and overcomes the "animal forces" that bind body and soul. These forces, which are connected directly with the subterranean spheres, can rise through the body and overwhelm the soul.[9]

Movement of the arms is mirrored in the activity of the legs when we make the same *A* ("ah") gesture by opening the legs and feet in a wider stance, connecting our whole being with the Earth. Forces from the Earth, which stream upward through the legs, are brought into balance and harmony by the mirrored activity of the upper body and arms. Steiner observes that we speak with our feet

and legs, sing with our arms, and think with the quiet, outer stillness of the head.[10]

> *A* ["ah"]...has to do with all those forces in human beings
> that make us greedy, that organize us according to animal
> nature; the "ah," in fact, lies nearest to the animal nature
> in humankind, and in a certain sense one can say that when
> the *A* ["ah"] is pronounced, it sounds from human animal
> nature. And, certainly, as spiritual investigation confirms,
> "ah" is the sound that was the very earliest to appear in both
> the phylogenetic evolution and the ontogenetic evolution of
> humanity. In ontogenetic evolution, it is somewhat hidden,
> of course; there is a false evolution as well, as you know.
> *A* ["ah"] was the first sound to manifest in human evolution,
> however, resounding at first entirely out of the animal nature.
> When we tend toward *A* ["ah"] with the consonants, we still
> call on the animal forces in us...the whole sound is actually
> formed accordingly. If we use the sound therapeutically, as it
> presented itself to our souls yesterday, we can combat what
> makes children, as well as adults, into smaller and larger ani-
> mals. With such exercises [using the "ah" sound and gesture
> in eurythmy], we can have very respectable results in making
> human beings less animalistic.[11]
>
> The person who assumes the task of observing speech will
> see that our confrontation with the outer world must involve
> living into the world vigorously, becoming selfless and living
> out into the world. In the vowels, we come to ourselves; in
> the vowels we go within and develop activity there. In the
> consonants, we become, in a way, one with the outer world,
> though in varying degrees. These degrees of unification with
> the world manifest in certain practices in language as well. In
> the development of consonants in eurythmy—particularly in
> reference to the sensory-suprasensory observation of which I
> so often speak when introducing eurythmy performances—it
> is necessary to consider whether one objectifies oneself. [12]

It is not possible to overcome and transform forces intellectually
or abstractly, but only through conscious engagement with them
within ourselves.[13] This is true with each vowel and diphthong

sound. The primary sounds *A* ("ah"), *E* ("ay"), *I* ("ee"), *O* ("oh"), *U* ("oo"), *Ei* ("ie"), *Au* ("ow") are connected directly to the planets Venus, Mars, Mercury, Jupiter, Saturn, Moon, and Sun. Each sound and its planetary forces are linked to the cardinal organs and are used to treat various disorders, disturbances, and diseases. (This is an extensive study[14] that will not be further elaborated here.)

The Consonants

Consonants are connected to the formative forces of the zodiac. Therapeutic eurythmy exercises for these sounds (individually or in combination with particular vowel sounds) are effective in treating all types of digestive and structural disorders. For example, the sound *R,* especially a rolling *R,* is effective in treating constipation and intestinal blockages. This is a physical problem that addresses the need for more activity and airy elements in the bowels. These exercises and sounds work within the whole body and stimulate the entire intestinal tract when performed in a specific way.

The forces of digestion and elimination, which are destructive forces, originate, in part, from the subterranean spheres, and are also connected with the nervous system and the brain.

> What appears in the brain as earthly matter has simply been excreted; it is excretion from the organic process. Earthly matter has been excreted to serve as a basis for the *I* ["ee"]. On the basis of this process in the metabolic-limb system (beginning with the consumption of feed and going on through the entire distributive activity of the digestion), a certain amount of earthly matter, of earthly nourishment, can be led into the head and brain.... However, food substance is not deposited only in the brain. Whatever is no longer capable of assimilation is deposited, along the way, in the intestines.[15]

The sound *L* promotes flexibility and movement when forces become stuck or sclerotic. It establishes harmony and strengthens the inhalation process and the life, or ether, forces. The *L* sound is found in many important sequences created by Rudolf Steiner to treat a variety of illnesses. It is a water sound that embodies transformation and metamorphosis. When used in a particular way involving "jumping" with the legs, the peristaltic action of the intestines is stimulated. In another exercise, the *L* can promote the change of teeth when a child is delayed at this stage of development.

THE ART OF THE SPIRIT SELF

"What the soul carries within itself of the true and the good is immortal in it" and is called the consciousness soul, or "the soul within the soul."[16] In humanity today, the consciousness (or spiritual) soul and the spirit self (manas) form a unity. The spirit self is so called "because it manifests as the 'I' ['ee' sound]"[17] It is the purified astral body, which is comprised of wisdom. The unchanged, "fallen" portion of one's soul is really a part of the outer world working within. It is exterior to the "real you"—the "I." When we inwardly observe our own world of desires, urges, fears, and so forth, we experience this world as outside of the "I." A passive element is always present in such activity.

The astral body is individualized through its permeation and transformation by the moral forces flowing from the "I." Thus, the spirit self is a product of the "I" and no longer the province of the gods; it is one's own achievement. All the suffering experienced along one's path of development may be transformed into wisdom, for suffering reborn in the "I" is wisdom. As the polaric counterpart to the fallen self, the spirit self is the first member of an objective higher self. The spirit self flows from forces of the Holy Sophia and of the Holy Spirit. Thus, it is also known as the Sophianic self.

The consciousness soul, as a metamorphosis of the physical body, thus has a connection to the mineral earth. In addition, purification of the soul requires bringing awareness to the energies in one's lower self that originate in the fire earth. The fire earth, also called the passion earth, is the seat of all lower passions, or animal passions, and sensations of pleasure and pain. To achieve some measure of progress toward developing the spirit self, one must transform portions of the subterranean spheres that lie within.

Note that the Sophianic higher self descends into the "I"; the "I" does not ascend or rise to meet it. The lower self is gradually mastered by the "I," which learns to become as indifferent to itself as it is to the phenomena of outer nature. If the "I" tries to achieve or experience the Sophianic self by rising to the next spirit level, by excarnating to meet it, its experience will be luciferic and ultimately produce only ahrimanic consequences. The higher members of human nature (spirit self, and so on) are accessed appropriately through the "I." Likewise, if eurythmy is not undertaken as an "I"-experience, it is in danger of becoming luciferic and self-indulgent, thus losing its effectiveness.

EURYTHMY EXERCISES FOR SPIRIT SELF (MANAS)

Three exercises specifically promote the development and incarnation of the spirit self: A-Veneration ("ah"), Hope-U ("oo"), and Love-E ("ay"). These are connected to the three principal Christian virtues: faith, hope, and charity (or love). Faith looks toward the past—the Father; love lives in the present—the Christ; and hope applies to the future—the Holy Spirit. Through proper practice, adding appropriate imaginative images or visualizations, we engender a strengthening and transformation of our soul forces. Everything done consciously in eurythmy movements and gestures becomes ensouled through the activity of one's "I" and imagination, thus "potentizing," or activating, the inherent forces in the movements.

Before undertaking these exercises, one should create the following picture in the mind's eye. As a human being, we stand between the celestial, or heavenly, worlds and the subearthly worlds of the interior of the Earth. The Sun is above our head as we stand erect at the outset of the exercise. The center of the Earth, where a new sun is germinating, lies directly beneath our feet. Christ, who once lived on the Sun, now lives as the Spirit of the Earth at its center, which is made of gold. Thus we may picture the polar extremes: the Sun and the Earth's center, each glowing with golden light. We stand positioned between them and, in fact, comprise the means by which these two realms will one day be reunited. Above is the regions of the etheric and astral worlds, the lower and upper devachan worlds. Below are the subterranean layers harboring the forces of opposition, those of selfishness, egotism, and evil. However, below the subterranean spheres, at the tenth telluric layer, is the center of the Earth, where the Resurrected Christ, the new planetary spirit, dwells.

A-Veneration: Faith.

The *A* ("ah") gesture takes us forward and upward into the world. Through this gesture, we receive the creative "breath of God" through the *H* sound, taking one back into the gesture of veneration; we are filled and permeated with life forces. *H is a wonderful sound of the spirit, where the out-breathing of the breath is hardly perceptible, while the movement or gesture can be expansive. H allows the soul to release into the spiritual space behind the body, freeing the soul from the sense-bound world of daily life. We throw off the burdens and fears of the day to create a space in the soul for deeper sleep and the renewing healing forces in the body.* This exercise strengthens the immune system and is done before bed to assist in an easy passage into sleep. It provides a counter to the negative effects of modern life on one's soul forces.

> Slowly, we free ourselves from the world of the senses and become submerged in the world lying behind us. If this is practiced often, the organic power of resistance will be

strengthened. Veneration for something great conquers one's own egotism.... It develops devotion in the soul, and in the body makes the organism capable of warding off external influences.[18]

HOPE-U

In the soul exercise Hope-U, we move from the open gesture of Hope in the space behind, the realm of inspiration, accentuated by placing our weight on the heels, into the movement of U ("oo"), pouring gathered forces down through our being from the crown of the head to the feet and into the Earth. This is a powerful gesture and experience re-enlivening and focusing forces of the "I" back into the body. "This means that the astral will act very strongly upon the etheric, and it can be said that it will have a beneficial warming effect on the breathing system." [19]

Because this exercise promotes a future evolutionary condition (the spirit self), the focus of the eurythmy movement is, until its final motion, directed toward the space behind the body. In the physical body, the back is the direction of the past, and the front is the direction of the future. We look ahead to see what's approaching; we look behind to see where we have been. In the ether body, the reverse is true. In the ether body, the future approaches from behind, and the past lies in front. Our higher self approaches and incarnates from above and behind. Hence, the direction and position of the Hope-U exercise is orientated toward the rear through the center of the body and in a downward motion with U. The front of the ether body (the gender of which is opposite to that of the physical body) is at the physical body's dorsal side; its backside is positioned along the front side of the physical body. This means that the etheric backbone, along which the seven foci of the chakra points are located, lies along the front. This etheric backbone, or energy "frontbone," is the focus of many movements in therapeutic eurythmy.

This vertical descent with the "U" gesture from the point above one's head (the highest point of which is the center of the Sun) to the bottom of the feet, pointing to the center of the Earth, precisely reflects the descending path of incarnation of Christ, from the time when he left the Sun, incarnated on the Earth (the mineral earth), and descended into the subterranean spheres during the Mystery of Golgotha. In this way, one replicates his journey, microcosmically, through the movements of the Hope-U exercise.

Love-E

The Love-E ("ay") exercise alternates between two opposite soul gestures. It shows an open gesture in which the loving forces from the heart pour out through the curved arms into the world. Then, before the arms are able to enclose, an *E* is created across the chest, drawing all of the soul forces back into the heart. This exercise brings balance and creates healthy boundaries for the soul. As Rudolf Steiner often mentioned, we need to establish healthy sympathies and antipathies to maintain the balance of the conscious "I" in the center. The Love-E exercise, when practiced in a sequence of ten times, pausing between each set, helps one develop an ability to stand balanced between sympathy and antipathy.

> Now we want to express what one could call the feeling of love toward something.... Imagine it [the movements] carried out ten times consecutively and accompanied by a powerful *E* ["ay"] between each of the movements, one after the other, with a small pause between.... You accompany the movements that you have learned as expressing feeling in eurythmy—it could be another feeling as well—with the movement of *I* ["ee"]. Here we have a strong influence that proceeds from the human etheric to act on the astral nature and has the effect of warming the circulation. It is something that really works on the circulatory system in a beneficial manner. One cannot say that it accelerates or retards the circulation; it affects it in a beneficially warming way.[20]

The experience of these three exercises is more important for us today than ever before. They not only assist us in transforming our nature, but also protect us in a world that tries to overwhelm, attack, and disillusion our very being. One has only to listen to the nightly news to feel the fear and hopelessness that strives to take root in our souls.

Because of these movements and their accompanying imaginations, awe and wonder descend into feelings of veneration and reverence, then descend further into one's will to become devotion. Devotion to the Divine is the foundation of all genuine spiritual development. Reverence leads to willing sacrifice and devotion. We try during this exercise to have such feelings and such willingness—at least briefly. This is not easily done, for depending on how awake we are during the exercise, we become aware of impediments and blocks in our nature that divert our energies and consciousness into cul-de-sacs of personal interests, concerns or worries. It is very difficult to maintain and sustain conscious thoughts and feelings of reverence and devotion without losing focus. The intention is to experience awe in thinking, reverence in feeling, and selfless devotion in the will, then to send the transformed energies from our heart center into the subterranean spheres and into the golden center of the Earth.

Eurythmy can assist us in the lifelong project of gaining control over our nature, so that we gradually cease being victims of our soul forces. We master our being and progress, from compulsion and reaction to gaining command over our nature. We become individuals of initiative. By gradually transforming our nature, we connect directly with the forces of the Sophia (Anthroposophia). To quote Rudolf Steiner's apocalyptic prophecy:

> You can see ... that human beings are related to all of these [subearthly] layers, for they continually radiate out their forces. Humanity lives under the influence of these layers and has to overcome their energies. One day when human beings have learned to radiate life and have trained their

breathing so that it promotes life, they will overcome the fire earth. When spiritually they overcome pain through serenity, they will overcome the air earth. When peace and harmony reign, the splintering earth will be conquered. When white magic triumphs, no more evil will remain on the Earth. Thus human evolution implies a transformation of the Earth's interior....In the end, when human powers have transformed the Earth, it will be spiritualized. In this way, human beings impart their own being to the Earth. So the will of human beings is connected with what happens on Earth. One transforms one's dwelling place and one's self at the same time. When people spiritualize themselves, they spiritualize the Earth as well.[21]

These ideas, which reveal our connection to the Earth and its subterranean energies, also open the door to the healing effects bestowed by eurythmy and therapeutic eurythmy when undertaken with such concepts in mind.

Chapter 6

THE MINERAL EARTH AS THE GATEWAY TO FREEDOM AND THE SUBTERRANEAN SPHERES:

THE MINISTRY OF JESUS CHRIST

PAUL V. O'LEARY

EACH OF US FEELS deep within the impulse to freedom. We want to control our thoughts and emotions and not act merely as a result of genetic determination and social indoctrination. Current scientific thought asserts that human behavior is determined by "nature or nurture," meaning our thoughts, emotions, and actions are either "programmed" from within or from without. We ask: But what about me? Where do I fit in? Heredity and environment may have shaped me, perhaps even most of who I am and what I have done. But is that all there is? What about freedom? Freedom is something I want, need, and can experience. Is my experience of freedom the illusion modern science teaches it to be? And, if freedom is an illusion, does that make me (my "I") an illusion, too?

This is not a treatise on philosophical or political freedom. I would, however, like to connect the idea of freedom with the preconditions required for freedom: the realms of evil and necessity. Only out of evil and necessity (lack of freedom) can freedom be born. The realm of necessity is, in the first instance, the realm of death, the mineral earth, the outermost layer of the subterranean spheres, where we spend our lives between birth and death. The remaining subterranean spheres are the realms of evil.

Each day, we confront the limitations imposed by our physical body; we have to eat, drink, sleep, digest, and eliminate. We are spirits confined to a material realm that restricts, even enslaves, us on all sides. We are constituted in this way owing to the presence of the mineral earth, the phase of human and planetary evolution that features a physical, solid component for the first time.

The physical body, which is formed in part by substances from the mineral earth (and must therefore die), provides the foundation for our freedom. We hope to show that the solidity of the mineral earth, and the spiritual cause that called it into existence, was as necessary a component to the creation of the free individuality—the ideal human being—as was the deed of Christ at the Mystery of Golgotha to create it.

Why does the mineral earth exist at all? What is it about "death" that makes it so important? What does Christianity have to say about such questions, and in what way is its central "miracle," the death and resurrection of Jesus Christ, relevant? Human freedom, death, necessity, and evil are all interconnected. This chapter will discuss some of those connections and the role played by the subterranean spheres, although the principal focus will be the mineral earth.

Before the Fall, human beings lived within the bosom of the gods in a state of complete lack of freedom, without individuality or personality, poured through and transparent for the impulses and directives of higher beings. Within this state of divine indwelling, there was no error, no secrecy, no deception or lies, and no personal life—only a group existence that reflected entirely the activity of the gods. We were all, more or less, the same. At a certain point, humanity was "infected" by the luciferic impulse of selfishness. Humanity absorbed evil and, as a result, was ejected from Paradise, losing the primal connection to the Godhead. Through the Fall, Earth condensed out of the spirit realms over long periods of time to become physical substance, and, owing to the presence of the mineral earth, humanity, too, acquired a physical body.

Through the absorption of self-love and consequent incorporation into matter, humanity began to experience pain, illness, and death. The mineral earth, as a realm of death, is an arena of rejected cosmic sacrifice, comprised of being that has been thrust out of the spiritual worlds and has condensed to physicality. The physical realm (mineral earth) acts as a veil, or barrier, that shuts humanity off from the direct perception of the spiritual worlds, from which it fell. It provides a neutral realm that can receive impulses from both the suprasensory spiritual worlds and the subsensory spiritual worlds, or subterranean spheres. Once imbued with selfishness, individual human karma began. Selfishness (evil) and its consequences provide the basis for the process of individuation, for the variety of human experience, and for freedom. Humanity fell from one state of nonfreedom (necessity) in Paradise to a subsequent necessity, permeated by the luciferic and ahrimanic forces that bind us. The "wheel of necessity" of Eastern spiritual traditions, by which we are imprisoned by our lower self and repeat our actions, is described by Jesus Christ: "Everyone who commits a sin (creates new karma) is a slave to sin (karma)" (John 8:34). Our present situation, however, allows the possibility of achieving true freedom. Lucifer gave us the ability to be indifferent toward others; Christ gives us the ability to be indifferent toward our self. Lucifer gave us the power to say "no" to others; Christ gives us the power to say "no" to our self.

> But without evil there could be no self-feeling, no free choice of good, no freedom. Good could have been realized without Lucifer, but not freedom. In order to be able to choose good we must also have the bad before us. It must dwell within us as the force of self-love. But self-love must become love of all. Then, evil will be overcome. Freedom and evil have the same original source.[1]

Thus, freedom and evil have a common source: the luciferic intervention. The resulting condensation of physical matter out of spirit blocked human perception of the gods so that humankind could develop individual, personal will, freed from the vision of the activity of the gods who created them.

Freedom could not be "given" to humanity as a gift of the gods, because even the gods cannot create a free being; if they did, the leading strings of their creativity would always remain attached and negate the possibility of achieving genuine independence.[2] A free being has to create itself. Hence, humanity has incorporated evil into its nature in order to evolve the free personality, the ideal human being. "The gods did not shrink from the evil, which alone could give the possibility of freedom. Had the gods avoided evil, the world would be poor, without variety.... For the sake of freedom the gods had to allow evil to enter the world."[3]

We human beings feel this dilemma every day. We are positioned between good and evil, between freedom and necessity.

> Human life, as far as it consists of experience of outer nature as well as of the inner life of soul and spirit, lies between two poles; and many of the thoughts that necessarily come to human beings about their connection with the world are influenced by the realization that these two polar opposites exist. On the one side, human life of thinking and feeling is confronted by what is called "natural necessity." We feel dependent on adamantine laws that we find everywhere in the outside world and that also penetrate through us, inasmuch as our physical and etheric organisms are part and parcel of this outer world. On the other hand, we are deeply sensory... our dignity as human beings could not be fully attained if freedom were not an integral element in our life between birth and death. Necessity and freedom are the polar opposites of our life.[4]

This battle takes place within us; we comprise the arena in which good and evil confront each other.[5] "In the middle, so to speak—for this requires a spatial image—is the surface of the Earth, the mineral plane, the region where the collision takes place between these opposing forces. For on the Earth's surface, a being has gradually developed who is the product of this polarity."[6] Through repeated Earth lives, we both create karma and have the opportunity to heal karma. We incur debts and pay off debts. Through this process and gradual permeation of our lower nature or natural selves with morality, we ascend along a lengthy path of development toward the ideal human being. "In reality, karma is our redemption through ourselves, through our own efforts as we gradually ascend to freedom through the series of incarnations."[7] Of course, no progress at transforming the lower into the higher, of creating our own free being, would be possible without the founder of Christianity, Jesus Christ. "You can achieve human dignity, but the one thing you should not forget is that you owe what you are to the one who restored to you your archetypal human form through the act of salvation on Golgotha. Humanity ought not to be able to embrace the idea of freedom without the idea of salvation through Christ."[8]

Historical Christianity has pointed to the "teachings" of Jesus Christ, or his "miracles," as evidence of his divinity and his mission as the Redeemer, without offering any in-depth analysis of "death," except to characterize his victory over death as the principal "miracle" among many. The Roman Catholic Church emphasizes Jesus' sufferings and atonement for humanity's Fall into Sin through the Passion and his death, with literally millions of icons of the crucified Christ adorning the altars and chests of its faithful. The Pentecostal movement, a form of evangelical Christianity, looks more to the personal experience of inner salvation and to the Holy Spirit. In the Eastern Church, on the other hand, awe and reverence for the ruling will of the Father predominates. None of these Christian confessions addresses the essential Mystery—overcoming death—as the Mystery that relates specifically to the planet we call Earth, and our individual and collective evolution as the future hierarchy of freedom and love. The very existence of the physical Earth is a consequence of the Fall of humanity, as is death itself. The Earth, as "earth," or as the mineral earth (soil, ground, mineral substance), and the other eight subterranean layers, comprise the realm of death and the forces of evil in which the Mystery of Golgotha took place. Only the esoteric Christianity of Rudolf Steiner's Anthroposophy provides keys to understanding the connections among death, evil, the ideal human being, and freedom, as they manifest in the earthly life of Jesus Christ.

The period between Jesus' baptism in the Jordan by John and Christ's resurrection and ascension, known as the "three years," features critically important junctures when Jesus Christ interacted with, then ultimately penetrated and transformed, the nine layers of the subterranean spheres. What follows is a commentary on many of the most important events involving these significant aspects. Because of the Mystery of Golgotha, Christ no longer lives in the sphere of the Sun. He became the spirit of the Earth, whose influence has begun to transform terrestrial realms and will eventually bring about the spiritualization of the entire planet, which is a very, very long process.[9]

BEFORE THE BAPTISM

The contrasting landscapes of the Holy Land reflect both Christ's past and future. The area in northern Israel surrounding the Sea of Galilee, which includes Mount Tabor (the Mount of Transfiguration) and the villages of Nazareth, Cana, and Capernaum, is a well-watered paradise of rolling meadows and green fields, a land of "eternal spring"; it provides an earthly image of the Sun sphere. The Galilean sunlight there reverberates with inner radiance and echoes the cosmic harmonies of its origin. This is the region Jesus called home.

Just sixty-five miles south of the Galilee and connected by the River Jordan lies Judea, a hilly, dry, stony region of moonscapes, particularly in the desert areas east and south of Jerusalem. In Judea lie the Dead Sea, Bethlehem, Hebron, the Baptism site, and a district of dormant volcanoes and volcanic vents.[10] The light in Judea, at its most intense, bakes the ground dry and spawns hallucinogenic waves of heat that ripple across the arid landscape. The Dead Sea itself is the lowest depression on the face of the Earth, in which the salt has become so concentrated that its waters are thick like gel, casting off salt that congeals into crystalline rocks that stand as sentinels along its shore. It is the land of death where Jesus Christ was crucified. Judea offers a picture of the mineral earth; it is barely permeated by the life forces of the vegetative world, where the fire earth and other subterranean layers push their way up to the Earth's surface.

These archetypal landscapes reflect the path taken by Christ in time and space; Jesus Christ left behind the celestial spheres of the Sun and radiant Galilee for the lunar landscape of Judea and his death, creating a new future for himself, for humanity, and for the cosmos.[11]

AFTER THE BAPTISM:
THE TEMPTATIONS IN THE WILDERNESS

Immediately after the Baptism, the new entity, Jesus Christ, retreated into the Judean desert for forty days to undergo the Three Temptations in the Wilderness. There, in the desiccated monotony of scrabble hills, he had few percepts from the world of outer nature to distract from the inner process of compressing his being, from its massive expanse as the Logos to incorporating and uniting with the threefold human sheaths of Jesus of Nazareth. The process of incarnation, which began a new phase at the Baptism, continued as a process of self-constriction experienced by Christ within the sheaths of Jesus of Nazareth as a "slow process of dying,"[12] leading up to and through the Mystery of Golgotha. It was a path of descent that continued into the mineral earth and beyond.

In the five lectures in which Rudolf Steiner specifically discusses the subterranean spheres,[13] he offers only a neutral description of the mineral earth: that it "is related to the interior [of the Earth] as an eggshell is related to an egg."[14] The mineral earth functions to close off human consciousness from the spiritual worlds, thus allowing the process of individuation.[15] Historically, as self-awareness arose, awareness of our relationships with the stars, nature, and other human beings disappeared. Group, collective consciousness declined; individual awareness increased, as did personal egotism. Humankind reached the ultimate stage of ego isolation and selfishness in our present age of the consciousness soul, along with the development of scientific atheism (recall Nietzsche's "God is dead" or Sartre's "Hell is other people") and existentialism. The consciousness soul needs the existence of the mineral earth, because it is the transformed physical body. As "the soul within the soul," it is also known as the observer, or spectator, soul. The death forces of the mineral world act as a mirror that reflects an independent inner life of the soul within the "I." "The highest manifestation of the 'I' belongs to the consciousness soul."[16]

"I"-consciousness and the experience of death go hand in hand, since both belong to and with the Earth. "Earth," as solid, mineral substance, is the new element in our current planetary evolution. It was not present during the ancient periods of Saturn, Sun, and Moon. The mineral kingdom is more transitory in nature than are the etheric (plant), astral (animal), and higher realms, because it appears only once (during Earth evolution) and will cease to exist during the future metamorphosis of our planet—the Jupiter, Venus, and Vulcan evolutions.[17] The future Jupiter evolution will recapitulate the Old Moon condition, the future Venus condition will recapitulate the Old Sun, and the Vulcan period will recapitulate the higher octave of ancient Saturn, whereas the Earth alone has no future recapitulations.

Christ's first encounter with the mineral earth, the realm of death, was in the Third Temptation in the Wilderness. As elucidated

by Rudolf Steiner,[18] the First Temptation concerned the astral body
and provided the encounter with Lucifer, who "showed him all
the kingdoms of the world in a moment of time" (Luke 4:5), and
promised him all their power and glory if he would only worship
him (Lucifer).

Lucifer and Ahriman worked in tandem in the Second
Temptation, in which the ether body of the new being Jesus Christ
was the object of attack. Whereas Lucifer sought to goad Christ's
pride (a fundamental quality inherent in the fallen astral body),
Ahriman sought to play upon the currents of fear found in the fallen
etheric body. Jesus Christ was led to the pinnacle of the Temple in
Jerusalem, where Ahriman threw down the challenge:

> If you are the Son of God, throw yourself down from here,
> for it is written, "He will give his angels charge concerning
> you, to preserve you" and "Upon their hands they shall bear
> you up, lest you dash your foot against a stone." And Jesus
> answered and said to him, "It is written 'You shall not tempt
> the Lord your God.'" (Luke 4: 9–12)

These Temptations were successfully overcome; nothing was
left uncompleted or unresolved in their encounter. But not so
with the Third Temptation, which involved only Ahriman, who
"said to Christ, "If you are the Son of God, command that this
stone become a loaf of bread." And Jesus answered him, "It is
written, 'Not by bread alone shall humankind live, but by every
word of God'" (Luke 4: 3–4). Steiner explains the significance
of this scene:

> Then the Christ being said, human beings do not live by
> bread alone, but by the spiritual forces that come from the
> spiritual worlds. No one knows this better than he, since he
> had just descended from the spiritual worlds. Then Ahriman
> said, "You may indeed be right, but that cannot prevent me
> from keeping a certain hold upon you. You know only how
> the spirit acts—the spirit who descends from the heights.
> You have not yet lived in the human world. There below, in

the human world, people must make stones into bread and cannot draw their nourishment from the spirit alone." That was the moment when Ahriman communicated something to Christ that could indeed be known on Earth, but could not yet be known by the god who had now come to Earth for the first time. He did not know that there below it was necessary to turn mineral substance—metal—into money, or bread. Ahriman had said that human beings on Earth below had to nourish themselves by means of "gold." That was the point through which Ahriman still retained power. And he said, "I shall use this power."

That is the true account of the Temptation. And so one thing remained unresolved at the Temptation. Not all of the questions were ultimately solved. The questions of Lucifer, yes, but not of Ahriman.[19]

He could not nullify Ahriman's attack completely. The fact that it could not be completely nullified is connected with the whole activity of the Christ impulse on Earth.

During the remainder of Earth evolution until the Vulcan period, the operations of the higher hierarchies cannot drive Ahriman completely from the field. Through spiritual effort, it will never be impossible to vanquish the inner temptations of Lucifer—the desires, cravings, passions and all that arises as pride, vainglory, arrogance. When only Lucifer attacks a person, he can be vanquished through spiritual effort. When both Lucifer and Ahriman attack a person, then, too, spiritual victory can be achieved. But when Ahriman is alone, his activity penetrates right down into the material processes of earthly evolution. In this case, he cannot be driven entirely from the field. Ahriman, Mephistopheles, Mammon (these concepts are the same) are hidden in gold and in everything that brings egotism into play in the material world. Inasmuch as some element of materialism must inevitably be part of human life, Ahriman has to be dealt with. . . . Thus, Ahriman could continue to work through the three years that Christ lived in the body of Jesus of Nazareth, could be near Christ on the Earth, and then creep into the soul of Judas and incite that soul to betrayal. What occurred through Judas is related to the question that remained only partially answered in the Temptation after the event at the Jordan.[20]

The Third Temptation, the encounter with the mineral earth, was overcome only through the Mystery of Golgotha. We all live our lives immersed within the Three Temptations, which manifest in contemporary life in the allure of power, sex, and money.[21] Modern society affirms each temptation by encouraging us to increase personal power; revel in "sex, drugs, and rock 'n' roll"; and, of course, "you can never have enough money." The Third Temptation is the only one we cannot fully conquer, because we encounter the realm of necessity in it. We must deal with it daily, repeatedly, for it never goes away. We must eat to stay alive. We all need money to live. It does not matter where the money comes from; we can earn it ourselves, or someone else may have earned it. Money may be given to us, or we may borrow or steal it. With each minute we exist in the realm of necessity, we incur a cost to be paid. Christ spent much of his time with "publicans and sinners" in order to familiarize himself with those who most needed to "turn stones into bread," those most involved in the deeper consequences of the Fall and most entangled in the power of necessity inherent in matter.[22]

Hence, Rudolf Steiner could describe money as "frozen sacrifice." Our labor and creativity are given over and returned to us "frozen" in the form of money. The deepest spiritual forces for good and for evil work through money, or "capital," leading Steiner to point out that the incarnation of Ahriman will be preceded by the domination of life by financial interests (the capital and credit markets), which has been the collective human experience for the last two hundred years.[23] Even worse was the development of "paper" money, followed by fractional reserve banking, which permits the creation of money (credit) out of nothing, and finally electronic money, which dominates economic life today. These phenomena are connected with the Third Temptation and its corollary, the mineral earth.

From the Temptations
to the Mystery of Golgotha

After the experience of the Baptism and then the Temptations in the Wilderness, Jesus appeared as a changed man. Simon's recognition of Jesus as "The Christ of God" (Luke 9:21) is considered very significant. However Simon (Peter) was not the first to recognize Christ as the "Holy One of God." Demonic beings who inhabit various realms of the subterranean spheres were the first to do so. Early in Luke's Gospel, we find, "In the synagogue, there was a man possessed by an unclean devil, and he cried out with a loud voice, saying, 'Let us alone! What have we to do with thee, Jesus of Nazareth? Have you come to destroy us? I know you, who you are, the Holy One of God" (Luke 4:33). Closely following in the same chapter is a similar scene: "And devils also came forth from many, crying out and saying, 'You are the Son of God.' And he rebuked them and did not permit them to speak because they knew that he was the Christ" (Luke 4:41). The chthonic beings were more awake than his own disciples were to the fact of Christ's presence on Earth.

On two well-known occasions, Jesus Christ employed "dust" of the mineral earth as a vehicle for karmic accounting. The story of "the woman taken in adultery" from John's Gospel has entered our collective Western consciousness as a scene of high tension and vivid drama.

> Then the Scribes and Pharisees brought in a woman who had been caught committing adultery. They stood her out in the middle and said to him, "Master [teacher], this woman was caught in the very act of adultery. Moses has commanded us in the Law that such a woman should be stoned. What do you say about that?" They asked him this to test him, so that they might find a reason to bring a charge against him. But Jesus bent down and wrote with his fingers on the ground. When they continued to ask him, he straightened up and said, "Let one among you who is without sin cast the first stone."

And once again he bent down and wrote upon the ground. When they heard what he said, they went away, the eldest first, then the rest, one after the other. Jesus was left alone with the woman still standing there in the middle. Then he stood up, and seeing no one but her, he said, "Woman, where are they? Has no one condemned you?" "No one, Lord," she said. And Jesus said to her, "Neither do I condemn you. Go your way and sin no more." (John 8:3–11)

The karmic consequences of her actions lay within the province of the Earth, to be resolved in future lives.

John also relates the story of the man born blind from birth. The theme again is karma, only this time a karma arising from the past.

As he [Jesus] went on his way, he saw a man who had been blind from birth. And his disciples asked him a question. "Master," they said, "who has committed sin so that this man was born blind? Was it he himself or his parents?" Jesus answered, "Neither this man nor his parents have sinned. Rather, he was born blind so that the workings of the kernel of divinity within him should reveal itself. We must do the work of him who sent me so long as daylight lasts. The night is coming when no one is able to work. While I am in the human world, I am a light unto humankind."

After saying this he spat on the ground and made a paste of earth and spittle. And He put the mixture upon the man's eyes and said to him, "Go and wash in the pool of Siloam" [which means "sent out"]. And so the man went away and washed as directed—and he came back seeing. (John 9:1–7)

Notwithstanding the literal language of the biblical text, Steiner asserts that the correct interpretation of Christ's words refers to the healing of past karma. As the sixth of the Seven Signs in John's Gospel, it demonstrates further intensification of the "I" principal.[24]

The point of emphasis for us is Christ's use of earth, both as dust on the ground and as a paste made of his saliva and earth—a mixture capable of carrying the loftiest forces of spiritual healing and karmic resolution. Our karmic bonds pass through both the Earth's interior and the heavens.

Humanity has always thought of Hell as being somewhere below the surface of the Earth. Part of our existence after death takes place within this subearthly realm. While our soul-spiritual nature passes through the Kama Loca state in the planetary and celestial spheres above the Earth, our "double" passes through the interior of the Earth.

> While individuals are in the Kama Loca state and receiving moral impulses to correct the wrongful acts they have committed, the "double" in the interior of the Earth is simultaneously receiving the reflection of those impulses, or antagonistic inspirations. Thus, when we are born once again on Earth, we arrive with the inner experience of the spiritual world of good and, in opposition to this, what our double has experienced in the realm of evil. Consequently, during the life between birth and death, we must overcome evil; we can never "free" ourselves of it merely by escaping from it. Evil that is not overcome in earthly life endures, and human beings will find themselves in close association with it repeatedly, until they have conquered it during the time between birth and death. This shows clearly that there is an unbroken current of evil. The threads of evil in humankind are drawn from one incarnation into the next through the strata of the Earth's interior, just as the threads of good in humankind are drawn through the incarnations by way of the heavenly spheres of Kama Loca and Devachan.[25]

Rudolf Steiner's conversations about this subject with Countess von Keyserlingk in June 1924 are remarkable:

> "The Earth's layers of the mineral world are permeated with the Kama Loca of our soul life."
>
> "Yes, that is correct," said Rudolf Steiner, who continued to read:

"There we meet everything that connects the mineral darkness to the Hell of souls. When we step out of the human world (which can occur even while the body continues to exist on Earth), we arrive in the land of the dead. Once those who have died have accomplished their Kama Loca, they rise to the starry worlds. I would think, though, that if it were possible to achieve a state of sinlessness in Kama Loca and, instead of rising upward, one were to remain in the depths, wouldn't the golden gates of the realm of fairyland open once more for the petitioning soul?"

Rudolf Steiner: "Yes, that is possible."

"And is the interior of the Earth made out of the gold that comes from the hollow cavity in the Sun and is destined to return there?"

Rudolf Steiner: "Yes, the interior of the Earth is of gold."[26]

This points to the existence a golden center of the Earth that lies below the ninth layer of the subterranean spheres, making ten chthonic layers in total.

THE MYSTERY OF GOLGOTHA

Christ incarnated on the Earth to incorporate it into his being. "Through the Mystery of Golgotha, the body of the Earth became the body of Christ."[27] "Since dying on the Cross, the divine, macrocosmic Christ being permeates the nine layers of the Earth. Only after penetrating through to the core does the Christ being, in a certain sense, fulfill his deed. The forces of Resurrection increase as Christ penetrates matter more deeply." All of Christ's "journey as Jesus of Nazareth—his betrayal, his torture, his suffering on the Cross—had as their purpose the events that happened in those three days." The Mystery requires and encompasses the full thirty-nine hours from 3:00 P.M. on Good Friday until 6:00 A.M Easter Sunday; it includes the death on the cross, the descent to the center of the Earth, and the resurrection. "What happened during [Christ's] descent into Hell can be given only as indications."[28]

One way to view the Mystery of Golgotha is to characterize it as the death of a being who had come from a world where there is no death and who had never experienced or had any knowledge of death. There is no death in the spiritual worlds, but only metamorphosis and transformation. For Christ, the experience of death was the new element in the Mystery of Golgotha. All that came before was preparation for it. Archetypal events within Christ's Passion were recapitulations of critical turning points within the previous embodiments of Earth: the ancient Saturn, Sun, and Moon conditions that preceded our present planet.

On ancient Saturn, there was no light, no air, no matter, but only different degrees of warmth or heat. Ancient Saturn evolved in darkness. The dynamics of evolution took place between the polarity of coldness and warmth. To quote Valentin Tomberg:

> What took place there was the act of a secret being in the middle of Saturn evolution (in the iciest cold), causing the transformation of that cold into the warmth of will. One has to imagine that the trial of Saturn evolution consisted in the fact that will was "banned," or immobilized, and that a being of Saturn evolution caused a turning point by offering the sacrifice of entering that immobility of icy coldness and "standing" there. Steadfastly "standing" within the persistent, motionless will led to the turn in Saturn evolution. When Jesus Christ was nailed to the Cross, it was a distant echo of this Saturn event when he said, "Eli, Eli lama sabachthani."[29]...Calling upon "Eli" recalls, or repeats, the event on Saturn that was the primordial crucifixion of the world.[30]

During the ancient Sun evolution, the dynamic was between the polarities of light and darkness.

The essence of happiness involves the fact that there is a "relationship." The essence of misery in the soul involves the possibility of complete loneliness in the world. The darkness of loneliness is the essence of misery....

The sacrifice that was offered when the archangels went through their human stage of development was this: one archangel had inwardly united with the being of Christ, and this union created a still point—the still point of complete aloneness within the overall experience of loneliness. The center of the radiant Sun was morally and spiritually fashioned when the Christ being plunged into the darkness of loneliness. In this way, the Sun radiated its own light from this center, while the center point itself was total darkness and loneliness. What happened then, during ancient Sun, was repeated during the Mystery of Golgotha. Just as the physical crucifixion was a repetition of the sacrifice that took place during Saturn evolution, the night in Gethsemane was a repetition of the sacrifice on ancient Sun. That night repeated what caused the turning point for ancient Sun evolution.[31]

On the ancient Moon, Christ accomplished another pivotal sacrifice that synthesized the conflicting opposites.

Most important for the ancient Moon period of evolution is the fact that the Moon had two sides; ancient Moon existence was also situated in a tension between two polarities. One side was turned toward the Sun, while the other side was dark. In *An Outline of Esoteric Science,* Rudolf Steiner describes the changes in consciousness of the Moon inhabitants. He describes how they had a consciousness directed toward the Sun on the light side and, on the dark side, had a pictorial consciousness. This led to the pendulum-like oscillation between a resounding Sun and a silent perception of the lunar environment. The danger that threatened Moon humanity then involved the fact that it could be torn apart into two separate kinds of humankind: one kind would have outer perception, and the other would have Sun awareness. Consequently a mystical humanity and a materialistic humanity would have eventually arisen on Earth. This would have begun on ancient Moon if a sacrifice had not again taken place. The sacrifice performed by Christ on ancient

Moon was essentially his union with the same archangelic being whom he had united with on ancient Sun. Thus, he went to the dark side of the Moon to awaken the memory of the Sun and eliminate the danger of forgetting. On ancient Moon, the sacrifice was that of descent into oblivion, so that memory could arise from oblivion. That sacrifice, too, was reflected in the events of Golgotha. At the Last Supper, when Jesus Christ was with the circle of his disciples, He broke the bread and gave it, saying, "Do this in memory of me" (do this to reawaken the memory of me). The Last Supper thus recapitulated the sacrifice on old Moon, the mystery of the resurrection of memory out of oblivion.[32]

The new element in the Mystery of Golgotha was Christ's unification with the mineral earth (death) and his descent into the Abyss within the subearthly spheres. Ordinary human beings experience a tableau-like image of their life for approximately the first three days after death. While the body goes one way, returning to the "dust" from which it was created, the spirit goes the other way, initiating the postmortem existence. Jesus Christ renounced the sight of His own life tableau, a sight that protects human beings from seeing the Abyss and the realm of Ahriman, thus allowing Christ to descend directly into the subterranean spheres. Whereas, at death, human beings split into temporal physical matter (the corpse that quickly decays) and the eternal spiritual part, Christ followed his body into the realm of death and continued in that same vertical direction into the interior of the Earth. While the body of Jesus died, the Christ spirit acquired a body: the planet as a whole. He had come to Earth precisely for this purpose, to save humankind from inevitable destruction through egotism. Descent into the subterranean spheres is a descent into the realms that are the source of selfishness, egotism, and evil.

The dramatic scenes in the Garden of Gethsemane on Holy Thursday evening and Good Friday morning saw Jesus Christ praying to stay in his body, not to die prematurely before he had fully penetrated the mineral realm, his own skeletal system. His last words "from the cross, 'It is finished,' do not refer to the sufferings that have been surmounted, but to the complete conquest over the power of death, which had been achieved."[33] Thus, the Resurrection can be understood only in conjunction with his union with the mineral earth (death) and his descent into Hell.

Death, from the spiritual point of view, constitutes cosmic substance, or cosmic being, that has been excluded from its actual purpose. It is "outside" the spiritual world of the hierarchies and exists only on the Earth. It is the rejected sacrifice of spiritual being that has been closed off from its proper place. Uniquely among all the aspects of our life on Earth, death alone stands within the maya of our daily existence in its full reality.

> In the whole world of Maya, one thing only shows itself in its reality: death. All other phenomena must be traced back to their reality. All other phenomena entering maya have reality behind them. Death is the single reality in maya, for it involves the fact that something was cut off from reality and taken into maya. That is why death is the one and only reality in maya.[34]

Only human beings truly experience death, and death can be experienced only on the physical plane. "I"-consciousness can likewise be experienced only in the physical-mineral realm. "Human beings have to acquire "I"-consciousness there [on the physical plane]. Without death, they could never find it."[35] Just as death is the only part of maya, having its full reality within maya, so, too, the Mystery of Golgotha is the only event that has no prototype in the higher worlds, and whose full reality takes place only in the realm of death, the Earth. Although all other events follow the esoteric principle "as above, so below," only the Mystery of Golgotha has no higher spiritual model or template, since it took place only on the physical plane. You will not find the spiritual archetype of the Mystery of Golgotha in the suprasensory worlds, because it is not there; it is only here on Earth. Therefore, comprehension of the

Mystery of Golgotha can take place only on the physical plane, the mineral earth, the first layer of the subterranean spheres.

> The death at Golgotha, which is enacted on Earth as the origin of all the subsequent Christ development, can only be understood in the physical body. Of all the facts important to our higher life, this alone is comprehensible in the physical body. It is then further developed and perfected in the higher worlds; but we must first have understood it while in the physical body. Just as the Mystery of Golgotha could never have taken place in the higher worlds and has no prototype there, but is an event that, since it includes death, is confined to the physical plane, so, too, must we comprehend it on this plane.... Here we have something that in itself belongs directly to the world of reality.[36]

The mineral earth, as the product of rejected cosmic sacrifice, was excluded from the "universal cosmic process." It was, so to speak, slipping away from the province of the "good" hierarchies and in danger of falling out of reach, beyond their control. Steiner describes this as a crisis in the "council of the higher hierarchies." They said,

> We are losing the possibility of letting our servants intervene in human souls. We have been unable to hold off Lucifer and Ahriman, and because of this we will be unable to influence evolution through our servants after this time. Then powers will arise in human souls that can no longer be guided by angels, archangels, and archai. Human beings are going beyond our reach owing to the powers of Lucifer and Ahriman.[37]

This sacrificial cosmic substance—cut off from its origin and in danger of being lost permanently to divine evolution—is the mineral earth and the remaining chthonic spheres that needed to be rescued. The "mood in heaven" was filled with a "great anxiety"[38] over this potential wrong turn in evolution. Hence, Rudolf Steiner could describe the Mystery of Golgotha in this way: "The gods have opened a window there in heaven, and for a brief season their affairs are conducted before human eyes."[39] This explains the extraordinary, even shocking statement (from one point of view): "Truly, as important as it was for humanity to receive the Christ, it was more important for the gods to have to let him go, giving him to the Earth."[40]

The Baptism in Jordan, when the Divine "I" entered the three sheaths of Jesus of Nazareth, may be viewed as Christ's conception in the earthly sphere. Christ's incarnation into Jesus' astral body is indicated by the Sermon on the Mount, where he poured forth wisdom upon wisdom, including the Beatitudes and the Lord's Prayer. His union with Jesus' ether body is pictured in the Transfiguration, when he appeared in his transformed etheric body before James, Peter, and John. The Christ did not incarnate fully into Jesus' physical body until the Mystery of Golgotha, which, including the descent into the subterranean spheres and the resurrection, constitutes his birth within the Earth planet. His death on Golgotha was his birth on Earth. "For the Christ being, the 'basic development pattern' for life in this world and in the afterlife is exactly opposite diametrically to the human one. Rudolf Steiner refers to this inversion in his lecture cycle, *The Fifth Gospel*."[41] The death of Jesus is also the birth of Christ, who for the first time acquires a physical body that, as underscored in this chapter, consists of the nine layers of the subterranean spheres, from the mineral earth to the Earth's core.

The topography of Jerusalem is characterized by the polar peaks of the lunar Mount Moriah (Temple Mount) and the solar Mount Zion, the location of the Upper Room of the Last Supper. "The greater polarity of Galilee and Judea finds a concentrated repetition compressed into a small area in the two elevations of Jerusalem."[42] Between the two is an ancient fissure in the surface of the Earth, where the crucifixion site Golgotha was positioned. Nearby was Christ's tomb, which today is enclosed by the Church of the Holy Sepulchre. The tomb was actually a small cave. Thus the god-man who was buried in the garden cave beside Golgotha was the same person physically (the Nathan Jesus) who had been born in a cave in Bethlehem thirty-three-and-a-third years earlier. His birth and burial were each within the Earth's crust, the first layer of the subterranean spheres.[43]

An earthquake occurred on Holy Saturday, and the Earth opened up, receiving the body of Jesus Christ as a communion. "An earthquake again tore open the original fissure that had been filled during the time of Solomon. Thus, the whole Earth became Christ's grave. The Earth took deep into herself the host administered to her."[44] Christ's long path of descent continued to its goal. "Only after penetrating through to the [Earth] core does the Christ being, in a certain sense, fulfill his deed. The forces of Resurrection increase as Christ penetrates more deeply into matter."[45]

Steiner points to the fire earth as the source of earthquakes, that chthonic layer that is in particular the abode of Ahriman. "He had to die into the Earth so that he could encounter Ahriman."[46] However, this particular earthquake may also be considered a "heavenquake," meaning the energy generated by his sacrificial death and descent into Hell forced open the telluric depths. In this light, we may picture forces flowing in reverse, from above downward, rather than from below upward.

> When the Mystery of Golgotha was accomplished, when the Christ had undergone death on the cross, He appeared in the world where souls lingered after death and set limits on Ahriman's power, illuminating the regions that the [ancient] Greeks had called "the kingdom of shades" with a spiritual bolt of lightning that showed its inhabitants that light was meant to enter it again. What was accomplished on behalf of the physical world through the Mystery of Golgotha cast its light into the spiritual world.[47]

The "nine layers of evolution of the Abyss are permeated by beings who, since the Saturn, Sun and, Moon periods, have remained behind and not followed the positive course of divine evolution."[48]

These are the luciferic, ahrimanic, and asuric hierarchies, who, respectively, fell from positive evolution during the old Moon, Sun, and Saturn periods of evolution. Along the path of personal development, individual human beings become aware of the personal abyss within their own selfish lower nature by penetrating the depths of the subconscious. The greater one's self-knowledge, the greater is one's awareness of and control over the instinctual life. Thus, the realm of the subterranean spheres may also be viewed as the Earth's subconscious.[49] The karmic debts of individuals and humanity as a whole have been deposited in the depths of the Earth.

> When the neophyte has been permeated by this bitter realization (it is bitter, since to see what is lying and active in these layers is a true test of the neophyte), something even more terrible is revealed.... These abysses are not only the accumulated crimes and failures of humanity, but also the karmic necessities to be met for balancing these crimes. These necessities consist of events in the future that, up to a certain point, have to be considered inevitable, and that, as a consequence, must happen in order to achieve karmic balance. This includes not simply the small, individual karmic necessities, but above all, the wider karmic interconnections of groups, nations, and the world. These future karmic necessities will have devastating consequences for the fate of millions of people and the highest integrity of soul and spirit is needed to withstand this "vision" without being extinguished by it.... These insights are essential for understanding the descent of Christ into the Abyss of the Earth. The possibility that the renewed Phantom of the Son of Man will rise from the grave is only then given when the descent into the core has been mastered and the ascent has been achieved. It is necessary to relate the essence of this Resurrection Body with the descent into Hell, for this is where it is created.[50]

Christ, who was previously located outside of the human "I," may be found today within the human "I," as reflected by Saint

Paul's words, "Not I, but Christ in me" (Galatians 2:20).[51] Christ entered the human "I" via the gate of death by reuniting with the Father. His own words describe this path: "I am going to the Father" (John 14:12–13). As a result, the Earth has become a seed for a new cosmic system and will ultimately be spiritualized. Just as a seed has a dry husk, or hull, made of dead material with new life contained within, likewise the Earth is a seed enveloped by its outer shell or crust (the mineral earth) with the future stages of its evolution contained within.

The new being who arose from the grave at Golgotha in his resurrection body, which Steiner also terms the "phantom," was the fulfillment and actualization of the "final ideal of the whole evolution of the world."[52] Steiner reflects, "Let us look out from what we have pictured as the beginning, middle, and end of humanity's evolution to the Mystery of Golgotha [as the midpoint of evolution, between ancient Saturn and future Vulcan]. We have the being who was incarnated in Jesus through the Mystery of Golgotha approximately in the middle of that cosmic time … [then] the being as God, which the human being as humanity will be at the end of Vulcan evolution." As the Alpha and Omega (Apocalypse 1:8), he contains within himself and shows that future humanity will contain "the whole divine world."[53] Part of this future world is the transformed interior of the Earth, which gives its name to the seventh incarnation of our Earth planet: Vulcan, or Volcano.[54] All of the other names for the planetary embodiments refer to heavenly bodies that correspond to planets of our solar system (Saturn, Sun, Moon, Mars-Mercury [Earth evolution], Jupiter, and Venus). But not Vulcan. Why? The Vulcan Mysteries refer to the highest mysteries of Earth evolution, which require the conversion, or redemption, of Earth's interior through human efforts. There is no planet Vulcan, since it already exists in a nascent state, concealed within the Earth. Vulcan will arise as the seventh and highest planetary condition of form when the Earth is "turned inside out," or spiritualized—"when the lowest evil is transformed into the highest good."[55] "Human evolution thus implies a transformation of the Earth's interior."[56]

The "final ideal of the whole evolution of the world" is the "ideal human being," pictured in the opening vision of the Apocalypse as the "Son of Man, with a long robe and a golden girdle around the loins; and his head and hair shining white as white wool or snow, and his eyes sparkling with fire. And his feet were flowing fire, as if glowing in a fiery oven,... and the radiance of his countenance was like the shining Sun" (Rev. 1:12–16). The ideal human is the purpose of this, our cosmic (zodiacal) system, which began on ancient Saturn and culminates with Vulcan. Hence, Rudolf Steiner's astounding statement that humankind [the ideal human being] is the religion of the gods.

> The gods had a vision of the ideal human being; the reality of this is not the physical human being of today, but a state of development in which the life of the human soul and spirit reaches its highest level in a physical human being whose potential is fully realized.
>
> Thus, the gods have the image of the human being before them as their highest ideal, their religion. In their mind's eye, they see, as if on the far shore of divine existence, the temple that is their supreme work of art, representing the human as the image of divine being.[57]

This ideal, realized in the Resurrection Body, or phantom, is both physical and spiritual. "The body that was really intended for human beings by the rulers of Saturn, Sun, and Moon—the pure phantom of the physical body, with all the attributes of the physical body—this is what rose out of the grave."[58] It is the synthesis of opposites into a new third, which is both physical and spiritual.[59] The form of the phantom, a threefold reflection of the Trinity itself, is made possible by the presence of the (mineral) earth. The physical body makes this possible, since the physical body represents the stage where a complete reconciliation between heaven and Earth could be brought about. When the human "I" is consciously united with the spirit, this is still only the first stage of that reunion; when that union also includes the astral body, the second stage is attained; and when the alliance between the "I" and spirit becomes strong enough to reach not only to the astral body, but also beyond the ether body and deep into the physical body, then the communion is complete. This is why the physical body was seen as the communion body by those who understood the Grail tradition.[60]

AFTER THE MYSTERY OF GOLGOTHA

In his article entitled "Subnature and the Second Coming," which is updated for this volume, Robert Powell sets forth a schedule of Christ's continuing descent into the nine spheres of the interior of the Earth and their counterparts within the human being (see table on facing page).

With the following example, Powell shows how the descent of the Christ into the various subterranean spheres elicits a corresponding counter-force within the Earth and within human nature, largely in the region of the subconscious will life. Christ's evolutionary path for transforming the Earth is one of continuing descent. So, too, in "Imitation of Christ," it is the path that we, ourselves, must follow. Although personal transformation (self-development) wears the guise of ascent through ever-higher regions of consciousness, if balanced progress is to take place it must be accompanied by a similar conscious descent into the chthonic realms of our own and the Earth's being. Therefore, Steiner could say, "We transform our dwelling place and our self at the same time. When we spiritualize our self, we spiritualize the Earth as well."[61]

CTHONIC SPHERE:	HUMAN SHEATH:	DATES
Mineral earth:	physical body	May 25, 1933– Apr. 1, 1945
Fluid (soft) earth:	ether body	Apr. 1,1945– Feb. 10, 1957
Air earth:	astral body	Feb. 10, 1957– Dec. 21, 1968
Form earth:	sentient soul	Dec. 21, 1968– Nov. 1, 1980
Fruit earth:	intellectual soul	Nov. 1, 1980– Sept. 11, 1992
Fire earth:	consciousness soul	Sept. 11, 1992– July 24, 2004
Earth mirror:	spirit self (manas)	July 24, 2004– June 5, 2016
Earth server*:	life spirit (budhi)	June 5, 2016– Apr. 14, 2028
Earth core:	spirit body (atma)	Apr. 14, 2028– Feb. 24, 2040

REFLECTIONS ON THE MINERAL REALM AND THE "I"

The mineral earth is different from the other layers of the sub-terranean spheres in many respects. It is the only fully material sphere hardened to dense physicality, whereas the other layers are spiritual (etheric, astral, or devachanic). As the crust, or shell, of the planet, it holds back the sub-earthly layers beneath it. It also appears only once (during our Earth evolution) and has no future recapitulations. As the realm of death, it bestows the potential for

freedom, allowing human beings to exist beyond complete dominion by divine forces, whether suprasensory or subsensory.

The mineral earth plays a neutral role relative to the other
chthonic layers, which are invested with qualities of evil. It is
capable of being penetrated by the celestial spheres and supports
life (the etheric), conscious awareness (the astral), and creative self-
awareness (Devachan). At the same time, it is a vehicle for telluric
energies and carries anti-life (fluid earth and air earth), anti-soul
(form earth, fruit earth, and fire earth), and anti-spirit (mirror
earth, explosive earth, and core earth).

In this quality, the mineral earth is like the human being, who
also contains a neutral realm within "objective" consciousness,
which is confined to the brain. Brain-bound thinking is dead, and
because it is lifeless, it may also be free. If our thinking were still
under the direct influence of the gods and actually participated in
the creative world process without our own initiative, we could
never free ourselves from divine powers. We would be overwhelmed
by forces greater than our own. Abstract, dead thinking provides
a neutral or "objective" platform from which we can achieve
suprasensory and subsensory consciousness by extending states of
awareness above and below the thresholds that hide the celestial
and subterrestrial regions. We can do so owing to the presence of
the mineral earth, which is the sine qua non required to create our
present bodily form and individual "I"-consciousness.

"I"-consciousness is a death process in human beings, requiring
the physical to sacrifice its life forces so that the mirroring process
can take place in the nervous system and allow self-awareness.
The mineral earth provides this resistance. The brain and skull
are the most mineralized (dead) portions of the physical body.
The brain even contains "brain sand" (a bona fide mineral deposit
excreted by the pineal body[62]), which is needed for the spiritual
to manifest in the physical. The ancient Hebrews were the last
Eastern (clairvoyant) race and the first Western (non-clairvoyant)
race, because a more mineralized physical brain was first developed

through them, providing the basis for brain-bound, intellectual consciousness.[63]

"I"-consciousness is "the essential Earth possession"; you cannot have one without the other.[64] We find in Genesis, "and there was no human (*adam*) to till the soil (*adama*). . . . Yahweh Elohim formed the human (*adam*) of dust from the soil" (Genesis 2:5–7). The name *Adam* and the word *soil*, or ground, have a common source. *Adam* in Hebrew is *'adam*, whereas "ground" is the Hebrew *ha-'dama*. In Earth evolution, the densification of spiritual substance into physical matter came about gradually. "Not until Genesis 3: 17 was there an *Adam*, which means 'hard human being.'"[65]

Yahweh reminded Adam and Eve of their terrestrial origin when expelling them from the Garden of Eden: "By the sweat of your face will you earn your food until you return to the ground, as you were taken from it. For dust you are and to dust you shall return" (Genesis 3:19). "Dust" is capable of receiving and incorporating energies from both the subterranean and celestial spheres.[66] Thus Adam's body could be created from "dust" and could be ensouled. This dual quality reflects our dual nature and the dualities (polarities) that meet (some would say "collide") within human nature: spirit/matter; angelic/demonic; inner/outer; life/death; percept/concept; and so forth. We form the arena where these cosmic oppositions meet, conflict, and resolve. We are both fruit and seed and form the bridge between the past and the future. Said differently, we are both the karma of the gods and the means of its solution, which can take place only within the "neutral" sphere of the mineral earth through our human "I" activity. In fact, the mineral realm is the polar reciprocal of the human "I."

> For this reason the minerals here on Earth are, in a certain sense, in a reverse situation to that of humankind. We have our "I" within us, enclosed within our skin. Each is a human center individually. Plants form a wider center; taken together, they form an earth center. In addition, the "I" beings of the minerals form the circumference of our cosmic

sphere. Wherever there is a human being, the human "I" is always the center. The mineral "I" is always at the periphery—exactly the reverse.[67]

The mineral realm is that of death and the Father. When Christ spoke to his disciples, "I am going to the Father" (John 14:12–13), he was foretelling his crucifixion. When he united with the mineral sphere through the Mystery of Golgotha, he reunited with the Father. The realm of space belongs to the Father, and space requires physical manifestation—the mineral realm. It is not accidental that an alternate name for the Father is the "Divine Ground of the World" or the "Ground of Existence"—with the word "ground" meaning both "foundation" and the "ground beneath our feet."

The Father sacrificed a portion of his being to create the mineral realm and at the same time the "I" as polarities through which freedom could be developed. Thus freedom, death, evil, "I"-consciousness, and the mineral earth are all intimately connected. The "I" needs to confront and incorporate forces of death within itself to develop fully the faculty for the consciousness soul. The "I" uses these death forces in the "dying and becoming" needed to transform the lower into the higher. It needs the confrontation with evil to mature fully and, via an awakened conscience, to break through to the experience of the true spiritual life through the consciousness soul.[68]

> The ground of the world has poured itself completely into the world. It did not remain outside of the world in order to control it externally; it has not withheld itself from the world but impels everything internally. Its highest form of appearance in the reality of ordinary life is thought and, with it, the human personality. If, therefore, the ground of the world has goals, they are identical with the goals that the human spirit sets for itself in life. We are not acting according to the purposes of the guiding power of the world when we search out one of his commandments, but when we act according to

our own individual insights; the guiding power of the world manifests in them. He does not live somewhere outside of humanity as will; rather, he has entirely renounced his own will so that everything depends on human will. Before we can create our own laws, we must abandon all concern about such matters as universal determinations that come beyond the human world.... Our philosophy is a philosophy of freedom, therefore, in the highest sense.[69]

Thus Rudolf Steiner summarizes the profound connections between death and freedom and indirectly, that our potential for freedom—as the future hierarchy of Freedom and Love—stems from the birth of the independent "I" within the realm of death through the Mystery of Golgotha.

The "Stone" as Spiritual Image of the "I"

The following are very brief indications of the depth of connection between the development of the "I" principal and the mineral earth. Each imagination is worthy of extensive treatment, far beyond what is offered here.

The Old and New Testaments offer the well-known image of the "I"—and Christ Himself—as a "stone." We read in the Psalms, "The stone the builders rejected has become the corner stone" (Psalm 181:22). This passage is quoted by Jesus Christ early in Holy Week in response to the Jewish Sanhedrin (High Priests, Scribes, and the Elders) who have challenged his authority. "Then Jesus said to them, Have you never read in the Scriptures: 'The stone that the builders rejected has become the cornerstone?'" (Matthew 21:42). Christ makes clear in plain language that he is the cornerstone they are rejecting.

St. Peter, formerly called Simon, was given his new name by Christ: petros is Latin for "stone," or "rock" (Matthew16:18).[70] Such a change of name occurs only a few times in the Bible, but when it does, it indicates a profound inner change in the individual.[71]

At the conclusion of the Sermon on the Mount, Christ offers one last parable of the "I." "I will show you what someone is like who comes to me, listens to my words, and acts on them. That one is like a person building a house, who dug deeply and laid the foundation on rock; when the flood came, the river burst against that house but could not shake it, because it had been well built. But the one who listens and does not act is like a person who built a house on the ground without a foundation. When the river burst against it, it collapsed at once and was completely destroyed" (Luke 6:47–49).

In his first epistle to the Corinthians, Saint Paul describes the experiences of the Jews during their forty years wandering in the desert. "All drank the same spiritual drink, for they drank from a spiritual rock, and the rock was the Christ" (1 Cor. 10:4).

John's Apocalypse also shows the duality of the "I" and its connection to the mineral earth. In its opening chapters, Christ dictates to John seven letters to seven churches, which refer to the seven cultural ages of the post-Atlantean epoch. The third letter, written to the church at Pergamos, offers two imaginations of the human "I"[72]:

> The one with the sharp, two-edged sword says this... "To the victor I shall give some of the hidden manna; I shall also give a white amulet [stone] upon which is inscribed a new name, which no one knows except the one who receives it." (Rev. 2:12, 17)

The "I" is a two-edged sword, since only the "I" is able to cognize and transform forces from the physical, mineral realm and the highest spiritual realms. Having a human "I" also means having the capacity to do both good and evil. The "I," lighting up within the soul, "opens its portals on two sides: toward the corporeal and toward the spiritual."[73] "The spirit develops the 'I' from within outward; the mineral world develops it from without inward."[74] This dual nature is expressed in its method of cognition, which receives sense impressions from the physical sensory world, and intuitions from the spiritual world. The "white stone" is also the "I," or I AM, which is the "new name, which no one knows except the one who receives it."

Many esoteric and spiritual writings refer to the "I" as a stone. For example, Christian Rosenkreutz, the founder of Rosicrucianism, became Knight of the Golden Stone in 1459.[75] Throughout the Middle Ages, alchemists spoke of the "Philosopher's Stone." It is the fourth stage of Rosicrucian initiation, and physically is the element carbon, from which human bodies of the future will be built.[76] The various states in which carbon is found—charcoal, coal, graphite, and diamonds (the purest carbon)—reflect spiritually transformative processes. The fibrous composition of charcoal shows its vegetative origin and, like coal, is dark and "dirty." Graphite is one of nature's softest minerals, whereas a diamond is its hardest. Graphite crystallizes in a hexagonal system, whereas diamonds crystallize in a cubic system. (For the esoteric significance of a crystal cube, see the final paragraph of this chapter.)

The Holy Grail itself is the "stone that fell from Lucifer's crown," the "I," which progresses from selfishness to selflessness by hollowing itself out through sacrifice and moral transformation.

> A wonderfully beautiful legend tells us that when Lucifer fell from heaven to Earth, a precious stone fell from his crown. This precious stone, so the legend proceeds, became the vessel from which Jesus Christ took the Holy Supper with His disciples. The same vessel received Christ's blood when it flowed from the Cross, and it was brought by angels to the Western world, where it is received by those who wish to come to a true understanding of the Christ principle. Out of the stone that fell from Lucifer's crown was made the Holy Grail. This precious stone, is in a certain respect, nothing but...the full power of the "I."[77]

The essence of Anthroposophy is concentrated in the Foundation Stone Meditation, given by Rudolf Steiner at the founding of the

General Anthroposophical Society during the Holy Nights of 1923. This event repeated, on a spiritual level, the laying of a physical foundation stone of the Johannes Bau [later the Goetheanum], September 20, 1913, in the form of a double pentagonal dodecahedron, shaped "as an emblem of the striving human soul immersed as a microcosm in the macrocosm."[78]

Coincidently or not, Rudolf Steiner's last name means "stone" in German.

Finally, the future Jupiter evolution is pictured in the Apocalypse as a stone—specifically, a crystal cube embedded with precious gems.

> [He] showed me the holy city Jerusalem coming down out of heaven from God. It gleamed with the splendor of God. Its radiance was like that of a precious stone, like jasper, clear as crystal.... The city was square, its length the same as its width.... The wall was constructed of jasper, while the city was pure gold, clear as glass. The foundations of the city were decorated with every precious stone; the first course of stones was jasper, the second sapphire, the third chalcendony, the fourth emerald, the fifth sardonyx, the sixth carnelian, the seventh chrysolite, the eighth beryl, the ninth topaz, the tenth chrysoprase, the eleventh hyacinth, and the twelfth amethyst. The Twelve gates were twelve pearls, each of the gates made from a single pearl; and the street of the city was of pure gold, transparent as glass. (Rev. 21:10, 11, 16, 18–21)

Forbearance is asked of the reader for the brevity and density of the topics covered in this chapter. Much more could be written, and a certain incompleteness is the result. For example, a different perspective would be cast if the descent of the Christ into the layers of the interior of the Earth were viewed as the transformation of the counter-spheres of evil. This connection between the "I" and evil—as the means by which the "I" is matured—has been largely omitted.[79] The options were to write either a quite lengthy exposition or a more compact "summary" presentation; the choice was made for the latter. On the other hand, no pretense is made that the subjects have been treated comprehensively. For our understanding is limited by the fact that "the human intellect is not adapted to grasp the greatest fact of human evolution"[80]: the Mystery of Golgotha.

Chapter 7

PARADOXICAL THOUGHTS
ON CHRIST AND SOPHIA
IN THE HUMAN MYSTERY OF THE EARTH

CHRISTOPHER BAMFORD

Christ went down to Hell for our salvation
and we should be careful frequently
to go down there, too.
                        —THOMAS AQUINAS[1]

The Sun, an enormous orb, rises from the
Earth's valley. A golden orb, it bears all lands,
seas, mountains within it. Made of gold wrested
from the Earth, it is the Sun, which once trav-
eled to the center of the Earth, now bringing
salvation. Now it is ascending. It bears with it
all that has united with the Sun's gold. It is his
body, his holy, risen body. Quickened, gold-
radiant, it ascends, leaving the old world to
its cinders.
                        —JOHANNA VON KEYSERLINGK[2]

RUDOLF STEINER IS INVARIABLY described as a "Renaissance" figure, a polymath, whose apparently encyclopedic knowledge seemed to cover virtually every field. Yet, considered as a whole, his spiritual research, vast as it is and dealing with the most varied themes and topics, has in fact a single interrelated focus, humanity and the Earth, and a single key or method of approach, the Mystery of Golgotha, "the turning point of time."

In our age of egotism and fundamentalisms, this requires a caveat. Though Steiner spoke frequently of the "Christian Mystery," giving various and often detailed accounts of different aspects of it—and almost universally applying it implicitly as a lens, or basic premise, through which to view other things—he did not create any kind of rigid "system" around it. Indeed, he strove consciously not to. Rather, on different occasions he illuminated different facets of the mystery. The whole picture cohered magnificently, but the spiritual reality was always explicitly larger and more indeterminate than the relatively determinate "snapshots" (the results of his spiritual research) that he presented. He gave a series of images of processes, so that others could think or meditate those processes and their implications. He did not purvey information. He knew that the certitude or truth of spiritual realities lies in their claim upon us, not in their literal expression. Spiritual realities claim us, not we them. To know an angel is to be seen by an angel, not to see one. By taking Steiner's or anyone else's images too literally, we are guilty of idolatry. Their claim upon us is unconditional, but our cognitions are always conditional and provisional; they are images, lightning flashes, of the truth to work with. While contemplating so great a mystery, therefore, one can only present images or metaphors in the hope that, in them and in the gaps between them, spiritual realities may begin to make a claim upon us, to which we may be called to respond with our being.

In fact, esoterically, as well as exoterically, the Mystery of Golgotha, while it is an absolutely real and a *historically* divine-cosmic-human-earthly event, eludes any kind of sensory certainty. One will never find the historical Jesus or material evidence of the Crucifixion or Resurrection. What occurred was/is, above all, suprasensory or spiritual, so that whoever will must seek to confirm it inwardly, through one's experience. Furthermore, as a spiritual event, the full, complete reality of the Mystery of Golgotha must always escape our theologies, philosophies, and spiritual research. Much, of course, may be known and may be discovered about the event, but much also remains hidden and will perhaps remain so for a long time. Nevertheless, over the centuries, some basic aspects—three, perhaps, above all—have become gradually clearer.

First, the Mystery of Golgotha revealed the reality that "the human, earthly world" is the place or state in which cosmos and divinity can begin to become one, thus announcing the possible universal redemption of all things.

Such redemption, in final analysis, is the "good news" of the reality that a being—the "I am," divine-spiritual Creator and Word, Life and Light, the Christ-Messiah—was "made flesh" and, by that passage, entered humanity and the Earth in a divine act accomplished in, through, and with Mary and Jesus. Through suffering and death on the Cross, as well as by descending to the "heart of the Earth" through burial, this divine-spiritual being—again, in, through, and with Mary-Jesus—penetrated, anointed, and renewed not just humanity, but through it also the Earth and the cosmos, even unto its spiritual and material depths. Then, through Resurrection from the dead, Ascension to heaven, and sending the Holy Spirit at Pentecost, this being sealed forever the union of the divine spiritual world, human nature, and the Earth. These three destinies became one: to build up the mystical body, whose seed had been planted. Thus, by Christ through Mary and Jesus, with the participation and support of the whole angelic world, the original intent of creation was restored: that the divine be all in all, the hidden treasure known.

So viewed, the Mystery of Golgotha is not only an event within humanity, or the Earth, but also what Rudolf Steiner called the central cult (or liturgical sacrifice) of the gods themselves, the focus of whose "religion" is none other than humanity and the Earth, and upon whose spiritual cooperation the gods depend for their own salvation.

Undertaken by the spiritual world through Christ-Mary-Jesus, the Mystery of Golgotha was thus undertaken not only for the "salvation" of fallen, skin-bound human beings, but also for the sake of all creation, the work of the gods, and not least, perhaps, even for the Divine, whose love and aspiration for self-knowledge rested in creation and in humanity. The One who had "made" all things came into his "own" and became "flesh" so that human beings, empowered to overcome their egotism and aid in overcoming the egotism of the world—cosmic egotism—might, through love, assume their true and destined cosmological function as cosmic beings and become selfless, participant coworkers with the divine, capable of raising the world and (in a sense) even the divine itself, who was now indeed one with it.

Implicit in this is the fact that the Mystery of Golgotha reveals a twofold quality. However you parse it, metaphysically, theologically, or anthroposophically, those events reveal the cooperative activity of two in the revelation of what we might call the "Human (or earthly) Mystery." Whether you call them divine and human, as in the traditional view, or Christ and Mary-Jesus, or Christ and Sophia, the same two are involved. One we may call the true, divine "I"; the other we call the (human) soul (and body.) But these are only approximations. What is clear is that it is now impossible to separate them. Call them Sophia and Christ; together they teach, suffer and are on the Cross; together they descend to the center of the Earth; and together they rise and ascend to heaven to sit on the right hand of God.

Here again is a mystery that cannot yet be fully told. In anthroposophic terms, it will not be understandable until the next, or sixth epoch. As Rudolf Steiner describes it, in that age, which we are approaching, each person will feel every other person's pain as one's own; everyone will undertand that humanity constitutes a single being; and religion will be a matter of indivual conscience: we will each have our own religion. Nevertheless, this age and its Sophianic Mystery is dawning and has been so for a while, beginning with the earliest Christian communities, continuing through the declaration of Mary as *Theotokos*, Mother of God, in 432 C.E., then rising into the great Marian (Alchemical-Grail-Templar) centuries of the Middle Ages, and finally taking conscious form in Jacob Boehme, Novalis, the great Russian Sophiologists (Vladimir Solovyov, Pavel Florensky, and Sergei Bulgakov), and Rudolf Steiner himself.

Hildegard of Bingen may give us some hints. For her, Sophia (who is Wisdom and Love, *Sapientia* and *Caritas*) unites Creator and creation, God and cosmos. Through her mediation, the divine manifests and may be known, for she lives in the encounter of God and creation, where the one stoops and the other aspires. She inhabits their mutuality. At the same time, she is creator and midwife, giving birth and aiding in giving birth. She makes possible not only creation itself, but also "births" the incarnation of creation in time realized through the Mystery of Golgotha.

For Hildegard, the new creation, made possible through the Mystery of Golgotha, was that for which the world had been made. Moreover, this event, the new creation, the union of divinity and humanity and the Earth, was made possible by the feminine in the form of a woman, Mary. But, for Hilegard, the feminine, Sophia, is not limited to Mary. It extends first to Jesus, the Humanity of Christ, "Jesus, our mother," and then by extension to the "Community," the "body of Christ," humanity, and the Earth, which is in turn one with the cosmos itself. Thus Jesus, the crucified Christ bearer, humanity, matter, the Earth, the cosmos, are feminized as Sophia. Sophia is the place where the heart of Christ, the divine Heart, must come to dwell. From this perspective, the hearts of Jesus and Mary are one heart, the heart of Sophia. At the same time, that heart is no other than the heart or center of the cosmos itself. Creating such a center in oneself by walking the path of Mary and Jesus, therefore, made possible the indwelling of the divine heart and the union of wisdom with love. Hildegard well understood that such inner work made possible the renewal of humanity's cosmogenic or Adamic function. For, once the soul was so purified or "enchristed" that it was one with Sophia (was Wisdom and Love), the being in whom it was purified was perfected in the three realms of Sophia, which are, traditionally, the perfection of the human state. Perfected in these, she became "Trismegistus," mistress of the three realms. Hildegard has a marvelous antiphon that describes these realms:

> O energy of Wisdom, encompassing all
> you circled, circling in the path of life
> with three wings; one flies on high
> one distills from the earth,
> and the third flies everywhere.[3]

Humanity for Hildegard is thus potentially Sophianic and contains the universe. "O human being, Look to humanity!" she writes. "For humanity contains in itself the heavens and the earth and all created things. It is one form within which all things are hidden."[4] For her, God's plan from the beginning was that humanity, being the center and created source of all creation, would help in actualizing the divine potentiality. In her Sophianic vision, the Incarnation was not a simple consequence of the fall. It would have occurred, even had we not fallen. "When God created the world, he decided in his eternal wisdom that he would become human."[5] All of which is to say that the relationship of divinity and humanity (or Sophia) is predestined and ineffably intimate—so intimate, in fact, that we might suspect Sophia (or humanity) as already being the Mother of God and giving birth to Christ in the spirit before creation. In other words, humanity is perhaps not only the Christ's created place but also his uncreated place.

Stated theologically and more circumspectly, Sophia is the bride, mother, and daughter of Christ. "The Eternal Bride of the Word of God," she is also "my father's house in which there are many mansions," the "Master" of the house being, of course, Christ himself. She is also Life, the common life of the Divine, the Spiritual, and Creation (which includes the cosmic, human and earthly), and thus she is mysteriously both created and uncreated. At the same time, she has a very particular relationship to humanity. "One in God, she is multiple in creation and is perceived in creation as the ideal person of the human being, our guardian angel," according to Pavel Florensky. As such, she is the guardian, patron, and person of the community of humanity and the Earth and the spiritual world, on both sides of the threshold. In this sense, then, she is the Body of Christ, which we build up through our selfless I–Thou relationships: the *uniting* spirit, the spirit of true community, who makes it possible that, when "two or three are gathered" in Christ's name, he is there. In other words, she is the principle of *theophany,* or *glory.* She reveals the divine. She is the container and unity of the divine ideas. And as such, again, she is related intimately to *humanity;* for it is *through human beings* that the presence of God, or theophany, is consciously realized cognitively in the universe.

According to Pavel Florensky[6] her motto is *"Omnia conjugo"* (I unite all). She brings together the highest spiritual world, the world of the stars, and the earthly world, proclaiming the good news that human and divine nature, divinity and cosmos, are no longer two but one, potentially at least. For, uniting with human nature and the Earth, with creation or evolution, divinity in this twofold way entered the evolving world to be immanent in it. As the early Christian Fathers recognized, the divine Persons of the One-in-Three and Three-in-One—the Father, the Son, and the Holy Spirit—though distinct, are indivisible. They cannot be separated. Through the Mystery of Golgotha, then, the entire Godhead entered the stream of world evolution so that now there is no longer any transcendent outside. It is omnipresent in *this* world, which is now the only world.

That divinity is no longer outside the world means that creation is *"turned inside out."* Outside is now inside, but with this difference: that there is no longer any outside. Though we would never suspect it, we now live in a non-exterior world, which awaits only our realization of it. As Rudolf Steiner shows in his *Philosophy of Freedom,* we need no longer seek causes or explanations beyond what we can experience; there is no beyond. Each thing in our experience can open to infinite depth and height. Such is the wisdom of the heart: humanity and the Earth, including the cosmos, contain all. All of creation awaits only the manifestation of a new humanity in Christ to be raised into its wholeness from the bondage of separation, isolation, meaninglessness, and death. In the words of St. Paul: "Creation waits with eager longing for the revealing of God's children.... The whole of creation has been groaning in pain and labor until now."[7] In other words, Earth and humanity have become the vessel and scene of a new, second, non-dualized creation.

In Steiner's work, this double focus of humanity *and* Earth presents a paradoxical picture of great complexity. However, the complexity, though real enough, perhaps only appears as such. It seems complex if we look at it from the outside, dualistically, trying to make a "system" out of it; by definition, however, reality is now one (non-dual, or monistic), *living*, and therefore not systematizable or "calculable." For his part, as the Mystery of Golgotha demands, Steiner was monistic from the beginning, never systematic or calculating, always discouraging his followers from trying to capture disparate aspects or fruits of spiritual research in "comprehensive" diagrams. In this, he followed those whom he called "the old philosophers," the alchemists—sole heirs to the wisdom of the Ancient Mysteries—always affirming the unity of their work; insisting that its "matter," in whose transformations they assisted, was one only and thus also not "other" than they themselves.

This "alchemical" tradition holds that the secret unity of all things may be found by meditating the living mystery that lies between seed and seed in the living plant that unfolds in time and to our eyes through the various stages of germination, rooting, sprouting, leafing, flowering, and fruiting: the multiplication of seeds. The alchemical work, which is simultaneously inner and outer, thus unfolds analogically in imitation of the cycle of the flowering plant. Goethe, for instance, intuited his *Metamorphosis of Plants* with the help of old alchemical texts and the Hermetic vision of Jacob Boehme, whose seven divine qualities of creation—from the abyssal seed, through duality, rotation, stillness, union, intelligible sound, to the new seed, tincture or entelechy—are exemplified in the plant as the image of Life itself, which unfolds through a series of expansions and contractions, polarizations and exaltations, dissolutions and coagulations, until the flower emerges and the new seed is announced. As God created the world in seven days, the path of a seed from germination to the realization of the fruit and the new seed falls into seven stages, none of which is quantitatively separable from another. From this perspective, the universe itself is a flowering plant; its seed is in heaven, its flowering on Earth, where new seeds are sown so that a new heavenly reality can germinate.

All this is to say that the Great Work, of which our present Earth is only a stage or state, is a whole, a unity, and participates in the whole or unity throughout. One may give the example, as Steiner does, of a man who, at fifty, still contains who he was when he was five, and at every moment participates in the whole that is his life. "Past" evolutionary stages are always accessible in the present. As Steiner says, "It is possible to see primeval events within the earthly life of the present."[8] The center is always the center of the whole. As in the flowering plant, each stage contains the whole, which Goethe called the "archetypal phenomenon," whose entelechy, or punctual essence, is always present as the "heart" of the process.

In general, however, it is often forgotten that our present Earth is, in reality, both a transitional stage, or moment, and part of a whole in which it participates and in some sense contains. Those who inquire, for instance, about the interior of the Earth usually have in mind only the interior of our present Earth. They forget the larger context. Steiner, however, with his customary precision, always calls our Earth the "Earth stage," or state, within the larger, cosmic spiritual development he generally refers to simply as "Earth evolution."

Earth, for Rudolf Steiner, thus often connotes the whole evolutionary process in the largest sense. He means that the Earth has gone through, and will still go through, different stages before it completes its evolutionary metamorphosis. As is well known, he calls these stages, or states of consciousness, the Saturn, Sun, and Moon stages, leading to our present Earth stage, from which in turn will further evolve or metamorphose the states he calls Jupiter, Venus, and Vulcan. Three things might be noted here.

First, it is not a completely foregone conclusion that the Earth will in fact complete this process or that it will do so successfully. Since what is at stake is always an evolution of consciousness (and consciousness implies "I" beings), at every moment the full realization of any stage depends upon the free collaboration of the beings involved. Nevertheless, paradoxically, it must be the firm, unshakeable ground of our conviction—our faith, hope, and love—that it will. Such "universal salvation" indeed is the meaning of these. In theological language, God will achieve the end of becoming "all in all."

Second, though we make these divisions, and distinguish many evolutionary stages, the process of evolution as such is, in fact, one, single, and whole.

Last, but certainly not least, though we call the process "Earth evolution," we could obviously just as well (perhaps even better) call it "anthropocosmic" or "cosmic-spiritual-human" evolution. The "archetype" in this case is *Anthropos* (the archetypal human being). In the Saturn stage, the seed of the human being is planted, and germinates; through Sun and Moon stages it grows into the cosmos; at the Earth stage, this cosmos flowers simultaneously, and indivisibly, as Earth and human "I" beings, through whom (with the gift of Christ), the seeds of a new human-spiritual cosmos are sown. As if this high vocation were not sufficient (though Steiner does not mention it), esoteric Christian tradition maintains that, within the initial seed hides another seed, that of divinity itself.

As Steiner presents it, then, *the evolution of the human being and the evolution of the Earth are a single process.* To follow the evolutionary unfolding of the human being—beginning with the germ of the physical body during the Saturn state, and moving through the creation of the astral during the Sun state and the etheric during the Moon state—is also to follow the embryonic stages of the creation of the Earth, from its center to its outer atmosphere.

The ongoing metamorphosis of humanity and the Earth is thus a single work; the future evolution of the Earth is part of the future evolution of the human being. Humanity, further, is called through Christ to bring the Earth with it in its evolution. But even that is to state it dualistically. Earth and humanity are one, and whatever is to happen will happen as one: Earth and humanity, a unity, a single Work.

This evolutionary process, like the alchemical process, is two-fold, described as "the materialization of spirit" and "the spiritualization of matter." In the alchemical work, which is the mirror or reverse image of creation, the alchemist first spiritualizes matter, and then materializes spirit, to create the Stone. In this, one collaborates with the Creator in the very process of creation, which includes two movements: a process of the gradual materialization or descent of spirit and an ascent of spirit, or a spiritualization of matter. Transposing this image to the evolutionary process itself as Steiner describes it, the turning point is Earth evolution and, within it, "the turning point of time" is the Mystery of Golgotha.

Such anyway is the view from the "turning point," which is where we are. Nevertheless we should hold in mind that the two movements (which we could also call "evolutionary" and "involutionary") are simultaneously present as the fundamental polarity at all points of the process. Evolution and involution (materialization and spiritualization) are always going on, just as there is always a periphery and a center, and their consequences always remain present until resolved in the ongoing process. It is to this reality that Steiner alludes in his references to beings who, as part of the evolutionary process, withhold their "sacrifices" and, hence, become "abnormal," or retarded. Traces, or residue, of such "egotistic" activity remain, awaiting evolutionary redemption at the involutionary center, which is now none other than the center of our Earth. The primacy of unity means that, at any given point in evolution, everything is present, which is to say that the interior, or center, of the Earth, the human being, and of the cosmos are, in some sense, one. It is in this sense that Basil Valentine, whose work Steiner studied deeply, resumed the essence of the alchemical work in the acronym V.I.T.R.I.O.L: *Visita Interiora Terrae Rectificando Invenies Occultum Lapidem*[9] ("Visit the Interior of the Earth and Rectifying You Will Find the Hidden Stone").

Undoubtedly, all this is difficult to grasp with ordinary thinking. Two of the last "Michael Letters," written at the very end of Steiner's life, will perhaps help begin to shed some light. "What is the Earth in reality in the Macrocosm?" (January 1925) begins by stating the problem: "*We are too close to the Earth in our inner lives to perceive its nature clearly.*"[10]

Having stated the situation, Steiner then turns first to what is well-known, at least to Anthroposophists: we receive the forces of our being as a gift from the extra-earthly cosmos (the actual macrocosm, but also Saturn, Sun and Moon stages of development). However, the forces that give us self-consciousness, and "I"-consciousness, come from the *Earth*.

But what is the meaning of the Earth? Steiner notes first that, the more deeply higher vision penetrates the *past*, the more the cosmos is alive (and hence incalculable). As humanity has separated itself out of this living incalculable element, the cosmos has become less alive. It is now more calculable. In other words, it has entered a death process. Indeed, in the cosmic present, it is essentially *dead*. But not only humanity arose, or separated. At the same time as humanity emerged, the Earth too arose. The two, in fact, are inseparable, as in fact they have been throughout.

Today, with "scientific" consciousness—that is, spatially, with observer consciousness—"we look on the Earth as a speck of dust, insignificant compared to the great universe of physical space." For spiritual vision, however, the picture is quite different: *The essence of the earthly realm stands as a new life-kindling element within the dead and dying macrocosm.*" Steiner explains: "As out of the plant seed, which spatially seems so small and insignificant, the whole great plant builds itself up again, as the old one falls apart in death, so out of the "speck of dust" of the Earth a new macrocosm will emerge, as the old one dies away."[11]

Several weeks later, he returns to the same theme in "The Human in its Macrocosmic Being" (March 1925). Again, he contrasts the polarity of periphery (or starry macrocosm) and center, or Earth. Contemporary humanity, he remarks, feels strongly related to the Earth, but weakly related to the stars. As regards the latter, however, if we become aware of our own etheric natures this will change, for etheric forces come from the extra-earthly, starry cosmos. Then he adds:

> *Those for the physical body radiate from the center of Earth*…. Everything that has to do with the forming of the "I" as the bearer of self-consciousness, must stream forth from the center of a star. The astral works from the circumference; what is related to the "I" radiates from a center. *As a Star, the Earth gives the impulse for the human "I" from its center.* Every star radiates from its center forces that mould the "I" of some being.[12]

By bringing together the physical body and the "I" in relation to the center of the Earth, Rudolf Steiner is suggesting of course that Christ, who is connected to both, has something to do with the theme of this book.

That the "interior of the Earth," like the Earth herself, is connected with the central Christian Mystery, the Mystery of Golgotha, is already indicated by the fact that, in the only lectures dedicated to the topic, Steiner connected knowledge of it—or research into it—to the practice and experience of the seven Stages of the Cross: Jesus Christ' journey from Holy Thursday to Easter Sunday. To accompany Jesus Christ inwardly and meditatively on this journey is to journey through the first seven layers of the Earth. Beyond these seven, according to Steiner, are two final layers, or a penultimate layer and the center, making nine, all interconnected and intimately related to humanity (and hence to the Earth as a living earthly human being). That this is so is not surprising, since evolution (creation), as we have seen, is evolution of the human being (and Earth), and the center of the Earth is the center of evolution.

We may imagine, therefore, that the layers represent an involutionary reflection of the entire spiritual evolutionary process. Clearly other factors, such as the evolutionary/involutionary course of embodied earthly self-conscious humanity, above its growing egotism, would also play a part in this. In other words, our Earth and its interior are a spiritual reality: a divine-cosmic-human state. Like all sensory phenomena, though the Earth is physical material for ordinary cognition (as are the planets and stars, for instance), such perceptions by their nature occlude the creative divine spiritual suprasensory activities whose aftereffects we objectify or reify as *things*. As Steiner says, introducing the topic, "What matters to us is to reveal ideas about how everything was created and came into existence. That is the spiritual aspect."[13]

As for the layers themselves, the first seven, generally speaking, as Steiner describes them, would seem to relate to the Sophia part of our story, while the last two suggest something more Christic. For the images that Steiner uses, from the seventh, "mirror earth," or reflector earth, through the sixth "fire" (lower soul life) earth, to the living matter, or *prima materia,* of the fifth, the "waters" of the fourth, the "life" of the third, and the "fluidity" of the second—as well as the contraction of the mineral in the first—are all "fallen" Sophianic images. In that sense, as we shall see, the "interior of the Earth" reflects "fallen" Sophia-Achamoth: what must be redeemed or rescued. As for the central core layers, which are explicitly (though negatively) creative, for their part, they represent "fallen," or "shadow," Christic elements.

At the same time, we must also note that in other places Steiner gives a much more positive picture of the interior of the Earth as containing the "Golden Land," the "kingdom of light within," the mysterious realm of Shambhala. This is not surprising; where the shadow is, the reality is, too. After all, the interior of the Earth is primarily a state, or condition, of consciousness. Unlike material objects, more than one of which cannot occupy the same space at the same time, many different states of consciousness can and do coexist. Furthermore, where Mary-Jesus-Christ goes, they still *are*. Descending to the center of the Earth, performing there the ultimate act of compassionate redemption, the heart of Mary-Jesus-Christ dwells there still: at once as altar, before which the most purified souls may worship, and as the golden fiery sun seed, or Christ spirit, of the new creation. Here we might note that, in Anthroposophy as in many esoteric traditions, in the new creation, the Earth is destined to become a Sun, or what the Manicheans called the *Terra Lucida*, the "Earth of Light." According to Steiner, this is a process of wisdom (Sophia, the very substance of the Earth) becoming love through transformation in the enchristed "I." The Manicheans likewise taught that human beings, as beings of light, are called to rescue the divine "sparks" mingled at every point in creation with darkness. The human task, according to Mani, is thus to engage each perception, thought, feeling, and act—every cognition—and, through the power of selfless love, the only means available to the Good, separate light from darkness, creating a "column" of Light, or Glory, whereby the whole Earth would be transformed gradually through humanity and become a Sun, a perfect human being of light. From this perspective, Christ's descent into the interior of the Earth on Holy Saturday and the accomplishment of his work of redemption there (where he remains) plants the seed from which the new creation may grow.

However confusing such statements may seem at this point, for the moment let us note only that, according to Steiner, those who wish to walk the "Christian-Gnostic path of initiation" (the Stages of the Cross) must first acquire four virtues: simplicity, self-containment (a hidden life), humility (we receive everything), and patient resignation and devotion toward everything we meet. These virtues are, in fact, traditionally associated with Mary and Jesus, while, as Steiner describes them, the stages of the Cross (the washing of the feet, the scourging, the crowning with thorns, the carrying of the Cross (or Crucifixion), the mystic death, the entombment (or burial), and the Resurrection) likewise involve, above all, the primacy of the Marian virtue of *service* in Christ's deed. Steiner speaks of our need to become servants, "the last," "the least," of all so that our entire life becomes a great bow of gratitude to the whole cosmos (divine, angelic, mineral, plant, and animal) without whom (or which) we would not exist, and who have given us all. Emptying ourselves in this way, as Christ and Mary-Jesus did, we receive the ability to experience the power of compassion that will allow us to follow Jesus Christ in his work of love through the Mystery of Golgotha and so enter as coworkers, continuers of the work of Mary-Jesus-Christ, into the great work of cosmic redemption, even unto the heart of the Earth.

None of this is surprising when we consider that Rudolf Steiner, using the simplest language, always framed Christ's deed through all the stages of Golgotha under the rubric of a unique multilevel cosmic-spiritual, human-earthly overcoming or "purification" of egotism, which is, essentially, the idolatry that prefers self to the divine.

The Mystery of Golgotha always served as a kind of "Rosetta Stone" for Rudolf Steiner. Occasionally, as in his lecture course *From Jesus to Christ*, one of his most remarkable, he says as much. In the fifth lecture, for instance, Steiner speaks about the reality of the physical body in relation to the Resurrection—the "resurrection body"—upon which, as St. Paul recognized, Christianity itself depends: "If Christ be not risen, then is our preaching vain, and your faith is also vain" (Corinthians 15:14). Describing how spiritual research may follow the astral and etheric bodies from incarnation to incarnation, he turns to the question of the physical body, which seems "simply to disappear into the physical world," despite the reality that its seed or germ was formed during the earliest (Saturn) phase of evolution, making it the oldest, and in some sense the *highest*, member of the human being.

Is it conceivable, he asks, that the part of us produced by the gods in the beginning and then worked on by them through each stage of creation, should simply vanish each time a person died? Can spiritual knowledge, he asks, add anything to Maya, or appearances? Not really, he admits. "When we study the description given by spiritual knowledge of human development after death, we find scarcely any notice of the physical body." In fact, generally speaking, with regard to the physical body, spiritual knowledge seems to give tacit assent to Maya. Then he adds in another surprising aside, "And in a certain manner, spiritual science entitles us to agree, *for the simple reason that anything more must be left to the deeper foundations of Christology*"[14] (italics added).

Cutting a long and complex evolutionary story short, Steiner then explains how the physical body, whose reality is the foundation for true "I"-consciousness (the two in some sense going together) cannot be the substances composing it, but must rather be the suprasensory "form," a transparent network of spiritual forces that exists as a kind of spiritual "texture," or vessel, for the "physical" forces and substances. This form he calls the "phantom." It is what the spiritual world created in the beginning. Over the course of time, as the "I" gradually incarnated (subject to the luciferic temptations consequent on the Fall), this "phantom," or form body, the true physical body, became increasingly buried in, or "disorganized," by the "matter" produced by the "I" becoming egotistic in humanity. The result is that the body ceased to be the true body (and in that sense) the Earth no longer the true Earth.

As Steiner notes, "Alchemists always insisted that the human body really consists of the same substance that constitutes the perfectly transparent, crystal clear 'Philosopher's Stone.'"[15] We may also note that these alchemists, who said, "our Work is made the way the World is made," always insisted, "Our Stone is Christ."

It is this body, the true human form and foundation of the "I" (and so of Christ, the divine-cosmic "I") that the Mystery of Golgotha restores to us; and so restores to us the possibility of true "I"-consciousness: namely, "not I, but the Christ in me." One meaning of this is made clear when Steiner describes the function of the physical body—and the phantom—as a "mirror." Before human beings can become conscious of the "I," it must be reflected: "If we had no mirror apparatus, we could not be conscious of our own selves."[16] This mirror is the physical body. To function effectively, a mirror must be completely pure, spotless, and clear. It must be a perfect "witness" and reflect images so perfectly that one cannot tell image from mirror. This mirror, the true body, or phantom (and in some sense, the Earth) changed radically, requiring restoration; otherwise, death would rule.

> The truth is that the human being, in the course of Earth evolution, lost the *form* of the physical body, so that humankind no longer had what the divine beings intended from the beginning. It is something we must regain; to do so, however, it had first to be imparted again. Moreover, we cannot comprehend Christianity unless we understand that, when the events of Palestine took place, the human race on Earth had reached a stage at which the decadence of the physical body was at its peak; because of this, the whole evolution of humanity was threatened with the danger that "I"-consciousness—the specific achievement of Earth consciousness—would be lost....Everything that depends on perfect reflection from the physical body would have become increasingly worn out.[17]

In other words, "The body that was really intended for human beings...the pure phantom of the physical body with all the attributes of the physical body—this it was that rose out of the grave."[18] Such, then, is the risen body in which Jesus Christ arose on Easter Sunday morning, and in which we can all share.

And so we reach the Triduum: the three days that constitute the heart of the Mystery of Golgotha.

On Holy Thursday, Jesus Christ celebrated the Last Supper and the washing of the feet; he was betrayed in Gethsemane and was arrested. Through the night and into Good Friday, he was scourged, crowned with thorns, tried, and then carried his Cross up to Golgotha, where, as he was crucified, his side was pierced and water and blood (his etheric substance) flowed out over the Earth, permeating, penetrating, and filling it as the Grail. Then he died. He became "Lord of the Earth." Taken down before sunset, he was placed in the tomb prepared by Joseph of Arimathea, and a stone was rolled into place to seal it. Thirty-nine hours followed ("the sojourn of Jesus Christ in the flesh in the tomb," his descent to Hell, the Dead, and the center of the Earth), during which He became "Lord of the Subterranean (subcosmic, subnatural) Realms." Ascending on Easter Sunday morning, he arose in his "resurrection body," or restored Phantom, a revelation of his "overcoming death" and becoming the "Lord of Life."

Called Holy (or Great) Saturday, this was the period traditionally during which "he descended into Hell" "in the heart of the Earth," just as he had prophesied in Matthew 12:20: "For as Jonas was three days and three nights in the belly of the whale, so shall the Son of Man be three days and three nights in the heart of the Earth."

These thirty-nine hours present perhaps the deepest, least-known aspect of the Mystery of Golgotha. Exoterically, there is little to go on, though the Orthodox liturgy for Great Saturday gives us some clues. We hear that "the angelic hosts were overcome with awe"; that "death was blinded" by Christ's splendor, its "gloom scattered" by his light. We hear that "Hell was wounded in the heart"; that "the second Adam, who dwells in the highest, has descended to the first Adam, even to the lowest chambers of Hell." We also have the suggestion that the "fallen" angels themselves were visited and redeemed, Satan overcome.

At the deepest level, Hell is where God is absent and love is rejected. It is where the Father "cannot reach," the further reaches of the abuse of freedom. At the same time, it is a kind of "mirrored reflection" of the chaos at the beginning of creation: the fallen Sophia, a second chaos or abyss. The Father, who will not prevent "evil"—which is at once the price of freedom and the goad of love—is at the same time determined to save all. Thus, through Christ's descent, he makes the abyss into a way.

However, the idea of Jesus Christ's descent into Hell, the depths of the Earth, does not appear officially in Christian tradition until the second half of the fourth century. Initially, there was a reference only to a "burial for three days" followed by a resurrection "from the dead," or "from among the dead." After its first mention in the orthodox Creed of Aquileia, it begins to crop up in different places, until it eventually enters the Roman Church from Gaul (perhaps with the blessing of the Celtic Church) during the ninth century, thereafter becoming part of the received text of the Apostles Creed.

The descent was clearly already and always part of the early Church's understanding of the Mystery of Golgotha, though biblical evidence is slight. Two passages in the letters of Peter have been interpreted as referring to it. In his first letter, Peter writes that Christ "was put to death in the flesh but made alive in the spirit, *in which also he went and made a proclamation to the spirits in prison*" (1 Peter 3:18–19), while in his second letter he writes, "The Gospel was proclaimed even to the dead, so that, though they had been judged in the flesh as everyone is judged, they might live in the spirit as God does" (1 Peter 4:6). St. Paul, for his part, places Christ's descent in precise parallel with his ascent for the sake of the new unity:

What does "he ascended" mean except that he also descended
into the lower [regions] of the Earth? The one who descended
is also the one who ascended far above all the heavens, that
he might fill all things. (Ephesians 4:9–10)

Much theological ink has been spilled in the debate over how
far Christ (Sophia-Christ, Jesus Christ) descended. Did he descend
only to rescue the "good" dead, the "saints" of Israel (Abraham,
Moses, the Prophets and so on)? Did he continue on deeper to rescue *all* the dead? Did He go further still, into unthinkable regions
of sinfulness and fallenness? And further still into abysses of
"evil" we can barely imagine? Did He transform all these states,
as Origen and Gregory of Nyssa believed, so that their purifica-
tory fires would in the end burn away all iniquity—even iniquity
itself—assuring the final *apocatasis,* or resoration, of all things?
Or does God pick and choose among his creation, saving some and
consigning others to eternal damnation? Today, surely we cannot
imagine a God, who is love and mercy, who would *not* seek to
redeem all? Finally, therefore, there can be no doubt; he descended
as far down as he ascended up. He went to the bottom as he went
to the top. How far apart such opposites lie or whether they in fact
coincide is another question.

Between the hill of Golgotha, geologically a continuation of
Mount Moriah (where Abraham took Isaac to sacrifice him), and
the garden on Mount Zion (where Jesus Christ was buried), one
may still see the traces of the vast primal fissure that tradition recognized as not only the gate to the underworld, but, more important, as the grave of Adam. An ancient Syriac text, *The Cave of
Treasures,* tells us that ,when Adam was about to die, he called his
son Seth to him, and, blessing him, requested to be embalmed and
his body placed in the Cave of Treasures, near Paradise, where
they still lived. And then with foresight, he requested that, when a
later generation would leave that vicinity, one be chosen "to carry
my body with him, and take it and deposit it in the center of the

Earth, for in that place shall redemption be effected for me and for all my children."[19]

Adam's body was thus the first to be buried in the Earth—at the center of the Earth—beneath Golgotha, called the "Place of the skull" after Adam's skull. Descending to the center of the Earth, Sophia-Christ, the second Adam, went in search of the first Adam. However, where the first Adam lies so also lies Adam Kadmon, the Spiritual Human being, the first of creation, for the center of the Earth, as we have said, is also the center of all, even the divine center. So there, too, we may imagine Christ-Sophia must have gone. More than that, where they went, there they are. For Jesus Christ is still washing our feet, being scourged, crowned with thorns, and carrying his cross. He is still being crucified. His blood and water still pours forth. He is still descending to the center of the Earth, where he remains even now. Likewise, he is also still rising and risen and ascending and sitting with God. Thereby he rescued and rescues all or, at least, made and makes possible the rescue of all. That is to say, he assured and assures still "universal salvation"—the absolute redemption of all things—within the limits of human freedom. The rest is up to us.

After forty days, sealing the deed, he ascended from Earth into Heaven. And ten days after that, with the disciples gathered according to tradition around Mary in an upper room, the Holy Spirit—the Comforter and Advocate that he had promised—descended through Mary in tongues of flame to sit upon each.

Such is the Mystery of Golgotha—or is it? In fact, it is difficult to draw strict boundaries around it, for ultimately it includes the universe.

From one point of view, we may take it to refer strictly to the events surrounding the Passion—from the Last Supper and the washing of the feet, through Gethsemane (and the betrayal), the subsequent stages of the Cross up to the Crucifixion, burial and resurrection to the Ascension and Pentecost. From another, anthroposophic point of view, we may take it to begin with the Baptism and the incarnation of the Christ into the body of the Nathan Jesus. In this case, the Mystery of Golgotha would also include such phenomena as the miracles, the teachings, and "I AM" sayings. Or we may take it to include the Annunciation, the birth(s) of Jesus and so on (including what Steiner calls "The Fifth Gospel").

We can go further back, at least one generation, as was done in the East and in medieval Christianity, to include the birth of Mary from Anna and Joachim; likewise, we can go forward to include the "reappearance of Christ in the etheric" and other, future "reappearances." This would confirm the views holding that the Mystery of Golgotha is ongoing, not to be completed until the end of times, and that, as potentially enchristed "I" beings, we are now called to participate in it. This, in turn, would suggest that the Mystery of Golgotha must also stretch all the way back to "creation" itself. From this perspective, the Mystery of Golgotha, the new creation, now repeats in time what occurred in the Godhead out of time and unfolded through the stages of creation (or evolution), which themselves can then be thought of as enacting the Mystery of Golgotha. In this case, perhaps, the descent in the tomb to the heart of the Earth would mirror a divine descent to the center of the Godhead. None of these can be ruled out. In some sense, all must be born in mind.

The early Christians certainly took the long view. When the events of the Incarnation occurred, few people noticed them beyond the small circles of the disciples and the women and friends around Christ. Fewer still understood. Among the first to try to understand the significance of what had happened out of their own experience were early so-called Gnostics such as Valentinus. They encountered and named Sophia as a pivotal coworker in Christ's deed, for they saw the Mystery of Golgotha, creation and redemption, as a drama of Christ and Sophia.

Valentinus's account of this drama is complex and mythological. He begins (according to one account) with a primal, unknowable two-in-one pair—incomprehensible Depth (*Bythos*) and ineffable

Silence (*Sige*)—who create the first seed, from which arises the first aeon, or syzygy, Mind (*Nous*) and Truth (*Aletheia*), from whom twenty-two others such as Word (*Logos*) and Life (*Zoe*), Humanity (*Anthropos*) and Community (*Ecclesia*), gush forth in pairs. The last to arrive is Sophia, the youngest. Like the other Aeons, Sophia enjoys the fullness of all life. But she feels frustration at her distance from the ultimate Source, the unknowable Origin. Impetuous, impatient, unwilling to wait, her passion to know overcomes her and she dives upward. Much happens to her; she has many adventures; and perhaps she would have reached her goal, but she encounters *Horos* (limitation), who separates her from her passion, dividing her, as it were, into two and throwing her passion down from the spiritual world. Thus Sophia becomes twofold: Sophia *Ouranos*, or Heavenly Sophia, above; "Achamoth," or Sophia *Prunikos*, Sophia the Whore, below. At the same time, another pair of aeons is brought forth: Christ and the Holy Spirit. These bring knowledge of the Father to the other Aeons, who then created as the "fairest fruit," Jesus, who will be the pair (one-in-two) of Sophia-Achamoth. This was before the Fall as we know it. The Fall itself is the fall of Sophia.

In time, left alone and cast out, Achamoth-Sophia suffered agonies of fear, despair, passion, and ignorance. Her suffering, however, was not ineffective, for it produced a false, alien, aborted world, whose very matter, soul, and spirit mimicked that of the Truth: the fallen world, the Earth we know, and the Earth whose interior Steiner has described for us. As Valentinus says in *The Gospel of Truth*:

> Ignorance of the Father brought about anguish and terror. And the anguish and terror grew thick like a fog, so that no one was able to see. For this reason, error became powerful; it fashioned its own matter....It set about making a creature, with all its might, preparing in beauty a substitute for the truth.[20]

Here, Sophia is clearly a figure of human nature, and the fall of her passion to know for herself—to be unwilling to wait, to want what she wants when she wants it, her "selfishness"—is a metaphor for the "Fall" of humanity. Clearly, too, though the description is epistemological, the reason for error goes deeper than mere epistemology and inculpates the whole human person. Essentially, her passion is egotism. Her egotism actually creates a false world, not just the illusion of it. Her egotism "creates" its own "matter."

But the drama is not over. While Sophia-Achamoth labors below in pain, anguish, and illusion, above, heavenly Sophia, together with Jesus and all the Aeons, looks down with pity, sadness, and compassion as the Sophia below labors in ignorance, suffering, and anguish. Finally, at the last moment, they decided to rescue her. They sent Jesus the celestial bridegroom, "a being of perfect beauty, the very star of the spiritual world, its perfect fruit,"[21] into the world she had made to rescue her and it.

The details here are not so important as the general outline: an evolutionary drama of Christ and Sophia, in which Sophia appears in two forms, unfallen and fallen, heavenly and earthly, reminding us of the two female figures in Revelation: the "woman clothed with the Sun, with the Moon under her feet, and on her head a crown of twelve Stars" (Rev. 12:1–2) and the so-called Whore of Babylon, "a woman sitting on a scarlet beast, arrayed in purple and scarlet, and bedecked with jewels and pearls, holding in her hand a golden cup full of abominations" (Rev. 17:3–4).

Here we must note that in Valentinus's cosmology Sophia seems to be related in some way to primordial cosmic human nature itself. Perhaps that is why he taught, according to a letter quoted by Clement of Alexandria, that when the angels were creating humanity they stopped in fear when the creature they had made uttered a cry greater than its creation seemed to justify; they suddenly realized that the "One above" had invisibly deposited in being a seed of "the substance above," revealing the hidden nature of the ground of all being. No wonder fear fell upon the angels. As he wrote: "Adam, being fashioned in the name of Anthropos, inspired fear of the pre-existent Anthropos, because he was in him. Therefore they were terrified, and concealed their work."[22] Consequently, Valentinus said, Christ called himself "the Son of Anthropos."

For Valentinus, then, the new revelation proclaimed that creation was creation in human nature: the world was brought forth from human nature; it fell through human nature; and through human nature in the end, it will return to God whence it came. Thus the true meaning of the microcosm-macrocosm analogy is not that not only is the human being a little cosmos, but also that the cosmos is a big human. Cosmic evolution in this view is the progressive unfolding, transformation, and mutation of the seeds planted in the original human archetype.

Who, then, *is* Sophia? Perhaps we have some understanding of Christ, but Sophia, without whom we may not be able to fully understand Christ, remains largely unknown, though we may recognize that she has something to do with our humanity, as does Christ. Sergei Prokofieff calls knowledge of her "an evolving mystery," evolving not only in our understanding, but also in herself; in some sense, she is an evolving being. Prokofieff writes that understanding of and insight into her "is even more foreign to our materialistic age than is the Christ mystery,"[23] alluding to the fact that this appropriation of her mystery is for the future.

At the same time, she has always been with us, clearly present throughout the ancient mysteries and central in all ancient civilizations, called by many names: Inanna, Astarte, Ishtar, Isis, Maat, Hathor, Nut, Neith, Demeter, Persephone, Artemis, Athena, Hecate, and in the Hebrew Scriptures, Asherah, who is Wisdom (*Hokhmah*), who will become Mary and gnostic Sophia. The list is endless. The more one seeks, the more one finds. These figures, all of whom are aspects of Sophia, represent various states of one primal being.

For the earliest Christians, however, Sophia was known from her presence in the Hebrew Scriptures, above all as *Hochma*,

Wisdom, in the so-called Wisdom books. Complex as she is, only a few points can be made. In the earliest account (Job 28), Wisdom, not yet a "being," is divine, immanent in creation as its language: its meaning, its life. A few centuries later, however, Proverbs 8 presents a different view. Sophia is now a being who addresses human beings, wanting them to find and follow her, and in return she promises her gift of wisdom. And then she gives her pedigree, which famously goes back to the beginning:

> The Lord created me at the beginning of his course
> As the first of his works of old...
> I was there when he set the heavens into space...
> I was with him as a confidant,
> A source of delight every day,
> Playing in front of him all the time,
> Playing in his inhabited world,
> Finding delight with humankind.[24]

Here we might note that *beginning* in its original meaning is not the chronologically past source, but rather "opens out"; *beginning* is the ever-present opening. The English word *begin*, in fact, comes from old Teutonic *be-ginnan*, to cut open, to open up, and is cognate with Old English to gape, or yawn, as in the mouth of an abyss. The beginning, then, is an opening up of the primal, unknowable mystery.

For this reason, Sophia has also always been found in the abyss ("the deep," "the waters"): "And the Earth was without form and void; and darkness was on the face of the deep. And the spirit of God moved upon the face of the waters" (Genesis I:2). From this point of view, she, who is at the beginning, is also the continuously available opening place: the stuff of creation, the wisdom out of which all things are made, as in Psalm 104:24: "You have made all things in wisdom." "That wisdom is the beginning, and in that beginning you have made heaven and earth," comments Augustine,[25] for whom this "wisdom" is "spiritual matter" of almost unbounded fluidity." This view of Sophia as the *prima materia* was also that of the alchemists. "The Virgin Mother," Fulcanelli writes, "stripped of her symbolic veil, is none other than the personification of the primitive substance, used by the Principle, the creator of all that is, for the furtherance of his designs."[26]

In another Wisdom Book, Jesus Sirach, Wisdom again speaks in the first person, explaining how *she runs through all creation*. She tells how she came forth from the mouth of the Most High, covering the Earth like a mist, yet dwelling in the heavens and taking her course through abyss, all the while holding sway over Earth and her peoples. Most important, she seeks a permanent dwelling place in human beings, her true home.

The Wisdom of Solomon, finally, gives us perhaps the most revealing metaphor or image. He writes:

> Like a fine mist she rises from the power of God,
> A clear effluence from the glory of the Almighty;
> So nothing defiled can enter into her by stealth.
> She is the radiance that streams from everlasting light,
> The flawless mirror of the active power of God
> *And the image of his goodness.*
> She is but one yet can do all things,
> Herself unchanging, she makes all things new.[27]

The key image is the mirror, which we have met before as the true function of the physical body. The alchemists were well aware of this. "The first matter, which the artist must chose in order to begin the work, is called the mirror of the Art."[28] The Cosmopolite, likewise, speaking of Sulphur, says, "In its kingdom there is a mirror in which the whole world is seen. Anyone looking in this mirror can see and learn the three parts of the Wisdom of the whole world."[29] Basil Valentine, perhaps the greatest alchemist of the Renaissance, writes, "The whole body of the Vitriol must be recognized only as a Mirror of the philosophical science....It is a Mirror in which you see our Mercury, our Sun and Moon, appear and shine; by which you can show in an instant and prove to Doubting Thomases the blindness of their crass ignorance."[30]

Sophia—Nature, the Earth, and the "body," or mirror—is thus simultaneously matrix and imaginatrix, mediatrix and workshop of creation, its place and its process. She is *Imagination*, the intermediary between the world of mystery and the visible world. She is the "deep in-between"; she is "spiritual matter." In her, incorporeal beings take body and sensuous things are "dematerialized." Through her, spiritual beings enact the evolutionary drama of the world. This being comes to us through history. She enters history, she incarnates. But there is a story here.

What exists as our Old Testament, which reflects the current version of the Hebrew Scriptures, is not "original." It was rewriten after the exile by the so-called Deuteronomist and represents the "second temple teaching": Moses and the Law and monotheism. The second temple was reconstructed in 515 B.C.E. after the exile on the site of the destroyed first temple—Solomon's Temple. It was this second temple that Herod expanded around 19 B.C.E. and was destroyed in 73 C.E.

The teaching of the first temple—Solomon's Temple, built around 1000 B.C.E. and destroyed by Nebuchadnezzar in 586 B.C.E—was very different from the strict monotheism of the second temple. It seems to have included three deities: El-Elyon, the Most High; his Sons, the Elohim, the "angelic host," the most important of which was Yahweh; and the Goddess Wisdom, called *Asherah*.

After the temple had been destroyed, refugees fled south, where they confronted Jeremiah. Asserting that the destruction had taken place because they had neglected the Queen of Heaven, they complained: "Since we left off to burn incense to the queen of heaven and to pour out drink offerings to her, we have wanted all things and have been consumed by the sword and by famine.... Before, we had plenty of food, and we prospered and saw no evil."[31] As the Book of Enoch tells us, "All who lived in the Temple lost their vision; and godlessly their hearts forsook wisdom; and the house of the kingdom was burned; and the whole chosen people was scattered."[32]

The rewriting was an evolutionary necessity. The Mystery of Golgotha demanded it. Indeed, just before the first temple was actually destroyed, there had been an attempted purge: King Josiah's reform. Josiah threw out the "idols," especially that of the Goddess: "And the high places that were before Jerusalem, which were on the right hand of the mount of corruption, which Solomon had built for Asherah...did the king defile" (2 Kings 23:17).

It is this rejected Wisdom-Asherah-Queen of Heaven we find in the Wisdom Books. She is the Virgin who will give birth to Emmanuel: one and the same, but rejected. Associated with the fragrant, fiery Tree of Life and with the anointing oil extracted from it, at the first stage of initiation (according to the scholar Margaret Barker), she gave light as the Tree of Life; later, in the Holy of Holies, she was given in the anointing oil, which opened eyes and gave eternal life. In fact, in Solomon's Temple she *was* the Holy of Holies. She was also the "Great Lady," "the Bright One," the Queen of Heaven," "the Mother of Yahweh," "the bread of the presence," the "Queen and Mother of the King," the Morning Star, the co-creatrix in the beginning, the tabernacle, the "living ark of God."

This being had left. She had returned to Heaven. In the Book of Enoch (42:2):

> Wisdom went forth to dwell among human beings,
> And found no dwelling place:
> Wisdom returned to her place
> And took her seat among the angels. [33]

Although Asherah-Wisdom has "left Jerusalem," a faithful group always awaited her return. Margaret Barker writes, "It would appear, then, that the figure whom the Enochian writers and Gnostics remembered as Sophia/Wisdom and the Kabbalists as Shekinah, had been known to her worshippers as the Queen of Heaven, and so deep were her roots in Israel's religion that her loss was never forgotten; on the contrary, her restoration was to be a sign of redemption."[34]

Many at the time of Christ, then, still remembered the first temple as the true temple and awaited the coming of Wisdom. The huge number of female figures found in Israelite sites, dating from the period leading up to the Mystery Golgotha, confirms this. Texts also speak in confirmation: Micah 5, for instance: "But you, Bethlehem-Ephrathah, too small to be among the clans of Judah, from you shall come forth for me one who is to be ruler of Israel.... Therefore, the Lord will give them up until the time when she who is to give birth has borne." And of course Isaiah 7:14: "Therefore, the Lord himself will give you the sign; the virgin shall be with child and bear a son and shall name him Immanuel."

Thus people understood that Sophia, who had dwelt with God, helping in the work of creation, and had lived with human beings and had been rejected through pride and arrogance, went away. They understood, too, that she was approaching once again. They sensed her coming; they wooed her. They felt her preparing her ways. Sophia would come to help human beings build her Temple once again.

She did return. In the eyes of many, she came in the being of Mary-Jesus, for, as the Middle Ages still understood, these two constituted a single being, whose union with Christ at "the turning point of time" infused the Universal Medicine that, healing spiritual, cosmic, and human egotism, would reopen the path to God's becoming all in all. Thus the double mystery of the restoration of humanity and the Earth (or cosmos) in humanity was accomplished through the twofold cooperation of Sophia (Mary-Jesus) and the Logos, Christ. Here perhaps is the real meaning of the mystery of the union of divinity and humanity in Christ through the Mystery of Golgotha.

The Mystery of Golgotha, begin it where you will, is this twofold. Its teaching on both sides, however, is single. It is nothing but a great assent, an unwavering "Yes"—an unconditional hospitality and obedience to any and all otherness—made possible, in

Christian terms, by a continual *kenosis* or self-emptying, as Paul explains in Philippians 2:6):

> Let each of you look not to your own interests, but to the interests of others. Let the same mind be in you that was in Jesus Christ, who, though he was in the form of God, did not regard equality with God as something to be exploited, but *emptied himself*, taking the form of a slave, being born in human likeness. And being found in human form, he *humbled himself and became obedient* to the point of death—even death on a cross.

In its simplicity and purity, this "Yes" overcomes and transforms the power of *negation*, under whose rule Earth, cosmos, and humanity sink ever deeper into egotism, death, and materialistic (brain) thinking. For all of these depend on negation. Consider ordinary thinking: it depends entirely upon negation. Objectification, comparison, and abstract dialectic are all founded in the power of "no," a fact mirrored in the death processes of the brain. As such thinking becomes global, it empowers negation to penetrate ever further into our being, until the egotism it creates infects (disorganizes) not just our thinking but also our soul and will lives, and even our true physical body, the phantom. As negation, "egotism" sets up a limited, finite self in opposition to the infinity of the "I" and the divine spiritual reality of the cosmos and other human beings. Hungering after certainties, shoring up its sense of being self-constituted and constantly feeding the illusion that it is its own master, the egotistic self seeks complete control and knowledge and will defend itself and its imagined boundaries to the death. Violence and mayhem, destruction and self-destruction, follow. Death is negation: the primary negation from which all others flow. "Overcoming death," therefore, means in principle the end of negation and all its forms of egotism. Death and negation clearly have a function: they allow a certain consciousness of individuality. However, between individuality and egotism lies a slippery path, one that, as Steiner frequently reminds us, could do us in. The false, egotistic self is, of course, an illusion, having nothing to do with individuality, but it is a most powerful illusion for, as Valentinus said of error (which we may read here as egotism), "It fashioned its own matter.... It set about making a creature, with all its might preparing in beauty a substitute for the truth"[35]—the Earth as we know it.

The new creation will grow as human beings, walking the way of Mary-Jesus and Christ, enter the world of assent and affirmation. We cannot yet imagine what a way of being incarnating assent would be like or what a logic that did not know negation would be like: what it would be to think, feel, and will without negation, in conscious obedience (thorough listening) and unconditional hospitality toward the spiritual world. Nor can we imagine the immense transformational capacity of such love to redeem all things. Nevertheless, we can begin by following those closer to us than we are to ourselves, who have gone before and accompany us now.

Mary's "yes," her hospitality and obedience, begins at age three when she enters the temple to live there, "fed like a dove, receiving her food from heavenly messengers." It continues through her assent at the Annunciation: "Behold the handmaid of the Lord; be it unto me according to thy word." All else depended upon this, for the entire spiritual world hung then upon her response. From this "Yes" turning point her whole life then unfolded in assent upon assent: from her "Magnificat"—"My soul doth magnify the Lord"—to the birth of Jesus; from her assent to Simeon's prophetic blessing—"Yea, a sword shall pierce through thine own soul also"—to her "keeping [Jesus'] sayings in her heart" after she "lost" him at the age of twelve in the temple; through all his years of the "Fifth Gospel" to his baptism by John and the descent of the Christ by the Jordan; through the three years of the ministry when, closer to him than any of the disciples, she "fed him out of her own substance"; to her witnessing collaboration in the mystery on Golgotha, the descent into the Earth, and the Rising on Easter morning.

The rest we must imagine, from the descent of the Holy Spirit to her life with the beloved disciple in the community at Ephesus and her dormition, or assumption.

All are ripe for meditation and practice, for multiple virtues are contained within her "Yes." Among them are faith, patience, purity, compassion, humility, loving kindness, inner wakefulness, sincerity, and active openhearted hospitality and obedience. In a sense, all these virtues are contained in a single virtue, simplicity, which comes only to those who have given themselves up and so can give themselves to others.

As for Jesus Christ (it is difficult to separate these), as the Gospels tell it he walks the same path of unconditional devotion to the will of the Father ("Not my will, but thy will be done"), unconditional forgiveness ("seventy-seven times"), turning the other cheek, loving our enemies, and above all loving one another as we have been loved; in a word, a life of continuous dying to self—dying on one's feet, upright, in daily life, every moment for the sake of the world. "Unless a corn of wheat fall into the ground and die, it abides alone: but if it dies it brings forth much fruit" (John 12:24–27).

All Gospel teachings agree in the fundamental teaching of self-emptying assent as the one thing necessary. Sigismund von Gleich intuitively understood this when, in his moving essay on the interior of the Earth (*The Transformation of Evil: And the Subterranean Spheres of the Earth*[36]), he proposed practice of the Beatitudes as the appropriate path for healing and transforming the Earth. The nine Beatitudes, which in a sense encapsulate the Way of the Cross and correspond perhaps to the nine inner layers of the Earth, or at least to nine layers of egotism, lay out in beautifully succinct form the essential Christian path of action for the overcoming of self and doing good.

Thus, by the way of assent, the "Yes," which both the logic of life (death is negation) and unconditional love (conditions, limits, also being negation), Jesus Christ, Sophia-Christ, the union of perfect humanity and divinity, penetrate creation to its furthest, least, densest, darkest point, and permeate all with Glory and Light. Together, they redeem creation and return to humanity the possibility of being the true image and likeness, uniting in itself creation and the Divine.

Love, which is assent, as the Manicheans taught, is the *only* means that Good has to transform or heal evil: the "evil" of egotism, or self-will. Good cannot punish; it can do no violence; it can only accept, love, and forgive unconditionally. Otherwise, it implicates itself in and becomes precisely what it seeks to undo. Such anyway was the medieval Cathars' understanding of what passed on Golgotha. They believed that the Creator had no recourse to the egotism, or evil, that endangered creation and even the Divine itself, but to respond with unconditional love: therefore the "Father" sent his own "Son" in an act of utter, unconditional love to transform all through that same love.

According to this view, whenever in the humblest, most modest, tiniest everyday things we submit in unknowing (so that we may know), emptying ourselves of self (so that we may be receptive to the true "I"), die to our finitude (so that we might become infinite), and embrace our littleness (so that we might be anointed with greatness), we continue Christ's work of redemption and raise the all-transfiguring, transformative seed now planted in the heart of the Earth. To do so is to walk the way of the Cross: to overcome egotism and to live for the sake of the world. It is to enter selflessly into suffering—that of the world, which is the suffering of God and is manifest moment to moment in the individual suffering of innumerable beings right into the heart of matter.

"What can one say of a soul, a heart, that is filled with compassion?" writes St. Isaac the Syrian. It is a heart that burns with love for every creature: for human beings, for birds and animals, for serpents and for demons. The thought of them and the sight of them make the tears of the saint flow. And this immense, intense compassion, which flows from the heart of saints, makes them unable to bear the sight of the smallest, insignificant wound in any creature. Thus they pray ceaselessly, with tears, even for animals…and for those who do them wrong.[37]

It may seem simplistic to assert that all that stands between universal redemption and us is the complete and utter victory over egotism, and that assent, or love, is the sole means. However, egotism—human, cosmic, and spiritual—goes extraordinarily deep, as does the power of assent. Both have the power to penetrate the whole creation, as egotism does already, perhaps right down to the center of the Earth. Everything at all levels hangs on overcoming the temptation to prefer self to the divine "I am." But Christ-and-Sophia, through their divine-human "Yes," now also permeate creation through the deed of the "turning point of time." Creation is turned inside out. Potentially restored, its restoration in time depends on our response to it.

By the path of self-emptying assent and hospitality, selfless love and overcoming egotism, Sophia and Christ together, as one, give us the possibility of fulfilling our divine destiny and becoming Sophianic-Christic beings. By becoming, in Meister Eckhart's words, Mary, and giving birth to Christ (or, we may say, becoming Sophia and giving birth to Christ), and following them inwardly through the sufferings and the transformations they enacted in and through the Earth on Golgotha, we may yet become coworkers with them in the Great Work of transforming the Earth into a Sun.

This is the Good News.

NOTES

INTRODUCTION

1. "The beings immediately above humankind,...when they return
    to their inner being, they have nothing independent, nothing self-
    enclosed, like the inner life of human beings. Nevertheless, they feel,
    shining and springing forth in their inner being, the forces and beings
    of the higher hierarchies above them.... Thus, what we human beings
    call our independent inner life does not really exist in them.... These
    beings could hide nothing within them as the product of their own
    thought and feeling, for whatever they bring about in their inner being
    must show itself externally. They cannot lie; they cannot be untrue
    to their nature so that their thoughts and feelings did not harmonize
    with the external world. They cannot have an idea within them that
    does not agree with the external world. For any ideas that they have
    in their inner being are perceived by them in their manifestation. Now,
    however, let us just suppose that these beings had a desire to be untrue
    to their own nature. What would be the result?...If they wanted to be
    untrue, they would have to develop something in their inner being that
    would be inconsistent with their own nature.... To do so, they would
    have to assume another nature.... Angels have no life of their own"
    (Rudolf Steiner, April 8, 1912. *The Spiritual Beings in the Heavenly
    Bodies and in the Kingdoms of Nature*, North Vancouver, BC: Steiner
    Book Centre, 1981, p. 89 ff).
2. Rudolf Steiner, October 1, 1905, lecture 6, *Foundations of Esoteri-
    cism*, London: Rudolf Steiner Press, 1983, pp. 41–42.
3. Romans 7:19, 24.
4. *Faust* part one, lines 775–776.
5. Hermes Trismegistus, *Corpus Hermeticum*, begins with these words.
6. Rudolf Steiner, March 24, 1920, lecture 4, *Spiritual Science and Med-
    icine*, Blauvelt, NY: Garber, 1989, p. 65. Cited in Karl König, *Earth
    and Man*, Wyoming, RI: BFGA, 1982, p. 267.
7. Quoted in Christopher Bamford, *An Endless Trace: The Passion-
    ate Pursuit of Wisdom in the West*, New Paltz, NY: Codhill Press,
    2003, p. 57.

8.   Rudolf Steiner, Nov. 22, 1906, *The Origin of Suffering; the Origin of Evil, Illness and Death*, N. Vancouver, BC: Steiner Book Centre, 1980, pp. 20–21.

9.   Ehrenfried Pfeiffer, October 10, 1958, *Subnature and Super-nature in the Physiology of Plant and Man: the True Foundations of Nutrition*, Spring Valley, NY: Mercury Press, 1981, p. 25.

10.   Christopher Bamford, "Paradoxical Thoughts on Christ and Sophia in the Human Mystery of the Earth" in this volume.

11.   Our soul lives within the two poles of thought and will. Thought is lucid, transparent, and fully conscious. Will is opaque, dark, and unconscious. We are awake in our thoughts, but asleep in our will. Thoughts relate to our nervous-sensory system and the outer world. Will impulses relate to our limbs and metabolism and arise from the inner depths. Feelings link the two and may be more conscious or more asleep, related more to outer perception or to inner dynamics. See Rudolf Steiner's lecture of April 29, 1922, in *The Human Soul in Relation to World Evolution*, Spring Valley, NY: Anthroposophic Press, 1984.

12.   Maureen Dowd, January 7, 2007.

13.   *New York Times*, May 29, 2007.

14.   "If, with the normal consciousness of today, the soul feels that it can produce only ideas that are maya in the face of living reality, and if it is not as a squeezed lemon, acknowledging only the science of today, then it feels empty in the face of the real world. It certainly feels it can reach the further limits of the world with its ideas.... Doing so must involve a feeling of being spread out through an endless expanse of space with a set of weak ideas. The farther we expand thence into space, the thinner our ideas become, and we find ourselves eventually before an empty and bottomless abyss. That is an ordeal that the soul has to face. Those who thirst for reality, who seek to solve the riddles of the world, the 'wonders of the world' along the lines of abstract science, eventually find themselves standing before the cosmic void with their ideas dissipated entirely into spiritual vapor. Then one's soul must experience an infinite terror in the presence of this void. One who is unable to experience this fear in the presence of the void has simply not advanced sufficiently to feel the truth about present-day consciousness....

      "There is another path open to the soul. It can descend into its own depths in such a way that it experiences the nature of its own organization. Under modern conditions of consciousness, the soul really experiences only what has been added to its organization on the Earth. What it received on the ancient Moon as astral body remains subconscious; it lights up in the etheric body, but in normal consciousness, it is not experienced. Even less does one experience what was acquired during the Sun evolution as the etheric body, or what through Saturn, Sun, and Moon evolutions one has received in the physical body. These are regions closed to human beings. However, countless generations of gods, or the spiritual hierarchies, have labored upon these closed regions. Indeed, when, through clairvoyant knowledge and esoteric training, we descend into these regions and penetrate behind our "I"-consciousness into our own being—when we encounter the astral, etheric, and physical bodies within us—then we come not to a vacuum, but to a condensed world [universal] substance. There, we encounter everything that has worked into us human beings throughout millions and millions of years by innumerable spiritual hierarchies. But when, through the serious cultivation of self-knowledge as given by esoteric training, we try to enter and learn how to plunge into the work of countless generations through millions of years, we do not encounter a pure form of what the gods have created. Human beings have stamped into it all that they themselves have experienced through the generations as impulses, desires, passions, emotions, and instincts. In the course of terrestrial incarnations, what one has developed in this way has united with what is present below in the astral, etheric, and physical natures. Together, they form a dense mass, and one first enters this dense mass. What we ourselves have done to our divine nature veils it from us.

"Thus, when we plunge into ourselves, we find the opposite of what we find when we expand into cosmic space. When we expand into the expanse of space, there is the danger of eventually encountering the void. When we descend into ourselves, there is a danger of entering increasingly dense regions that we ourselves have condensed through impulses, desires, and passions. Just as we feel the matter of our consciousness scatter and disintegrate when we go out into cosmic distances, likewise, when we plunge into our own soul's depths, we feel increasingly pushed back. We feel like a rubber ball resuming its shape after being squeezed. We are repeatedly repulsed when we try to penetrate into our own inner being. We can be very clearly aware of this. It is not just that our impulses, desires, and passions—which we encounter first when we penetrate ourselves—seem horrifying to us when we meet them face to face. However—added horror—at every moment they seem to be trying to capture us. They become strong and powerful; their will nature comes to the fore. In ordinary consciousness, we may not obey one or another impulse or instinct, but as soon as we descend a little way into ourselves, those instincts develop their full strength and we must surrender to them. Repeatedly, the will of our lower nature grips us, and, more than ever, we are thrown back upon ourselves. That is the other danger; when we plunge into ourselves, we are confronted, as it were, by the density of our impulses and instincts.

"Thus we have to face formidable dangers. If we expand into universal space, we are in danger of dissolving with our consciousness into nothingness. If we plunge into ourselves, we are in danger of surrendering our consciousness to the impulses and instincts within us and of falling prey to the worst possible egotism. Those are the two poles, and between them lay all vicissitudes of soul—fear of the void and the collapse into egotism. All other ordeals are variations directed against what we may call dissolution into nothing, or against surrender to egotism. Even higher knowledge is dangerous in this connection;...when, in the esoteric life, we delve into our own inner being, we are overcome by the thought that we are, in fact, the aim and goal of the gods, that the gods have labored to create us. Here we confront the great danger of falling into immeasurable arrogance" (Rudolf Steiner, *Wonders of the World, Ordeals of the Soul, Revelations of the Spirit,* London: Rudolf Steiner Press, 1963, pp. 175–179).

15. Rudolf Steiner, June 12, 1906, "Earthquakes, Volcanoes and the Human Will," in *The Interior of the Earth: An Esoteric Study of the Subterranean Spheres,* London: Rudolf Steiner Press, 2006, p. 22. See also, "Human beings who, out of their own cunning free will, have become black magicians by placing spiritual forces in the service of their own egotism" (Rudolf Steiner, May 20, 1909 *Reading the Pictures of the Apocalypse,* Hudson, NY: Anthroposophic Press, 1993, p. 128).

16. See Erwin Schrodinger, *What is Life?* (with *Mind and Matter* and *Autobiographical Sketches*), New York: Cambridge University Press, 1967.

17. See, for example, James Lovelock, *Gaia: A new Look at Life on Earth,* Oxford, UK: Oxford University Press, 2000.

18. Christopher Bamford, "Paradoxical Thoughts on Christ and Sophia in the Human Mystery of the Earth," in this volume.

19. London: Temple Lodge Publishing, 2005.

20. London: Rudolf Steiner Press, 2006.

21. Rudolf Steiner, April 16, 1906, "The Interior of the Earth and Volcanic Eruptions," in *The Interior of the Earth: An Esoteric Study of the Subterranean Spheres,* London: Rudolf Steiner Press, 2006, p. 12.
22. See "Excerpt from a Memoir by Countess Johanna Keyserlingk," in *The Interior of the Earth,* p. 113.
23. Ibid, p. 109. Regarding the subterranean altar of Michael, see Rudolf Steiner's lecture of June 17, 1924, *Agriculture Course: The Birth of the Biodynamic Method,* London: Rudolf Steiner Press, 2005.
24. Ibid, p. 110.
25. Rudolf Steiner, September 23, 1921, lecture one, *Cosmosophy: Cosmic Influences on the Human Being,* vol. 1, Spring Valley, NY: Anthroposophic Press, 1985, pp. 7, 9, 10, 13.
26. "At the beginning of the Saturn evolution (or rather, before it began), there was a single etheric stream for the whole of humankind and for the whole of Earth's evolution. At the very moment when the Saturn evolution started, a split occurred in the cosmic powers.... This duality in the whole of cosmic activity began only with the moment when Saturn began to develop.... The totality of the divine spiritual beings who influenced evolution when the development of the planet Saturn began split in two; thus, we now have one evolutionary stream, which is involved directly in everything that takes place through Saturn, Sun, and Moon evolutions, down to our Earth, and another stream side-by-side with this main one.... Thus, we have indicated two realms of gods: two spiritual realms, one of which plays a direct role in all that takes place successively in the Saturn, Sun, and Moon periods of evolution, the other holding itself aloof, so to speak, and intervening only indirectly....

    "You will get a better idea of this by first looking at the human being. Consider the human soul; it thinks. What does it mean to think? It means bringing about thoughts.... Now, human beings with their thoughts, even as beings of soul, are still at a relatively subordinate stage of world organization. However, the beings we just referred to as gods and divided into two streams are at a far higher stage. Imagine for a moment that we could not only grasp our thought purely as thought, but that the human soul was so strong that its thought could immediately become a being.... Imagine that we could not only think thoughts, but that each thought brought forth a being. In this way, you can understand what takes place within the divine spiritual world. The gods who were living in complete harmony—the perfect unity that existed among them before Saturn—represented themselves; they thought. However, their thoughts were not like human thoughts, which we must call unreal. They were beings; they were other gods. Thus, we have generations of gods whose reality is original, and others who are merely the representations—the *real* ideas—of the gods associated directly with the Saturn, Sun, and Moon evolutions. They are the gods who surround the world sphere in the course of its development through the Saturn, Sun, and Moon evolutions.

"Thus we have two categories of gods: one is the thought world of the other. One of them, in fact, relates to the other as our thoughts relate to our real soul existence. What have we thus far usually called the gods who are merely the thoughts of the others? Owing to certain of their characteristics, we have called them luciferic beings.

"In a sense, what happens in our souls is a complete picture of this macrocosm. Only the pattern prefigured in the macrocosm occurs reversed in us. In our microcosm, we bear a copy of the division between the ranks of the gods, of whom one class is original and the other born out of this original class, existing so that the original gods may represent themselves to themselves. From this, you can see well that there must be a great difference between these two categories of gods. The difference is quite obvious through the fact that our entire self—including all that is unconscious in us, the whole comprehensive self from which our bodily organization has also sprung—derives from the original generation of gods. However, what we experience and what we can span with our everyday consciousness arises from the generation of gods who are only the thoughts of the original gods. Our being comes to us from two sides. Our organization as a whole, with all that is unconscious in us, comes from the original generation of gods. What lies in our awareness comes from the other side, the generation of gods who hover only around the Saturn, Sun, and Moon evolutions. Hence, when we closely examine our own life of ideation, we feel that the idea or mental representation is, in a higher sense, only the youngest daughter, as it were, of a line of gods. We feel the unreality, the merely notional transience, the elusiveness, of our conscious life. This also dawned upon the pupils of the Greek mysteries.... Those Greek pupils became clear that they must disregard their formal consciousness and turn to the ancient gods, also called the gods of the underworld—gods in whose nature Dionysus shared, for only thus would they be able to acquire knowledge of the true human being....

"The fact is that, of the divine stream that hovered over the Saturn, Sun, and Moon evolutions, up to a certain point of time only what I have just described could enter human life. It flowed into human consciousness from outside, so to speak, without human beings descending into their inmost being, the region of the lower gods. Moreover, what flowed inward in this way was incapable of ever reaching true universal reality. It was not possible to reach the true world reality through external knowledge. In order to reach that, it would have been necessary for something to be instilled into what (through the long ages of the Saturn, Sun, and Moon evolutions) had entered our normal consciousness from without—something that was not just the thought life of the subearthly, chthonic deities, but something that was itself a reality" (Rudolf Steiner, August 25, 1911, in *Wonders of the World, Ordeals of the Soul, Revelations of the Spirit*, London: Rudolf Steiner Press, 1963, 145 ff).

27. Rudolf Steiner, March 12, 1909, *Goethe's Secret Revelation and the Riddle of Faust* Whitefish, MT: Kessinger, 2003, pp. 113 ff.

28. Sylvia Francke, *The Tree of Life and the Holy Grail: Ancient and Modern Spiritual Paths and the Mystery of Rennes-le-Château*, London: Temple Lodge, 2007, p. 45, citing Rudolf Steiner's lecture of November 2, 1917, "The Problem of Faust" typescript R.55, Rudolf Steiner House Library, London, pp. 5–6. These concepts explain the mysterious phenomena of the Black Madonnas that appear worldwide. The "blackness" of Rea "is reminiscent of the darkness of ancient Saturn, the primal origins of matter" (Francke, p. 46).

29. See Edward Reaugh Smith, *The Burning Bush: Rudolf Steiner, Anthroposophy, and the Holy Scriptures: Terms & Phrases*, Great Barrington, MA: Anthroposophic Press, 1997, chart I-22, p. 584.

30. See endnote 38.

31. "We have the physical world, the astral world, lower Devachan, and higher Devachan. If the body is thrust down even lower than the physical world, it comes into the subphysical world, the lower astral world, the lower, or evil, level of the lower Devachan, and the lower, or evil, level of the higher Devachan. The evil astral world is the province of Lucifer; the evil lower Devachan is the province of Ahriman; while the evil higher Devachan is the province of the Asuras. When chemical action is driven down beneath the physical plane—into the evil devachanic world—magnetism arises. When light is thrust down into the submaterial—which is today, a stage lower than the material world—electricity arises. When what lives in the Harmony of the Spheres is thrust down even farther, into the province of the Asuras, an even more terrible force—one that cannot remain hidden much longer—is generated." Rudolf Steiner, October 1, 1911, *The Etherization of the Blood*, London: Rudolf Steiner Press, 1985, p. 40.

32. Ibid. See Rudolf Steiner *The Etherization of the Blood.*

33. Rudolf Steiner, January 2, 1920, in *The Light Course,* Great Barrington, MA: Anthroposophic Press, 2001. In another lecture, Steiner connects the egotistical forces pouring up from below with the electrical forces in outer nature and within the human will. "Human beings will mature by being able for a time to develop in the lower ego bearer, through rampant egotism, what is even more harmful.... For those having spiritual insight into world evolution, this electrical age is at the same time a challenge to seek greater spiritual depth, or genuine spiritual deepening. To the force that remains outwardly unknown to sensory observation there must be added the spiritual force in the soul, which lies as deeply hidden as the electrical forces, which also has to be awakened. Consider the mysterious nature of electrical power. Galvani and Volta first drew it out of its secret hiding places. Moreover, what lives in the human soul and is explored by spiritual science also lies hidden. *Both must come together, like North and South poles.* Just as surely as the electrical force, the force hidden in nature, is drawn out, the force hidden in and belonging to the soul that is sought by spiritual science will also be drawn forth." See lecture of September 30, 1916, *Geisteswissenschaftliche Erläuterungen zu Goethes "Faust"* (Spiritual-scientific explanations to Goethe's *Faust*), bdn., band 2, *Das Faust-Problem* (GA 273).

34. Rudolf Steiner, September 18, 1924: *Broken Vessels: The Spiritual Structure of Human Frailty,* lecture 11, Great Barrington, MA: Anthroposophic Press, 2003, pp. 153ff.

35. For this and the previous quote, see Rudolf Steiner *The Foundation Stone Meditation,* London: Rudolf Steiner Press, 2005.

36. Rudolf Steiner, *Verses and Meditations,* London: Rudolf Steiner Press, 1961, p. 58.

37. From Steiner's lecture of April 16, 1906, op cit.

38. "When one force begins to work in the universe another force, opposed to the first, arises at the same moment. Everything that happens in the world is subject to the law of polarity." See Adolf Arenson's essay "The Interior of the Earth" in *The Interior of the Earth: An Esoteric Study of the Subterranean Spheres,* London: Rudolf Steiner Press, 2006, p. 94; see also Sigismund von Gleich, *The Transformation of Evil: And the Subterranean Spheres of the Earth,* London: Temple Lodge, 2005.

39. Rudolf Steiner: December 5, 1920. "Light and Darkness: Two World Entities," *Colour,* London: Rudolf Steiner Press, 2005, pp. 87 ff.

CHAPTER 1: EVIL, OUR DANCE PARTNER...

1. Beatrice Portinari (real name Bice di Folco Portinari, 1266–1290) was a woman who lived in Florence, Italy, the muse for Dante Alighieri's *Vita Nuova*. She also appears as his guide in *Paradise*, the last book of *The Divine Comedy*, and in the last four canti of *Purgatory*. There, Beatrice takes over as guide from the Latin poet Virgil because Virgil, a pagan, cannot enter Paradise and because, being the incarnation of beatific love as her name implies, it is she who leads into the Beatific Vision. For Dante, Beatrice is the symbol for Divine Love.

2. Rudolf Steiner, "Evil and the Power of Thought," *The Golden Blade*, London: Hawthorn Press, 1955, pp. 1–11.

3. Adam Bittleston, "Christopher Fry and the Riddle of Evil," *The Golden Blade,* Forest Row, UK: Hawthorne Press, 1955, pp. 12–22.

4. Rudolf Steiner, *Autobiography: Chapters in the Course of My Life*, Great Barrington, MA: SteinerBooks, 2006.

5. Jakob Streit, *And There Was Light*, Fair Oaks, CA: AWSNA Publications, 2006, pp. 7–9.

6. Rudolf Steiner, *Lucifer and Ahriman*, London: Rudolf Steiner Press, 1976.

7. Barry Fell, *America BC: Ancient Settlers in the New World*, New York: Simon & Schuster, Pocket Books, 1989.

8. Rudolf Steiner, *Founding a Science of the Spirit*, London: Rudolf Steiner Press, 1999.

9. The following is a brief road map of life exercises based on spiritual science:

    1. Discipline of the thinking-through exercises in strengthening concentration (see Steiner's *Practical Training in Thought*).

    2. Nourishment of the feeling life through exercises supporting compassion; studies of art, and/or music, drama, poetry, eurythmy, and so forth (see Steiner's "Six Basic Exercises").

    3. Guidance of the will life through painting, through will exercises including modeling, wood and stone carving, knitting, and so forth (see Steiner's basic exercises in *How to Know Higher Worlds*).

    4. Attention to one's own moral development (also called life guidance)—the taking on of oneself to develop moral intuitions and ethical individualism (see Rudolf Steiner's *Intuitive Thinking as a Spiritual Path: A Philosophy of Freedom*).

    5. Interest in the social life—the effort needed to see the striving forces in other people, to become aware of the "spiritual essence"

in the other person (see the *Mysteries of Social Encounter* by Dieter Bruell and the "Social Ethic" by Steiner).

6. Cultivation of real interest and love for the world and nature.
7. Regular meditative activity; see Steiner's *How to Know Higher Worlds* and Jörgen Smit's *Steps toward Knowledge Which the Seeker of the Spirit Must Take.*
8. The study to understand the sevenfold nature of the human being.
    1. Physical body, the temple of our being
    2. Etheric body, the realm of formative forces
    3. Astral body, the expression of pleasure and pain
    4. "I," the individual center or guiding point of our being
    5. Spirit self, the urge to do things better
    6. Life spirit, the recognition of one's own destiny
    7. Spirit body, the attainment of a complete and pure form
    (see Steiner's *The Foundations of Human Experience*)
    An example of working with the four lower bodies can be found in the field of education:
    - The *etheric body* of the teacher (through order and regulation) works on the *physical body* of the child.
    - The *astral body* of the teacher (through expressions of joy, sorrow, art, tragedy) works on the *etheric body* of the child and balances the life forces.
    - The "I" of the teacher (the bearer of ideals) works on the *astral body* of the child. The teacher must fire the imaginations of the children.
9. Creation of a sense of joy every day; this inner joy comes from the discovery of the core essence that rules our lives.
10. Development of an interest in esoteric Christianity; see Steiner's *Christianity as Mystical Fact.*

10. Rudolf Steiner, "Supersensible Aspects of Historical Research," *Evil: Selected Lectures*, London: Rudolf Steiner Press, 1997.
11. Ibid., p. 133.
12. No pertinent discussion of evil can disregard the Holocaust. While living in Germany during my twenties, I met an amazing older woman, radiant in her being and gracious in her manner. While on a walk she shared some of her biography with me as a response to my questions about the serenity of her being that she projected to others.

    As a young girl, she lived in Potsdam outside of Berlin. Her father was a biodynamic farmer who was recognized for his diligence to work. The farm was a model of efficiency and order. One day during breakfast he announced that this particular day was to be a family holiday. After the necessary chores with the animals, a great picnic was to be held at the farm pond under the spreading oak tree. Laughter, swimming, games, and close family conversation echoed under the bright autumn sky.

Nine days following there was a loud banging on the door during the night and a truck full of uniformed soldiers from the Gestapo escorted the family to a concentration camp where they were incarcerated. A strong young girl, my new friend was separated from her family and placed on work detail. One of her jobs was to extract the gold from the teeth of dead people before they were cremated. While doing this task she came upon the bodies of her parents and aunts.

I asked her about the rage she must have felt at this unbelievable evil. She acknowledged it and went on to tell me that her desire to live was so strong that she was forced to contain it. I asked her how she could have possibly managed that, and she explained that she endured by repeatedly recalling the imagination of the day they had all stopped their regular tasks and had the picnic. Many times a day she would withdraw inward into this cherished memory, feel the warmth of the sun, the joy of her family, and the goodness they experienced. In this way she survived a tremendous evil.

13. Discovered in 1998, "dark energy" refers to the continued and speeded-up expansion of the universe. This energy is the opposite of gravity. Ironically, dark energy causes expansion because it has strong negative pressure. If you were to drop this book and it soared upward toward the ceiling, it would signal an unexpected force to you. In the same way the galaxies' accelerated expansion signaled the presence of an unknown force to astrophysicists. They named this force "dark energy" because it cannot be seen and remains in the dark. In the standard model of cosmology, dark energy currently accounts for almost three-quarters of the total energy of the universe.

See "The Cosmic Triangle: Revealing the State of the Universe" in *Science*, May 28, 1999.

14. Ibid., p. 94.

15. Sigismund von Gleich, *The Transformation of Evil*, London: Temple Lodge, p. 7, 2005.

16. Rudolf Steiner, *The Interior of the Earth*, London: Rudolf Steiner Press, 2006, p. 103.

17. Wolfgang von Goethe, *Faust* 1, scene 2, lines 775–80.

18. Rudolf Steiner, *The Interior of the Earth*, London: Rudolf Steiner Press, 2006, p. 103.

19. David Mitchell, "The Etheric Geography of North America," in *The Riddle of America*, edited by John Wulsin, Fair Oaks, CA: AWSNA, 2001, pp. 21–54.

This chapter explores, in an imaginative manner, the physical geography, morphology, and resultant culture of North America. There are practical exercises (pp. 49–52) that anyone can take on to deepen a connection with where one lives to give one a "sense of place."

20. Rudolf Steiner, "Rosicrucian Training, The Interior of the Earth, Earthquakes and Volcanoes," September 4, 1906.

21. Kees Zoeteman, *Gaiasophy: The Wisdom of the Living Earth*, Hudson, NY: Lindesfarne Press, 1991.

22. See the *Waldorf Science Newsletter*, vol. 13, no. 23, winter 2007, AWSNA.

23. Fritjof Capra, *The Tao of Physics*, Berkeley: Shambhala Publications, 1975.

24. Chet Raymo, *Science Musings*, Sept. 17, 2006, http://sciencemusings.com/2006/09/through-glass-darkly.html.

25. James Lovelock, *Gaia, A New Look at Life on Earth*, New York: Norton, 2000.

26. http://soundmedicine.iu.edu/archive/2003/quiz/humanWorth.html.

27. David Mitchell, "The Teaching of Science," Wilton, NH: Research Institute for Waldorf Education, *Research Bulletin 9*, vol. 2, 2004.

The steps toward phenomenological thinking are: (1) Stimulation of the senses; (2) Astute observation; (3) Rigorous training in thinking; (4) Allowance for extended periods of "not knowing" while inwardly listening; (5) Phenomenological thinking.

First, the phenomena are carefully observed. Second, the rigors and the laws of thinking as well as previously gained concepts in science are considered and the phenomena are contemplated. Third, everything up to now is laid to rest, the mind is cleared, and the phenomena themselves are allowed to speak. The student quietly observes what comes forward while keeping the mind from straying. Finally, the student will write what the phenomena reveals in his life of thought. This activity opens one up to new possibilities.

This type of thinking is freed from the senses and allows the universe to speak through to the individual. It is a type of thinking that is truly moral and can be the fertile ground for the "new" science of the twenty-first century.

28. Op cit, p. 6.

29. Sir George Trevelyan, "An Archive of His Life and Work," http://www.sirgeorgetrevelyan.org.uk/tht-death.html.

30. *Scientific American,* October 1997.

31. www.oregonstate.edu/dept/ncs/newsarch/2003/Dec03/bacteria.htm.

32. www.space.com/searchforlife/seti_rocks_030731.html.

33. Bill Bryson, *A Short History of Nearly Everything,* New York: Broadway Books, 2003, pp. 214–215; and http://scsc.essortment.com/projectmohole_rdry.htm.

34. http://jersey.uoregon.edu/~mstrick/AskGeoMan/geoQuerry8.html.

35. www.sciencedaily.com/releases/2006/06/060603092903.htm.

36. Rudolf Steiner, *The Occult Movement in the Nineteenth Century,* lecture 9, London: Rudolf Steiner Press, 1992.

37. Rudolf Steiner, *The Interior of the Earth,* p. 79.

38. Rudolf Steiner, *Founding a Science of the Spirit,* London: Rudolf Steiner Press, 1999.

39. For further information refer to the *The Leading Edge,* the journal of the American Society of Exploration Geophysicists.

40. Rudolf Steiner, *Founding a Science of the Spirit.*

41. See both Rudolf Steiner's *The Interior of the Earth,* pp. 3–18, 21–23, 25–27, 30–32, 96–101, and Sigismund von Gleich's *The Transformation of Evil,* pp. 37–40 for the sources of this information.

42. The Mandelbrot set is a set of points in the complex plane that forms a fractal. Mathematically, the Mandelbrot Set can be defined as the set of complex c values for which the orbit of 0 under iteration of the quadratic map $x2 + c$ remains bounded.

43. Rudolf Steiner, *Anthroposophical Leading Thoughts: Anthroposophy as a Path of Knowledge: The Michael Mystery,* London: Rudolf Steiner Press, 1973.

44. Rudolf Steiner, *The Interior of the Earth,* p. 49.

45. Although I admit to being somewhat skeptical of some of the commercial applications to curing pain with magnets, there is a positive study published in the November 1997 issue of *Archives of Physical Medicine and Rehabilitation.* Investigators at the University of Houston taped half-inch magnets to the sore spots of twenty-nine people with post-polio pain and attached identical but fake magnets to a comparison group of twenty-one patients. Neither set of patients knew who was getting the real magnets.

    All the patients were asked to rate their pain on a scale of one to ten, with ten being the most severe. Those wearing the real magnets reported a reduction in pain from a level of 9.6 to 4.4. But the twenty-one people treated with sham magnets said their pain dropped only from 9.9 to 8.4.

How might magnets produce such an effect? Some proponents suggest that magnets boost circulation, bringing more blood and nutrients to the targeted area. That's the theory advanced by Ted Zablotsky, M.D., President of BioFlex Medical Magnetics, a firm that sells magnets for medical uses.

The lead researcher from the University of Houston study, family physician Carlos Vallbona, M.D., raised a different possibility. "It's possible that the magnetic energy affects the pain receptors in the joints or muscles or lowers the sensation of pain in the brain," he said. But the bottom line is that no one understands how magnets could act as medicine. "We do not have a clear explanation for the significant and quick pain relief observed by the patients in our study," Vallbona said.

46. Adapted and borrowed from John Davy's "Man and the Underworld," *The Golden Blade*, 1980, pp. 45–60.

47. George W. Bush, State of the Union Address, January 31, 2006, available from www.whitehouse.gov/news/releases/2006/01/20060131-10. html, Internet, accessed February 1, 2006.

48. Owen Barfield, "The Time Philosophy of Rudolf Steiner," *The Golden Blade*, 1955, p. 76.

49. This quotation, from Goethe (quoted in "Cellular Politics" by Everett Just and Richard B. Goldschmidt in *The Biology of the Cell Surface*, University of Pennsylvania Press, Philadelphia. 1988, pp. 7–8) uses the same language to describe the nucleus and cortex of the cell.

50. Rudolf Steiner, *Anthroposophical Leading Thoughts*, letter of April 12, 1925.

51. Friedrich Benesch, *Easter*, Edinburgh: Floris Books, 1978, p. 13.

CHAPTER 2: AS ABOVE, SO BELOW...

1   *Warmth Course* (14 lectures, Stuttgart, March 1–14, 1924, CW 321), Spring Valley, NY: Mercury Press, 1988; *Agriculture Course: The Birth of the Biodynamic Method* (8 lectures, Kobierzyce, Poland, June 7–16, 1924, CW 327), London: Rudolf Steiner Press, 2005.

2. The "Michael Letters" are a part of Rudolf Steiner's *Anthroposophical Leading Thoughts: Anthroposophy as a Path of Knowledge: The Michael Mystery* (written 1923–1925, CW 26), London: Rudolf Steiner Press, 1998.

CHAPTER 3: SUBNATURE...

1. The sidereal zodiac is the original zodiac of the Babylonians, Egyptians, Greeks and Hindus. It is defined in my book *History of the Zodiac*, San Rafael, CA: Sophia Academic Press, 2007.

2. Robert Powell, *Hermetic Astrology II: Astrological Biography*, Sophia Foundation Press, 2007, pp. 327–353. This hardback edition is a reprint of the 1989 paperback edition, which is available from the Sophia Foundation of North America in Palo Alto, CA: http://www.sophiafoundation.org.

3. Robert Powell, *Chronicle of the Living Christ*, Great Barrington, MA: SteinerBooks, 1996, p. 415.

4. Rudolf Steiner, *The Evolution of Consciousness*, London: Rudolf Steiner Press, 1966, pp. 185–186.

5. Robert Powell, *History of the Planets* (San Diego: Astro Communications Services, 1989), p. 4.

6. See the diagram of Christ's ascent and descent in my book *The Christ Mystery*, Fair Oaks, CA: Rudolf Steiner College Press, 1999, p. iv.

7. Rudolf Steiner, *The True Nature of the Second Coming*, Rudolf Steiner Press, 1971, lecture January 25, 1910.

8. See Robert Powell, *Christian Hermetic Astrology: The Star of the Magi and the Life of Christ*, SteinerBooks, 1998, pp. 271–292; and Robert Powell, *The Christ Mystery*, Rudolf Steiner College Press, 1999, pp. 57–126.

9. From the official website of the Los Alamos Laboratory: http://www.lanl.gov/history/atomicbomb/index.shtml

10. There is an extraordinary mystery here: that the entrance into the atomic age coincided with the onset of Christ's second coming. This onset began on (or around) April 25, 1932, and just twelve days previously, on April 13, 1932, there took place the disintegration of the nuclei of lithium through bombardment by artificially generated protons, first carried out by John Cockcroft and Ernest Walton at the Cavendish Laboratory, Cambridge.

11. Rudolf Steiner, *At the Gates of Spiritual Science*, Rudolf Steiner Press, 1970, lecture of September 4, 1906. See also Rudolf Steiner, *The Interior of the Earth*, Rudolf Steiner Press, 2006.

12. Rudolf Steiner, *Rosicrucianism Renewed: The Unity of Art, Science, and Religion*, SteinerBooks, 2007.

13. Rudolf Steiner, *The Four Seasons and the Archangels*, Rudolf Steiner Press, 1968, p. 66.

14. Johanna and Adalbert von Keyserlingk, *The Birth of a New Agriculture*, London: Temple Lodge Press, 1999, pp. 84–86.

15. Rudolf Steiner, *The Christ Impulse and the Development of Ego Consciousness*, Great Barrington, MA: Anthroposophic Press, 1976, pp. 112–113.

16. Further aspects of Christ's path to the Mother are described in Robert Powell, *The Most Holy Trinosophia*, Steiner Books, 2000.

17. See note 10.

18. Two further examples are Professor Joseph Rotblat and Group Captain Leonard Cheshire, who witnessed the A-bomb explosion over Nagasaki as Churchill's official observer, and later, following a Christian conversion when someone said to him, "*God is a person and you know it,*" devoted his life to providing proper homes for the disabled (there are now some 265 Cheshire homes in forty-eight different countries around the world).

19. Wolfgang Weihrauch, "Natas-Satan: Texts Spoken Backwards on Rock Albums," *Flensburger Heft*, no. 19 (on the theme of music), Flensburg, Germany, 1988, pp. 167–173.

20. "Asclepius, Book III," *Hermetica*, vol. 1, Boulder: Shambhala, 1982, p. 335.

21. Jessica Locke Del Greco, "LSD Research: An Overview," http://mindmined.com/public_library/nonfiction/jessica_locke_del_greco_LSD_research.html.

22. The same cruelty is apparent in the Chinese annexation of Tibet, in contradistinction to the boundless compassion of the Mahayana Buddhism of the Dalai Lama and the Tibetan Buddhists.

23. Rudolf Steiner, *Cosmic and Human Metamorphoses*, Blauvelt, NY: Garber, 1989, lecture of February 27, 1917.

24. This quote by Rudolf Steiner is translated from Werner Schäfer's book, *Rudolf Steiner über die technischen Bild- und Tonmedien*, Bremen, Germany: Verein für Medienforschung und Kulturförderung, 1999, p. 12. Translated by Robert Powell.

25. Shakespeare, *The Merchant of Venice*, act IV, scene 1.

26. Rudolf Steiner, *At the Gates of Spiritual Science*, Rudolf Steiner Press, 1970, pp. 140–141. See also Rudolf Steiner, *The Interior of the Earth*, Rudolf Steiner Press, 2006, pp. 32–33.

27. Ibid.

28. This is the *Parsifal question*, so called because, in the Grail story of *Parzival* by Wolfram von Eschenbach, it was the question that Parsifal put to his ailing uncle Amfortas, who was healed as a result of the asking of this question.

29. Rudolf Steiner, *The Book of Revelation and the Work of the Priest*, Rudolf Steiner Press, 1998, p. 149.

30. Judith von Halle, *Das Abendmahl* ("The Last Supper"), Dornach, Switzerland: Verlag am Goetheanum, 2006, pp. 103–106.

31. "Considerations on the Glorious Stigmata of St. Francis" in *The Little Flowers of St. Francis*, book 2, chapter 9, London, 1963, pp. 129–130.

32. Rudolf Steiner, *The Book of Revelation and the Work of the Priest*, Rudolf Steiner Press, 1998, pp. 154–156.

33. See the following articles in the *Christian Star Calendar 2006*, Sophia Foundation of North America, 2005, pp. 3–14, 26–32; Robert Powell, "Zoroastrian Roots of Star Wisdom"; Wain Farrants, "The Continuing Influence of the Grand Conjunction of 1962: An Imagination for the 21st Century," See also the *Christian Star Calendar 2007*, Sophia Foundation Press, 2006, pp. 33–39; Wain Farrants, "The Reign of Antichrist: the Unlawful Prince of the World."

34. Judith von Halle, *Und wäre Er nicht auferstanden...*, Verlag am Goetheanum, 2005, p. 104 (English translation, *And If He Had Not Been Raised...: The Stations of Christ's Path to Spirit Man*, London: Temple Lodge, 2007).

35. Rudolf Steiner, *Karmic Relationships*, vol. 2, Rudolf Steiner Press, 1956, pp. 248–249, 254.

36. Robert Powell, "The Coming of the Kalki Avatar," *Christian Star Calendar 2002*, pp. 12–14.

37. Robert Powell, *Hermetic Astrology I: Astrology and Reincarnation*, Sophia Foundation Press, 2007, pp. 58–66. This hardback edition is a reprint of the 1987 paperback edition, which is available from the Sophia Foundation of North America in Palto Alto, CA: http://www.sophiafoundation.org.

38. The year 814 was also the start of the period of the Archangel Raphael (814–1169) connected with the 355-year rhythm of the planet Mercury and this was the time of the founding of the Mysteries of the Holy Grail associated with the figure of Parzival, whom Rudolf Steiner brings into connection with the time of Charlemagne.

39. Rudolf Steiner, *Background to the Gospel of St. Mark*, Rudolf Steiner Press, 1968, p. 153.

40. Robert Powell, *The Most Holy Trinosophia*, pp. 110–121.

41. Rudolf Steiner, "Vom goldenen Kalb" (lecture "Concerning the Golden Calf" held in Berlin on March 22, 1912; *Aus den Inhalten der esoterischen Stunden*, vol. 2, pp. 352.

42. Harrie Salman, *Die Heilung Europas*, Schaffhausen, Switzerland: Novalis Verlag, 1999, p. 14.

43. Rudolf Steiner, *The Book of Revelation and the Work of the Priest,* Rudolf Steiner Press, 1998, p. 231.

44. *Shoreline* (1991), pp. 25–52. A revised version of this article was published as chapter 3 in my book *The Christ Mystery,* Rudolf Steiner College Press, 1999.

45. Jesaiah Ben Aharon, *The Spiritual Event of the Twentieth Century: The Occult Significance of the 12 Years from 1933–1945 in the Light of Spiritual Science,* Temple Lodge Press, 1993, p. 32.

46. Ibid., p. 46.

47. Rudolf Steiner, *Rosicrucainism Renewed: The Unity of Art, Science, and Religion,* SteinerBooks, 2007; includes the Seven Apocalyptic Seals drawn by Clara Rettich, based on Steiner's designs.

48. Robert Powell, "Sophia and Venus," *Christian Star Calendar 2004,* pp. 7–14.

49. Robert Powell, *Hermetic Astrology I: Astrology and Reincarnation,* pp. 307–328.

Chapter 3: Postscript

1. David Tresemer with Robert Schiappacasse, *Star Wisdom and Rudolf Steiner* (Great Barrington, MA: Steiner Books, 2007) is a fruit of the work of the Boulder astrosophical research group, especially of David Tresemer's research into the significance of each degree of the zodiac expressed in images. Another fruit is the book *Signs in the Heaven: A Message for Our Times* by William Bento, David Tresemer, and Robert Schiappacasse, Hygiene, CO: Chapbooks, 2000.

2. Rudolf Steiner, *Christ at the Time of the Mystery of Golgotha and Christ in the Twentieth Century,* London: Rudolf Steiner Press, 1966, pp. 32–33. An entire paragraph from the German version of this lecture (held in London on May 2, 1913) was omitted from the English edition and has therefore been translated [by RP] and inserted here. The German original of this paragraph is in the volume *Vorstufen zum Mysterium von Golgatha* (Dornach, Switzerland: Rudolf Steiner Verlag, 1990), pp. 46–47.

3. My Ph.D. thesis has been published under the title *History of the Zodiac* (San Rafael, CA: Sophia Academic Press, 2007).

4. Rudolf Steiner, *Christ at the Time of the Mystery of Golgotha and Christ in the Twentieth Century,* London: Rudolf Steiner Press, 1966, pp. 34–35.

5. Rudolf Steiner, *From Jesus to Christ,* London: Rudolf Steiner Press, 1973, p. 46.

6. Robert Powell, *Chronicle of the Living Christ* (Great Barrington, MA: Steiner Books, 1996), p. 455. In the English edition, this figure is given incorrectly as 1:53 trillion, which has been corrected to 1:435 billion in the German and Italian editions.
7. Rudolf Steiner, *Mysterienwahrheiten und Weihnachtsimpulse* ("Mystery truths and the impulses of Christmas"), lecture of December 23, 1917 (GA 180). This lecture is entitled *"Et incarnatus est."* GA refers to the number in the Complete Works (German edition) of Rudolf Steiner's works.
8. Ibid., lecture of December 26, 1917.
9. Ibid., lecture of December 23, 1917, entitled *"Et incarnatus est."*
10. See the diagram in my book *The Christ Mystery* (Fair Oaks, CA: Rudolf Steiner College Press, 1999), p. iv.
11. Rudolf Steiner, *The Course of My Life,* New York: Anthroposophic Press, 1951, p. 276; currently published as *Autobiography: Chapters in the Course of My Life, 1861–1907,* Great Barrington, MA: SteinerBooks, 2006.
12. Rudolf Steiner, *From the History and Contents of the First Section of the Esoteric School 1904–1914,* Great Barrington, MA: SteinerBooks, 1998, pp. 369–370.
13. Rudolf Steiner, *Karmic Relationships*, vol. 1, lecture of February 17, 1924, London: Rudolf Steiner Press, 1972, pp. 41–42.
14. Rudolf Steiner, *From Jesus to Christ*, London: Rudolf Steiner Press, 1973, pp. 46–47.
15. Rudolf Steiner, *Concerning the History and Content of the Higher Degrees of the Esoteric School, 1904–1914,* Agyll, Scotland: Etheric Dimensions Press, 2005, pp. 369–370 (also published as *From the History and Contents of the First Section of the Esoteric School 1904–1914,* Great Barrington, MA: SteinerBooks, 2008).
16. Ibid., p. 395, footnote 2.
17. Rudolf Steiner, *The True Nature of the Second Coming*, London: Rudolf Steiner Press, 1971, lecture of January 25, 1910, in which Steiner indicates the importance of the years 1933, 1935, 1937.
18. See diagram in my book *The Christ Mystery,* Fair Oaks, CA: Rudolf Steiner College Press, 1999, p. iv.
19. Ibid.

Chapter 5: Transforming Subearthly...

1. See Rudolf Steiner, *Eurythmy as Visible Music,* London: Rudolf Steiner Press, 1977, and *Eurythmy as Visible Speech,* London: Rudolf Steiner Press, 1984.
2. Rudolf Steiner, August 26, 1923. *A Lecture on Eurythmy,* London: Rudolf Steiner Press, 1967, p. 8.
3. "The human being is a bridge / Between the past and the existence of the future." Rudolf Steiner, December 24, 1920, *Truth-Wrought-Words,* Hudson, NY: Anthroposophic Press, 1983, p. 143.
4. "He [Rudolf Steiner] said, moreover, that he would need this new art of movement if, for example, matters were to be introduced to people that are so profound that they could not be expressed in words at all." Rudolf Steiner speaking to Clara Smits, quoted by Sergei O. Prokofieff in the introduction to his chapter 4, "The Foundation Stone Mediation in Eurythmy (An Esoteric Contemplation)" in *May Human Beings Hear It!* (London: Temple Lodge Publishing, 2004), p. 261.
5. All are contained in the volume entitled *Curative Eurythmy,* London: Rudolf Steiner Press, 1983.
6. Rudolf Steiner, *Theosophy,* New York: Anthroposophic Press, 1971, p. 36.
7. Rudolf Steiner, *Occult Science: An Outline,* London: Rudolf Steiner Press, 1969, 2005.
8. Rudolf Steiner, citation not available.
9. The forces of human and animal reproduction originate in the ninth layer of the subearthly spheres. See Rudolf Steiner, *The Interior of the Earth,* London: Rudolf Steiner Press, 2006, p. 13.
10. Rudolf Steiner, *Eurythmy as Visible Speech*, p. 224. The comment is summarized from a verse. "I seek within me / The Strength of Creative Working / The Power of Creative Life. / It tells me / The heavy weight of Earth / Through the Word of my feet. / It tells me / The forming power of the Air / Through the Singing of my hands. / It tells me / The strength of Heaven's Light / Through the Thinking of my Head. / So the World in Man / Speaks, sings, thinks."
11. Rudolf Steiner, April 14, 1921, *Curative Eurythmy*, p. 33.
12. Ibid. p. 27.
13. "We can say we are approaching nearer to free will only when we have succeeded in mastering the influences of Lucifer and Ahriman, and we can obtain the mastery over the luciferic and ahrimanic influences only by means of knowledge (cognition)." Rudolf Steiner, May 28, 1910, *Manifestations of Karma,* London: Rudolf Steiner Press, 1969, p. 250.

14. The "cardinal organs" and their planetary complements are: Venus, kidneys; Mars, gall bladder; Mercury, lungs; Jupiter, liver; Saturn, spleen; Moon, brain and reproductive organs; and Sun, the heart.

15. Rudolf Steiner, quoted by Karl Koenig in *Earth and Man,* Wyoming, RI: Bio-Dynamic Literature: 1982, p. 270.

16. Both quotes are from Rudolf Steiner, *Theosophy,* p. 24.

17. Ibid. p. 30.

18. Dr. Kirchner-Bockholt, *Fundamental Principles of Curative Eurythmy,* London: Rudolf Steiner Press, 1977, p. 35.

19. Rudolf Steiner, *Curative Eurythmy* op cit, p. 55.

20. Rudolf Steiner, April 16, 1921, *Curative Eurythmy* op cit, p. 55.

21. Rudolf Steiner, September 4, 1906, *The Interior of the Earth* op cit, pp. 32–34.

CHAPTER 6: THE MINERAL EARTH...

1. Rudolf Steiner, November 22, 1906, *The Origin of Suffering; the Origin of Evil, Illness and Death,* North Vancouver: Steiner Book Centre, 1980, pp. 20, 21.

2. "Why should a triangle have only three angles? Perhaps a god might take a triangle not having three angles? There would be just as little sense in thinking of a triangle without three angles, as in supposing that the gods might have created freedom without the possibility of evil and suffering. Just as three angles are necessary to a triangle, so the possibility of evil...is necessary to freedom." Rudolf Steiner, November 14, 1911, *The Inner Realities of Evolution,* London: Rudolf Steiner Publishing Company, 1953, p. 50.

3. Ibid.

4. Rudolf Steiner: December 29, 1922, *Man and the World of Stars: The Spiritual Communion of Mankind,* Great Barrington, MA; Anthroposophic Press, 1963, p. 141. For an in-depth discussion of necessity and freedom and how they interact within human nature see four lectures of Rudolf Steiner, published as *Necessity and Freedom,* Anthroposophic Press, 1988.

5. No evil is ascribed to the physical world as such, which acts to shut off human consciousness from the spirit. "Evil cannot be explained in physical terms since it is in fact a misuse of forces which belong to the world of spirit!...*I would like to emphasize that those who believe that evil can be ascribed to the entanglement of our soul in the material world are mistaken. It is important to realize that the spiritual qualities and capacities of the human being are the source of evil.*"

Rudolf Steiner: January 15, 1914, "Evil Illumined through the Science of the Spirit," in *Evil: Selected Lectures*, London: Rudolf Steiner Press, 1997, p. 31.

6. Adolf Arenson, "The Interior of the Earth" found in *The Interior of the Earth: an Esoteric Study of the Subterranean Spheres*, Rudolf Steiner Press, 2006, p. 207.

7. Rudolf Steiner, June 13, 1906, *An Esoteric Cosmology*, lecture 17, Blauvalt, NY: Spiritual Science Library, 1987, p. 118.

8. Rudolf Steiner, October 14, 1911, lecture 10 in *From Jesus to Christ*. This translation from citation in Judith von Halle's *And If He Had Not Been Raised*, London: Temple Lodge Publishing, 2007, p. 13.

9. "Christ becomes more and more the Earth Spirit. The true Christian understands the words: 'He who eats my bread treads me underfoot.' He considers the body of the Earth to be the body of Christ. The Earth as a planetary body is the body of Christ; of course at present this is only at its beginning. Christ still has to become the Earth Spirit. He will unite Himself fully with the Earth, and when the Earth later unites with the Sun the great Earth-Spirit Christ will be the Sun Spirit." Rudolf Steiner, June 30, 1908, lecture 12, *The Apocalypse of John*, Anthroposophic Press, 1977, p. 221.

10. For these and further characterizations of the topography of the Holy Land see Emil Bock's *The Three Years*, London: Christian Community Press, 1969.

11. "Our cosmos" refers to the cosmic system encircled and enclosed by our zodiac, which began with ancient Saturn and shall culminate with the future Vulcan evolution.

12. Rudolf Steiner, January 9, 1912, "Esoteric Studies: Cosmic Ego and Human Ego: the Nature of Christ the Resurrected" (printed privately for the members of the College of Spiritual Science at the Goetheanum).

13. Four lectures in 1906 and one lecture in 1909, collected in the volume *The Interior of the Earth: An Esoteric Study of the Subterranean Spheres*, Rudolf Steiner Press, 2006.

14. Rudolf Steiner, September 4, 1906, "Rosicrucian Training, the Interior of the Earth, Earthquakes and Volcanoes," found in *The Interior of the Earth: An Esoteric Study of the Subterranean Spheres*, Rudolf Steiner Press, 2006.

15. Ibid., p. 30. See also lecture of January 1, 1909, "Mephistopheles and Earthquakes," ibid., p. 42. "The physical world in these circumstances became like a veil, a thick cover, over the spiritual world. Man could not, nor can he to this day, see directly into the spiritual world...the

entire physical world became like a dense rind closing off the spiritual world."

16. For this and the previous quote "the soul within the soul," see Rudolf Steiner, *Theosophy*, Chapter One, part 4, Anthroposophic Press, 1971, pp. 29, 24.

17. See generally Rudolf Steiner, *An Outline of Esoteric Science*, chapter 6, "Present and Future Evolution of the World and Humanity," Anthroposophic Press, 1996.

18. Rudolf Steiner, October 5 and December 18, 1913, *The Fifth Gospel*, Rudolf Steiner Press, 1968.

19. Rudolf Steiner, October 5, 1913. *The Fifth Gospel*, Rudolf Steiner Press, 1968, p. 96.

20. Ibid., December 18, 1913 p. 157.

21. Or: the will to power, sensuality and addictions generally. The fact of having a physical body means certain iron necessities cannot be overcome at this stage of our evolution.

22. Rudolf Steiner, October 5, 1913. *The Fifth Gospel*, op cit, pp. 97, 98.

23. Rudolf Steiner, October 27, 1919. *The Incarnation of Ahriman*, Rudolf Steiner Press, 2006, pp. 26, 27.

24. Rudolf Steiner, July 2, 1909. *The Gospel of John and its Relation to the Other Gospels*, Anthroposophic Press, 1982, pp. 176 & 177. "Hence we read, not the man's parents have sinned, nor has his own personality—the personality one ordinarily addresses as 'I'; but in a previous incarnation he created the cause of his blindness in this life. He became blind because out of a former life the works of the God within him revealed themselves in his blindness. Jesus Christ points clearly and distinctly to karma—the law of cause and effect.... As he pours His force into the I Am—as thus the exalted divinity of Christ communicates Himself to the divinity in man—the human being receives the force enabling him to heal himself from within. Now Christ has penetrated to the innermost being of the soul. His force has acted upon the eternal individuality of the sick man and strengthened it by causing His own force to appear in the individuality, thereby influencing even the consequences of former incarnations."

25. Valentin Tomberg, *Anthroposophical Meditations on the Old Testament*, Chapter 7, "The Karma of the Israelites," found in *Christ and Sophia*, SteinerBooks, 2006, p. 83.

26. See "Esoteric Conversations" in *The Interior of the Earth: An Esoteric Study of the Subterranean Spheres*, Rudolf Steiner Press, 2006, pp. 112–113. This comports with Steiner's description of "the ninth

layer, which lies immediately around the Earth's center" (page 12 in *The Interior of the Earth*).

27. Judith von Halle, *And If He Had Not Been Raised...*, London: Temple Lodge, 2007, p. 43.

28. For this and the previous three quotes, see Judith von Halle ibid., pp. 78, 79, 87.

29. "My God, my God, why have you forsaken me?" Matthew 27:46.

30. Valentin Tomberg, "The Four Sacrifices of Christ and the Appearance of Christ in the Etheric," lecture 1, in *Christ and Sophia*, SteinerBooks, 2006, pp. 360–361.

    For a different translation and interpretation of the phrase *"Eli, Eli, lama sabachthani"* see Rudolf Steiner's lecture of April 1, 1907, found in *The Christian Mystery*, Anthroposophic Press, 1998, p. 102, where Steiner translates the sentence as "My God, My God, how you have glorified and spiritualized me." See also the commentary of Judith von Halle about this interpretation in *If He Had Not Been Raised*, pp. 66 ff.

31. Tomberg, ibid., p. 361.

32. Ibid., pp. 361, 362.

33. Emil Bock, *The Three Years*, op cit, p. 227.

34. Rudolf Steiner, December 5, 1911, *The Inner Realities of Evolution*, Rudolf Steiner Publishing Company, 1953, p. 80.

35. Ibid., p. 82.

36. Ibid., pp. 84, 85.

37. Rudolf Steiner, December 18, 1913, lecture 7, *The Fifth Gospel*, Rudolf Steiner Press, 2001, p. 218.

38. Ibid., pp. 218.

39. Rudolf Steiner, December 18, 1913, lecture 7 in *The Fifth Gospel*, 1968, p. 151.

40. Ibid., 151. Cited sentence is this author's translation of the original German text: *"Wahrhaftig, bedeutender noch als es fur die Menschen war, dass sie den Christus aufnehmen konnten, war es fur die Gotter, dass sie abgeben mussten den Christus und die Erde."* Two other published translations of this sentence are found in the previously quoted editions of *The Fifth Gospel*. In the London 1968 edition, the sentence reads: "In truth it meant even more for the Gods to be obliged to give over the Christ to the Earth than it meant for man to be able to receive Him." In the 2001 edition the sentence reads: "Truly, it was even more important that the gods had to let Christ go, giving him to the Earth, than that humanity was able to receive the Christ."

41. Judith von Halle, op cit, p. 78.
42. Emil Bock, *Kings and Prophets*, chapter 8, Floris Books, 2006, p. 81. Bock continues. "...this casts a light on the Hebrew name of the holy city. Yerushalayim is neither singular nor plural, but a dual form. Even through the name one can perceive that Jerusalem is a twin-formation, a city of duality and cosmic opposites which meet here." The Tyropean Valley (a popularized name of the Hebrew *teraphon*, meaning the tear, or what has been torn) was a deep gorge, or cleft, between Mt. Zion and Mt. Moriah. It had been filled in largely by Solomon (Kings 11:27), but significant remnants of it remained at the time of Christ. Its fissure ran deep into the Earth and emitted volcanic fire, gasses and steam phenomena, and in pre-Solomonic time the gorge appeared as a gateway to hell. Gehenna, the Arabian name for Hell, is still the name of the western border of this gorge, lying outside the Old City walls, and was the site of the fire altar of Molech, associated with infernal cults of black magic. Old City Jerusalem is riddled with grottos, caves, corridors and passages in the subterranean rock. The Teraphon Gorge is only the main vein of the whole system of fissures and gaping chasms. The "pools" mentioned in the Bible—Gihon, Bethesda and Siloam, were fed heated, chemically rich waters from the interior depths of the Earth just as natural mineral baths are to this day.
43. Jesus Christ was buried in a cave within the mineral earth. The Nathan Jesus, who ultimately became the Christ Bearer, was born in Bethlehem in a cave within a hillside. The term "manger" used in the Gospel of Saint Luke (chapter 2) refers to a place where animals were sheltered from the weather. The hillside in Bethlehem, comprised of calcareous rock, offered a number of natural caves which were expanded into shelters for both man and beast. Thus, the picture of the Christ Child surrounded by various animals may well be correct; the image of a wooden "manger" or human-made structure typically found in churches or in public spaces is incorrect. The Grotto of the Nativity may still be visited today by descending a staircase within the Nativity Church in Bethlehem and entering a network of tunnels and caves, one of which was the scene of the birth of the Nathan Jesus.
44. Emil Bock, *The Three Years* op cit, p. 229.
45. Judith von Halle, op cit, p. 78.
46. Ibid., p. 79.
47. Rudolf Steiner, *An Outline of Esoteric Science*, Anthroposophic Press, 1997, p. 274.
48. Judith von Halle op cit, pp. 82, 83.

49. The term *subconscious* is preferred over *unconscious*, as clearly it is a realm of consciousness and one that lies below, or "sub," our ordinary day consciousness.

50. Judith von Halle, op cit, pp. 84, 85.

51. The full quote is "I have been crucified with Christ, and yet I am alive; yet it is no longer I, but Christ living in me."

52. Sergei O. Prokofieff, *May Human Beings Hear It!* p. 590. Chapter 9: "The Foundation Stone Meditation, Karma, and Resurrection."

53. Ibid., p. 590.

54. The word used by Rudolf Steiner for the seventh Condition of Form is *Vulkan*, German for "volcano." It derives from Vulcan, a smith and the Roman god of fire, volcanoes, blacksmiths, manufacturing in metals, and technology generally. His forge was believed to be located beneath Mt. Etna in Sicily. In the Middle Ages, he became a patron deity of Alchemy. For Paracelsus, he was synonymous with the alchemist-physician's manipulation of fire and the transforming power and creative potential of the invisible "*anthropos*" slumbering within every human being. His counterpart in Greek mythology is Hephaestus. Today the word *vulcanology* still refers to the scientific study of volcanoes and volcanic phenomena.

55. Valentin Tomberg, *Anthroposophical Meditations on the Old Testament*, Chapter 10, "The Babylonian Captivity and the Wisdom of Zoroaster, found in *Christ and Sophia*, SteinerBooks, 2006, pp. 124 ff.

56. Rudolf Steiner, September 4, 1906, "Rosicrucian Training, the Interior of the Earth, Earthquakes and Volcanoes" found in *The Interior of the Earth: an Esoteric Study of the Subterranean Spheres*, Rudolf Steiner Press, 2006, p. 32. The same lecture also published in *At the Gates of Spiritual Science*.

57. Rudolf Steiner, April 10, 1914, *The Inner Nature of Man and Our Life between Death and Rebirth*, Rudolf Steiner Press, 1994, p. 80.

58. Rudolf Steiner; October 11, 1911, lecture 7, *From Jesus to Christ*, Rudolf Steiner Press, 1991, p. 128.

59. Judith von Halle discusses this new concept in several ways in *Secrets of the Stations of the Cross and the Grail Blood*, London: Temple Lodge, 2007, pp. 79–84.

60. Valentin Tomberg, *Anthroposophical Meditations on the New Testament*, Chapter 3, "The Beatitudes in the Sermon on the Mount," in *Christ and Sophia*, p. 195.

61. Rudolf Steiner, September 4, 1906, "Rosicrucian Training, the Interior of the Earth, Earthquakes and Volcanoes," *The Interior of the*

Earth: an Esoteric Study of the Subterranean Spheres, Rudolf Steiner Press, 2006, p. 34.

62. The pineal body, or gland, is a small, pea-sized endocrine gland located between the two hemispheres of the brain near the center of the brain. It is connected with the two-petaled, sixth chakra, also called the "third eye." It is the only brain structure that does not manifest in pairs. While its principal excretion is the hormone melatonin, it also produces a gritty material called "brain sand," which consists chemically of calcium phosphate, calcium carbonate, magnesium phosphate and ammonium phosphate. Quoting Steiner: "It is actually in this mineral deposit that the spirit body is situated. And this immediately shows that what is living cannot harbor the spirit, but that the human spirit needs something non-living as its center point, which means that above all else it must be a spirit with independent life." October 28, 1923, lecture 6, *Man as Symphony of the Creative Word,* Rudolf Steiner Press, 1999, p. 99.

63. When the Lord finished speaking to Moses on Mount Sinai he gave him the two tablets of the Testimony, the tablets of stone inscribed by the finger of God (Exodus 31:18). "Anthroposophy shows us that the two 'stone tablets' were the increasingly mineralized and highly evolved right and left sides of the human brain." Edward Reaugh Smith, *David's Question,* Anthroposophic Press, 2001, p. 100, footnote 5 in the essay "As Above, So Below."

64. Rudolf Steiner, January 9, 1912, "Esoteric Studies: Cosmic 'I' and Human 'I'": The Nature of the Resurrected Christ" (available online at http://steinerbooks.org/research/archive.php). Steiner elaborates that only those beings who were at the stage of developing their fourth principal "could win a physical body for itself on the Earth; for the conditions which the Earth presents for the development of a physical fleshly body can be furnished only in conformity with its entire earthly relationship to a fourth human principal. Only that being could acquire a physical body for himself who wished to develop his fourth principle as 'I.'"

65. Edward Reaugh Smith, *The Burning Bush,* p.19. See also page 111 of the same work.

66. For more on this point see Valentin Tomberg's *Anthroposophic Meditations on the Old Testament,* chapter 8, "Moses," in *Christ and Sophia,* p. 99.

67. Rudolf Steiner, August 6, 1908, *Universe Earth and Man,* Rudolf Steiner Press, 1987, p. 43.

68.   Rudolf Steiner, October 26, 1918, "Supersensible Aspects of Histori-
      cal Research," in *Evil: Selected Lectures by Rudolf Steiner,* Rudolf
      Steiner Press, 1997, pp. 131–134. "Their [the forces of death] real
      and primary function is to endow us with the capacity for developing
      the consciousness soul.... The forces that, as a secondary effect, cause
      our death are really destined to implant, to inject into our evolution
      not the consciousness soul itself, but the capacity to develop the con-
      sciousness soul.... For this to happen we must wholly unite our being
      with the forces of death during the fifth post-Atlantean epoch.... This
      lies within our power. But we cannot unite with the forces of evil in
      the same way.... These forces of evil are active in the universe. We
      must assimilate them, and by so doing we implant in our being the
      seed which enables us to have conscious experience of the spirit....
      They exist to enable people at the stage of the consciousness soul to
      break through to the life of spirit."

69.   Rudolf Steiner, *Goethe's Theory of Knowledge: An Outline of the
      Epistemology of His Worldview,* SteinerBooks, 2008.

70.   "You are Peter, the Rock, and upon this rock I will build my
      church."

71.   Abram/Abraham; Sarai/ Sarah; Jacob/Israel; Naboth/Elijah; Levi/Mat-
      thew; Saul/Paul; Lazarus/John.

72.   See Rudolf Steiner, May 13, 1909, *Reading the Pictures of the Apoca-
      lypse,* Anthroposophic Press, 1993, p. 91.

73.   Rudolf Steiner, *Theosophy* op cit, p. 32.

74.   Ibid., p. 30.

75.   Rudolf Steiner, May 22, 1907, *The Theosophy of the Rosicrucian,*
      Rudolf Steiner Press, 1981, p. 8.

76.   Rudolf Steiner, May 19, 1907; "The Rosicrucian Initiation," in *Rosi-
      crucianism Renewed,* SteinerBooks 2007, p. 284.

77.   Rudolf Steiner, August 23, 1909, lecture 1, *The East in the Light of
      the West,* Spiritual Science Library, 1986, p. 4.

78.   F. W. Zeylmans van Emmichoven quoting Rudolf Steiner in *The
      Foundation Stone,* "Introduction," Rudolf Steiner Press 1963.

79.   The development of the "I" from a passive to an active entity takes
      place through its encounter with evil. See Rudolf Steiner: "Evil is
      the fault proceeding from the ego." *The Lord's Prayer,* Anthro-
      posophic Press, 1970, p. 20. "The path to spiritual perception
      involves a certain kind of martyrdom; for the moment we separate
      out our soul and spirit from the body and begin to be participa-
      tors in the world of spirit, we look back on our life with all its
      imperfections and realize that these follow us like the tail follows

a comet.... So we can see that our very first steps of ascent into the world of spirit are accompanied by an experience of evil and imperfection.... The common trait of all evil is nothing other than egotism." *Evil: Selected Lectures by Rudolf Steiner,* Rudolf Steiner Press, 1997, pp. 24–25.

80. Rudolf Steiner, October 11, 1911, lecture 7, *From Jesus to Christ,* Rudolf Steiner Publishing Company, 1956, p. 94.

CHAPTER 7: PARADOXICAL THOUGHTS...

1. Thomas Aquinas, *Expositio Symboli* 932, cited Hans Urs von Balthasar, *Mysterium Paschale,* Erdmans 1990.

2. From Johanna von Keyserlingk (tr. Christiane Marks), *Erlöste Elemente.* J. C. Mellinger, 1991, unpublished.

3. Barbara Newman (introduction, translation, commentary) *Hildegard of Bingen: Symphonia,* Ithica, NY: Cornell University Press, 1988.

4. See Heinrich Schippperges, *Hildegard of Bingen: Healing and the Nature of the Cosmos,* Princeton: Markus Wiener, 1997.

5. Ibid.

6. Pavel Florensky, tr. Boris Jakim, *The Pillar and Ground of the Truth: An Essay in Orthodox Theodicy in Twelve Letters,* Princeton, NJ: Princeton University Press, 1997.

7. Romans 8.22.

8. Rudolf Steiner, *Anthroposophical Leading Thoughts,* London: Rudolf Steiner Press, 1975.

9. Cited Titus Burckhart, *Alchemy: Science of the Cosmos, Science of the Soul,* Louisville: Fons Vitae, 1997.

10. Rudolf Steiner, *Anthroposophical Leading Thoughts.*

11. Ibid.

12 Ibid.

13. Rudolf Steiner, *The Interior of the Earth,* London: Rudolf Steiner Press, 2006.

14. Rudolf Steiner, October 11, 1911, *From Jesus to Christ,* London: Rudolf Steiner Press, 1978.

15. Ibid.

16. Ibid.

17. Ibid.

18. Ibid.

19. For *The Cave of Treasures,* see http://www.sacred-texts.com/chr/bct/index.htm.

20. "The Gospel of Truth," in *The Nag Hammadi Library*, New York: Harper and Row, 1977.
21. See Werner Forster, *Gnosis: A Selection of Texts I. The Patristic Evidence*, Oxford: Oxford University Press, 1972.
22. Ibid.
23. For this and the previous quote, see Sergei O. Prokofieff, *The Heavenly Sophia and the Being Anthroposophia*, London: Temple Lodge, 1996.
24. Proverbs 8: 22–31.
25. Cited Catherine Keller, *The Face of the Deep: A Theology of Becoming*, London: Routledge 2003.
26. Fulcanelli, *Le Mystère of the Cathedrals*, London: Neville Spearman, 1971.
27. Wisdom of Solomon 7: 25–27.
28. Fulcanelli, *The Dwellings of the Philosophers*, Boulder, CO: Archive Press, 1999.
29. "The New Chemical Light," in *The Hermetic Museum*, vol. II, London: Robinson and Watkins, 1973.
30. Cited Fulcanelli, *The Dwellings of the Philosophers*.
31. Margaret Barker, *The Great High Priest: The Temple Roots of Christian Liturgy*, London: T and T. Clark/Continuum, 2004.
32. *The Book of Enoch*, tr. R. H. Charles, London: SPCK, 1974.
33. Enoch 42:2.
34. Margaret Barker, *The Great Angel: A Study of Israel's Second God*, Louisville, KY: Westminster/John Knox, 1992.
35. "The Gospel of Truth," in *The Nag Hammadi Library*.
36. Sigismund von Gleich, *The Transformation of Evil: And the Subterranean Spheres of the Earth*, London: Temple Lodge, 2006.
37. From *The Ascetical Homilies of Isaac the Syrian*, cited in Hilarion Alfeyev, *The Spiritual World of Isaac the Syrian*, Kalamazoo, MI: Cistercian Publications, 2000.

BIBLIOGRAPHY & RELATED READING

Bamford, Christopher, *An Endless Trace: The Passionate Pursuit of Wisdom in the West*, New Paltz, NY: Codhill Press, 2003.

———, Peter Lamborn Wilson & Kevin Townley, *Green Hermeticism: Alchemy and Ecology*, Great Barrington, MA: Lindisfarne Books, 2007.

Klocek, Dennis, *The Seer's Handbook: A Guide to Higher Perception*, Great Barrington, MA: SteinerBooks, 2005.

———, *Weather & Cosmos*, Fair Oaks, CA: Rudolf Steiner College Press, 1991.

Mead, G. R. S., *Pistis Sophia: A Gnostic Gospel*, Great Barrington, MA: Garber Communications, 1984.

Pogačnik, Marko, *Christ Power and the Earth Goddess: A Fifth Gospel*, Forres, Scotland: Findhorn Press, 1999.

———, *The Daughter of Gaia: Rebirth of the Divine Feminine*, Forres, Scotland: Findhorn Press, 2001.

———, *Earth Changes, Human Destiny: Coping and Attuning with the Help of the Revelation of St. John*, Forres, Scotland: Findhorn Press, 2001.

———, *Healing the Heart of the Earth: Restoring the Subtle Levels of Life*, Forres, Scotland: Findhorn Press, 1998.

———, *Nature Spirits & Elemental Beings: Working with the Intelligence in Nature*, Forres, Scotland: Findhorn Press, 1995.

———, *Sacred Geography: Geomancy: Co-creating the Earth Cosmos*, Great Barrington, MA: Lindisfarne Books, 2008.

———, *Turned Upside Down: A Workbook on Earth Changes and Personal Transformation*, Great Barrington, MA: Lindisfarne Books, 2004.

Powell, Robert, *The Christ Mystery: Reflections on the Second Coming*, Fair Oaks, CA: Rudolf Steiner College Press, 1999.

———, *Christian Hermetic Astrology: The Star of the Magi and the Life of Christ*, Hudson, NY: Anthroposophic Press, 1991.

———, *Christian Star Calendar*, Palo Alto, CA: Sophia Foundation of North America (annual publication).

———, *Chronicle of the Living Christ: The Life and Ministry of Jesus Christ: Foundations of Cosmic Christianity*, Hudson, NY: Anthroposophic Press, 1996.

————, *Divine Sophia, Holy Wisdom*, Palo Alto, CA: Sophia Foundation of North America, 1995.

————, *Hermetic Astrology I: Astrology and Reincarnation*, Palo Alto, CA: Sophia Foundation of North America, 2006.

————, *Hermetic Astrology II: Astrological Biography*, Palo Alto, CA: Sophia Foundation Press, 2007

————, *History of the Zodiac*, Palo Alto, CA: Sophia Foundation of North America, 2006.

————, *The Most Holy Trinosophia: The New Revelation of the Divine Feminine*, Great Barrington, MA: SteinerBooks, 2000.

————, *The Mystery, Biography, and Destiny of Mary Magdalene: Sister of Lazaraus John & Spiritual Sister of Jesus*, Great Barrington, MA: Lindisfarne Books, 2008.

————, *The Sign of the Son of Man in Heaven: Sophia and a New Star Wisdom*, Palo Alto, CA: Sophia Foundation of North America, 2007.

————, *The Sophia Teachings: The Emergence of the Divine Feminine in Our Time*, Great Barrington, MA: Lindisfarne Books, 2007.

Prokofieff, Sergei O., *The Encounter with Evil: And Its Overcoming through Spiritual Science*, London: Temple Lodge, 1999.

————, *The Heavenly Sophia and the Being Anthroposophia*, London: Temple Lodge, 2006.

————, *May Human Beings Hear It!: The Mystery of the Christmas Conference*, London: Temple Lodge, 2004.

————, *The Mystery of John the Baptist and John the Evangelist at the Turning Point of Time: An Esoteric Study*, London, Temple Lodge, 2005.

Steiner, Rudolf. *Anthroposophical Leading Thoughts: Anthroposophy as a Path of Knowledge: The Michael Mystery*, London: Rudolf Steiner Press, 1998.

————, *At Home in the Universe: Exploring Our Suprasensory Nature*, Great Barrington, MA: Anthroposophic Press, 2000.

————, *Evil: Selected Lectures*, London: Rudolf Steiner Press, 1997.

————. *The Fifth Gospel: From the Akashic Record*, London: Rudolf Steiner Press, 1998.

————, *The Incarnation of Ahriman: The Embodiment of Evil on Earth*, London: Rudolf Steiner Press, 2006.

————, *Inner Experiences of Evolution*, Great Barrington, MA: SteinerBooks, 2008.

————. *The Interior of the Earth: An Esoteric Study of the Subterranean Spheres*, London: Rudolf Steiner Press, 2006.

————, *Isis Mary Sophia: Her Mission and Ours,* Great Barrington, MA: SteinerBooks, 2003.

————. *Lucifer and Ahriman*, GA 191, New York: Anthroposophic Press, 1993.

————, *An Outline of Esoteric Science,* Hudson, NY: Anthroposophic Press, 1997.

————, *The Reappearance of Christ in the Etheric: A Collection of Lectures on the Second Coming of Christ,* Great Barrington, MA: SteinerBooks, 2003.

————. *The Spiritual Hierarchies and the Physical World: Zodiac, Planets & Cosmos,* Great Barrington, MA: SteinerBooks, 2008.

Tomberg, Valentin, *Christ and Sophia: Anthroposophic Meditations on the Old Testament, New Testament, and Apocalypse,* Great Barrington, MA: SteinerBooks, 2006.

————, *Lazarus, Come Forth!: Meditations of a Christian Esotericist on the Mysteries of the Raising of Lazarus, the Ten Commandments, the Three Kingdoms & the Breath of Life,* Great Barrington, MA: Lindisfarne Books, 2006.

von Gleich, Sigismund. *The Transformation of Evil: And the Subterranean Spheres of the Earth*, London: Temple Lodge, 2005.

von Halle, Judith, *And If He Had Not Been Raised...: The Stations of Christ's Path to Spirit Man,* London: Temple Lodge, 2007.

About the Authors

 CHRISTOPHER BAMFORD is the editor-in-chief of SteinerBooks and its imprints. A Fellow of the Lindisfarne Association, he has lectured, taught, and written widely on Western spiritual and esoteric traditions, and is the author of *The Voice of the Eagle: The Heart of Celtic Christianity* and *An Endless Trace: the Passionate Pursuit of Wisdom in the West.* He has also translated and edited numerous books, including *Celtic Christianity, Homage to Pythagoras,* and *The Nobel Traveller.*

 DENNIS KLOCEK is an artist, scientist, gardener, and alchemist. He received an MFA with a thesis on Goethe's Color Theory and is director of the Consciousness Studies Program at Rudolf Steiner College in Fair Oaks, California. He is an international lecturer and the author of: *Bio-dynamic Book of Moons; Weather and Cosmology; Drawing from the Book of Nature; Seeking Spirit Vision,* and *The Seer's Handbook.* Dennis is also known as Doc Weather to those who visit his web site www.docweather.com for weather predictions and articles on climatology.

 DAVID MITCHELL has been a Waldorf teacher for thirty-six years. He was a class teacher and one of the founding teachers of the Pine Hill Waldorf School in Wilton, New Hampshire, and then taught Life Sciences, Shakespeare, Geometry, Blacksmithing, Woodworking, and Stone Sculpture in Waldorf High Schools for twenty-six years. He is an adjunct professor at Antioch College and has served as a leader in the Association of Waldorf Schools in North America in various capacities since the 1980s. In 1997, the Amgen Corporation selected him as one of the top two teachers in the state of Colorado. Currently, he is the chairman of publications for AWSNA and serves as the co-director of the Research Institute for Waldorf Education. He has edited scores of books over the years and is the author of *Will-Developed Intelligence*, *Windows into Waldorf*, *The Wonders of Waldorf Chemistry*, *25 Plays*, and *Resources for Waldorf Teachers*.

PAUL V. O'LEARY is a retired real-estate appraiser and lawyer who specialized in forensic appraisals and the appraisal of conservation properties. He has written, taught and lectured extensively on real-estate economics and appraisal for the Appraisal Institute, the Massachusetts Board of Real Estate Appraisers, the American Society of Appraisers, and the Massachusetts and United States Bar Associations, and is a faculty member of the Lincoln Institute for Land Policy in Cambridge, Massachusetts. Paul was instrumental in bringing to publication *The Transformation of Evil* by Sigismund von Gleich (2005) and the collection of Rudolf Steiner's lectures on the subterranean spheres, which appeared under the title *The Interior of the Earth: An Esoteric Study of the Subterranean Spheres* (2006).

MARKO POGAČNIK is an artist and geomancer from Slovenia. Starting from conceptual art and landscape art, he developed lithopuncuture (a method of ecological healing for places and landscapes) in the early 1980s. He designed the cosmogram on the Slovenian coat of arms. His books include *Venice: Discovering a Hidden Pathway*; *Sacred Geography: Geomancy, Co-creating the Earth Cosmos*; *Turned Upside Down: A Workbook on Earth Changes and Personal Transformation*; *Earth Changes, Human Destiny*; *The Daughter of Gaia: Rebirth of the Feminine*; *Nature Spirits & Elemental Beings: Working with Intelligence in Nature*; *Christ Power & the Earth Goddess: A Fifth Gospel*; and *Healing the Heart of the Earth: Restoring the Subtle Levels of Life*.

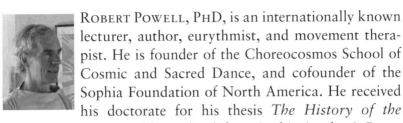

ROBERT POWELL, PHD, is an internationally known lecturer, author, eurythmist, and movement thera- pist. He is founder of the Choreocosmos School of Cosmic and Sacred Dance, and cofounder of the Sophia Foundation of North America. He received his doctorate for his thesis *The History of the Zodiac*, now available as a book from Sophia Academic Press. His published works include *The Sophia Teachings*, a six-tape series (Sounds True Recordings), as well as the follow-ing books: *Divine Sophia—Holy Wisdom*, *The Most Holy Trinosophia and the New Revelation of the Divine Feminine*, *The Sophia Teachings*, *Chronicle of the Living Christ*, *Christian Hermetic Astrology*, *The Christ Mystery*, *The Sign of the Son of Man in the Heavens*, *The Morning Meditation in Eurythmy*, and the yearly *Christian Star Calendar*. He translated the spiritual classic *Meditations on the Tarot* and co-translated Valentin Tomberg's *Lazarus, Come Forth!* He is co-author with Lacquanna Paul of *Cosmic Dances of the Zodiac* and *Cosmic Dances of the Planets*. He teaches a gen-tle form of healing movement: the sacred dance of eurythmy (from the Greek, meaning "harmonious movement") as well as the cosmic dances of the planets and signs of the zodiac, and through the Sophia Grail Circle he facilitates sacred cel-ebrations dedicated to the Divine Feminine. Robert offers workshops in Europe and North America and, with Karen Rivers, co-founder of the Sophia Foundation, leads pilgrim-ages to the world's sacred sites (1996 Turkey; 1997 Holy Land; 1998 France; 2000 Britain; 2002 Italy; 2004 Greece; 2006 Egypt; 2008 India)—see www.sophiafoundation.org.

RACHEL C. ROSS is an educator and eurythmist of wide experience. She holds a diploma in Artistic and Pedagogical Eurythmy from the London School of Eurythmy, a diploma in Therapeutic Eurythmy from the Medical Section of the Goetheanum in Dornach, Switzerland, and has a Masters of Science in Education from Sunbridge College in New York. Rachel specializes in treating children with developmental disorders and learning disabilities. She has been involved as a developmental specialist designing and implementing programs, training staff, teaching, and consulting to Waldorf and public schools. Rachel is a faculty member and codirector of the Waldorf Resource/Remedial Teacher Training Programs in Spain, Brazil, Ireland and Toronto, Canada. These trainings are in partnership with the Association for Healing Education. Rachel maintains an active practice in therapeutic eurythmy and remedial movement therapy. She is a traveling consultant to many Waldorf and private schools nationwide. Her forthcoming book, *Adventures in Parenting,* is from the Association of Waldorf Schools of North America (AWSNA).